War

a

Travelin

Traveling with Kids

Leslie Forsberg
Michelle Duffy

PO Box 16102
Seattle WA 98116
www.dispatchtravels.com

Wanderlust and Lipstick: Traveling with Kids

Published by:
Dispatch Travels
PO Box 16102
Seattle, WA 98116

ISBN 10: 0-9787280-7-6
ISBN 13: 978-0-9787280-7-6

Illustrations: Elizabeth Haidle

Library of Congress Control Number: 2008943344

Purchase additional copies online at:
www.WanderlustAndLipstick.com

Printed in the U.S.A.

*To my daughter, Kirsten, a seasoned travel pro
who makes every trip a joyful journey.*

LESLIE FORSBERG

*To my Murphs, all three of you,
long may we travel together.*

MICHELLE DUFFY

CONTENTS

FOREWORD

I wish I could say that my love of travel stretched back to when my parents whisked me off to Europe or South America when I was a toddler. But we never traveled abroad as a family. Instead, we occasionally packed up the car and made summer road trips—from the East Coast to the Southwest, and from New Jersey to Virginia, Georgia, and Alabama: all places where we had extended family.

For me it was a time to see beyond my limited world of Georgia (as a toddler) and New Jersey (where I spent my school days). While the details are fuzzy, I do remember our drive to New Mexico when I was three years old. My three brothers and I were piled in the back of a station wagon, and we tossed peanuts into our Coke bottles and sipped on the soda as we drove through the barren state of Texas. Later, when I was nine or ten, I vividly remember driving through the Blue Ridge Mountains of Virginia with my mom, cousins, and aunts, visiting the Luray Caverns in the Shenandoah Valley and stopping in on Aunt Lover (yes, that's what we called her), whose jukebox I was always fascinated with, and whose recipe for chocolate cake I still bake today.

Though I'm sure my parents could never have guessed what I would grow up to be, through these trips, they were directly responsible for my deep-seated wanderlust today.

In this book, you're going to read stories from, among others, a mom who spent two months in India with her sons, another who rock climbed the mountains of Switzerland with her daughter, and one who traveled with her son to Nepal. But equally important are the women (and often their spouses) who've taken their children to camp in the great outdoors, to enjoy theme parks, and to visit family in neighboring states.

No matter how far or near your travels with your children take you, the experiences are sure to make an indelible impression on them. With luck—and some guidance from you—they will take the knowledge they learn from those trips and develop a better understanding of the world and of themselves. They might even, like me, develop a passion for travel that stays with them forever.

A huge and heartfelt thank-you to both Leslie and Michelle for the amazing job you did in writing this book. Your unique perspectives and passion for traveling with your kids has made this a guide that I'm proud to include in the Wanderlust and Lipstick series.

For more information on travel in general, visit Wanderlust and Lipstick (www.WanderlustAndLipstick.com), and for a perspective on travel with kids, visit Michelle's blog at WanderMom (www.WanderMom.com).

Travel Well,

Beth Whitman

INTRODUCTION

Travels with Leslie

Traveling has always been in my blood. Maybe it is because I grew up on an isolated farm. I always had the sense that just beyond the far fields there was an exciting world, just waiting for me to come and find it. A stint as an exchange student to Mexico, living with a family at the heart of Mexico City, gave me a taste of the exotic flavors and colors outside of my white-bread world. Then I spent three months backpacking solo through Europe, and that was it—I was smitten.

Years later, I was a single mom, working long, tiring days, with little vacation time. Determined to fulfill my need for travel and share the fun with my preschool daughter, I took her along on weekend getaways that usually involved packing the car, calling friends of friends for couches to sleep on, and heading out to territories unknown—to us, at least. It wasn't easy. The prospect of packing up all of the many "required" kid items and dealing with all of the logistics sometimes seemed daunting, especially on those nights long past the bedtime of most, as I dug through a mountain of laundry deep in the dim recesses of my basement to find the only pair of stretch pants Kirsten hadn't yet ripped at the knee. (She was in the midst of a "doggy" phase, and of course, doggies romp around on all fours.)

Sometimes, as kids do, my daughter chose not to participate in a particular day's adventure. I always found a way to make our journey happen, even if it meant loading a forty-pound, three-year-old into a baby backpack and doing that hike anyway, her feet swinging at my knees. Inevitably, any reluctance melted away with each stride on the trail, until we were both excited about the wonders revealed with each bend of the path.

As my daughter grew, our travel experiences grew, filling family photo albums and offering up rich material for dinner-table chats. Then my travel-happy husband joined us, and our family trips took an international turn. Today, as a teenager, my daughter doesn't have boy-band posters on the walls of her room; instead, she displays nearly a dozen maps of the world. She devotes hours to poring over them and loves to talk about the geography and cultures of countries far across the globe.

While writing this book and talking with other moms about their family travel experiences, I learned that I was far from alone in my passion for sharing adventures on the open road with my child. In conversations that grew from a handful to dozens, I talked to moms who have also made travel a priority in their lives, no matter what it took. Some of the moms had undertaken far more exotic and challenging trips than most of us could ever imagine. One couple quit their jobs and traveled throughout Southeast Asia for a year with their children—who were only two, four, and six at the time!

Many others take their kids along on voyages of discovery to national parks in their own state, or to resorts around the world. It's really not about the distance traveled; it's about those little moments when your child makes a connection she wouldn't have without firsthand experience. It's that "aha" moment, when you see her eyes glow, and just for a second you know that this experience will broaden her understanding of the world and eventually, added to other experiences, will make a difference in the person she is becoming.

As a parent, this is an adrenaline rush like no other.

I hope that you find within the pages of this book the encouragement and practical advice to help get you out the door and off on your own grand travel adventures, however big or small they may be. And I hope that the experiences of the many wonderful moms who shared their lives with me as I worked on this book will bring a smile to your face and a skip to your step. Happy travels!

Leslie Forsberg

Travels with Michelle

When I was four, I disappeared from our home on the outskirts of a small town in Eastern Ireland. My poor mother, busy with my two younger siblings, was utterly distraught when she noticed that I was missing. Thankfully, before she could raise any alarm, the doorbell rang, and I was returned to her by an ambulance driver from the local hospital, who had found me confidently striding along the road, swinging my lunchbox in my hand. I was intent on going somewhere and had taken provisions with me to make sure I didn't get hungry along the way.

That story has been retold to family and friends many times because it encapsulates my personality perfectly: I pick a goal, I focus on it, and I go. Because I love to travel, my goals have often been travel related. First thing I did when I completed university? Backpacked around Europe. My gift to myself after my first year of working? A solo trip to Egypt. Rarely have I considered why I shouldn't go somewhere (even at four years old). Thankfully, my husband Andrew is a willing partner in these pursuits. I'm lucky we met when we did, since at the time, he was planning to emigrate to Australia. Instead, we got married, got green cards, and emigrated to the U.S.

When Cillian, our older son, was born just over a year later, one of the first things we planned as we adjusted to being parents was to take him "home"—i.e., home to Ireland—to meet his grandparents, aunts, and uncles. I can honestly say that I didn't even consider whether or not this would be difficult, or what, if anything, I would need in terms of specialized equipment. In researching for this book, it seems that this "why not?" approach to traveling long distances with very young children is common among the women I interviewed who are immigrants to the U.S. The importance of family far outweighs any fears or worries about traveling with children.

And so, because of the pull of family, my children have traveled frequently between the U.S. and Europe. With this type of travel under our belts, trips to Peru, Mexico, Hawaii, and Australia were easy to plan and tremendous experiences for all of us. I find that each trip we take makes traveling easier, as I learn more about what works and what doesn't work in terms of all the practical details such as transportation, equipment, packing, entertainment, and accommodation. The point of this book is to share what I have learned with you and to encourage you to follow my example with your children and to just go, to explore, to teach, and to experience the world with them and through their eyes. Trust me—it will be completely different than anything you have experienced before. Realize, of course, that with this book in hand, you'll be better prepared than I ever was.

I wasn't looking to write a book about traveling with children, but I was excited when Beth approached me to participate in this project. Prior to this book, I had written a couple of technical papers, which were well-received in my role as a Project Manager at Amazon.com. I initially thought Beth was asking me to share travel tips, stories, and ideas to help *her* write the book! But, loaded with experience in more technical forms of writing, and with a boatload of travel experience behind me, I forged ahead. I am deeply indebted to Leslie, my co-author, for teaching me the finer points of travel writing and for being patient with my fumbles along the way. And I owe thanks to Beth for her patience in guiding me through this project. It's been a wild ride.

Finally, I need to thank my husband Andrew and my children, Cillian and Brendan, for their patience with me as I worked on this project. Brendan, I think I owe you at least fifty bedtime stories. Cillian, you are and always will be an amazing individual. Andrew, *m'anam cara,* where will we go next?

Michelle Duffy

1.

WHY TRAVEL WITH CHILDREN?

*A*S *parents, we want the best for our children. And one of the best gifts we can give them is the love of learning about people and places around the world. By taking your children with you on your travels, you'll get to see each other in a new light; you can revel in their joy as they experience new wonders and stretch their wings; and you'll create lifetime memories in the process!*

Creating Global Citizens • LF

Our kids learn geography at school, but there's so much more to the world than the two-dimensional outlines of countries in textbooks. It's up to us as parents to help our children learn about other cultures by experiencing them firsthand. Exposure to other cultures helps our children become globally savvy citizens. The world holds an abundance of fascinating cultures, some closer to home and others farther afield.

Dizy B. embarked on a three-month adventure in Central America with her thirteen-year-old son, Christopher. In the process, they learned about Central American history by talking to local people—and Christopher got to indulge his passion for big-wave surfing at beaches along the way.

For Paula B., travel with her children is a way of life. When her kids were only two, four, and six, she and her husband set out with them to Southeast Asia for an entire year. Since then, the family annually goes somewhere exotic, often for a month or more. They've traveled across Bali, Ghana, Sri Lanka, and the Philippines, among other countries.

Forging Personal Connections • LF

No matter how isolated the region you might visit with your kids, you'll find that traveling with children opens up far more doors than traveling alone, as a single, or as a couple. "The locals recognize that you aren't the typical tourist—you're a family," Paula B. says. "In many cultures, family is so highly regarded that you're taken in."

In the city of Ulcinj, Montenegro, Laura F. and her husband were having a meal with their three-year-old daughter, Eden. The restaurant owner's young daughter, Dija, came over to show Eden her dog. Then the owner's son joined in, and he

Sarah C.'s Story

We like to do things that connect our kids with the local culture. On a trek in Peru, we visited Lake Titicaca, where some islands are actual islands and some are manmade islands constructed of floating reeds. Each island has a distinct, well-preserved culture.

We went to the Amantaní Day festival on Amantaní Island. Families were sitting on blankets having picnics, eating chicken and all sorts of root vegetables, including lots of potatoes. The islanders had a parade, and every organization in town took part in the procession—tailors, first-graders, bakers in traditional clothing—and then the mayor of Puno, the biggest city on Lake Titicaca, marched past.

Reporters were taking pictures, but since we were the only foreigners, they all wanted to take pictures of my family! Everyone hung out around the square, and the kids played a soccer game, kicking around an empty plastic bottle. My kids joined right in. Then the children kicked the bottle in front of the cathedral, and the women there wouldn't give it back. So someone tossed out another plastic bottle. Our kids were so much a part of the moment, running around with the locals and having a great time.

and Eden became instant friends. When the kids wanted to play in the pedestrian-only street outside, the waiter said, "No problem, I'll go with them." Dave and I sat and enjoyed a quiet meal like we hadn't on the whole trip, with the view of the sea and amazing food."

Laura strives to connect with people from other cultures. "This is why I travel: to see the differences, yet feel the similarities. To be reminded that we're all cut from the same cloth, regardless of our spot in the world. Feeling at home so far away from home—that is the magic of travel for me."

Laura F.'s Story

Truly the coolest part of traveling with kids is how they provide an entrée into practically any culture. We have met more people on the road with Eden than we ever did before she was born.

People in China went absolutely nuts over her when we first visited, when Eden was four months old. They love kids, and I don't think they had seen many Caucasian babies. People would literally pick her up out of my arms and carry her off into their houses. We wouldn't see her again for ten or fifteen minutes. The first time it happened, we were at a truck stop eating lunch, and the waitress disappeared into the kitchen with Eden. I started getting nervous and eventually went back there to see what was going on. Eden was sitting on a waitress's lap, with the rest of the kitchen staff fawning over her. It was so sweet.

One woman took her into her house and fed her watermelon. Eden wolfed it down and just smiled up at the lady for more.

Nurturing Lifelong Curiosity • LF

Children have an innate wonder about our world, which is expressed most vociferously when they're preschoolers, and we're peppered with scores of *why* questions every day. While this phase can be pretty exhausting, as parents struggle to explain the physics of rainbows with our paltry recollections of science classes from decades ago, it's also really exciting. At times like this, a parent knows that her child is fascinated by the world and is learning at an astonishing rate.

The information children process shapes who they will eventually be—what they believe in, and what is important to them. Traveling with our children adds to their knowledge base and stimulates them to keep learning. Travel creates individuals who have a lifelong fascination with discovery.

Kimm S., who traveled to Japan with her young daughter, speaks some Japanese. When she addressed people, her daughter looked at her with surprise. "Just to hear these words come out of her mother's mouth was a huge surprise to her," Kimm said. "She looked at me with awe—and that doesn't happen very often!"

Today numerous moms—with or without partners—are heading out to fascinating places, with wheeled luggage in one hand and a baby in a carrier on their backs or a tot holding their other hand. It's not all smooth going. It takes planning and dealing with the issues that arise once there, but as any who have traveled to far-flung places with their kids will say, it's well worth it.

Dawn L.'s Story

I went to Malaysia with my six- and eight-year-old daughters. One of the things I hadn't expected is that my kids weren't all that excited about going. When I told them about the trip, their response was "Can't we just stay home? It's a long time on the airplane." When we got there, they complained, "It's hot here, and it smells." I started questioning myself. Was it worthwhile to bring them? Why did I drag them here?

We were staying in a condo, and one day when we had some down time, my kids set up a restaurant in the kitchen, selling Malaysian foods. They even posted a price list with ringgits converted to dollars, and they were accurate! I laughed when I saw the sign they made that said, "help wanted, full time or part time," since we had seen lots of signs like that in restaurant windows.

The kids were "selling" mangosteens, *roti* (a traditional Indian flat bread), *nasi* (rice), and a lot of cereal. (They had found a type of cereal we don't get at home that they loved.) Their restaurant made me laugh, and I realized that they really did "get" travel.

Weaving a Rich Fabric • LF

I think of the countless daily interactions we have with our children as the threads in a piece of fabric. Each time we offer the opportunity for learning or exploring, we add one more colorful thread to the mix. Travel, because it is more intense than everyday life, can very quickly add to the abundance of experiences that fosters a child's positive emotional and intellectual growth.

Jeanne D.'s Story

My daughter, Mozart, was six when we were on a round-the-world trip, and a friend arranged for us to visit Berber children in the Sahara. We made plans for Mozart to play her violin for these kids, who had never seen or heard one. They live a very simple life, in mud huts with no running water, far from civilization. Mozart so looked forward to the trip and was more nervous about that concert than she has ever been, because she really wanted to play well "for the children."

We arrived by camel to a gathering of sixty Berber children, who greeted her with applause and French songs, in a nomad tent with the mind-blowing, great orange dunes in the background.

We had carried with us healthy snacks for the kids—fresh fruit and other foods—in big bags on the camels, like Santa Claus. After the concert, Mozart and the local kids ran through the oasis together, played outside, and visited some of the kids' homes.

When you add up the experiences of the overnight in this wonderful village—a rare rainbow as we arrived, yummy food, and the sweetest people you could ever meet—this was an experience that is burned into us as an out-of-this-world kind of dream.

Building Family Bonds • MD

Traveling is a great way to spend high-quality time together as a family. Nowadays, in most families, parents work, and children's after-school time is filled with homework, scheduled activities, and play dates. There's not a lot of time or energy left over on the evenings and weekends. The long school vacations in the summer can be a scheduling headache for working parents. The two or three weeks of true vacation time, when the family gets to spend time together away from the busyness of everyday life, are critical. It's a time to reconnect and enjoy each others' company.

Marie W. has taken many cross-country car trips with her six children, who now range in age from ten to twenty-three. She says, "At home, we focus on supporting each other in pursuing individual interests." Things change when she drives from one side of the country to the other, with her car filled with children and luggage and all the other things they need. These trips, she says, "force us to be together as one unit." Traveling together has proven to be a powerful way for her family to get to know one another on a different level than happens in the course of everyday life. "It can be excruciating to be stuck together in the car for days on end, but the memories make it all worthwhile."

Traveling is about full days of being a family unit together, including the joys—and stresses—that journeys can bring. When you are away from home, you can see how your children relate and react to different places, different cultures, and different foods. Your children have time to play together, deepening their relationships as siblings and friends. Travel presents opportunities for you to have extended one-on-one time with your child and to nurture your relationship together.

Melanie E.'s Story

I was really nervous before my trip to Los Mochis in Mexico. I hadn't met my husband's family yet, but I was going to stay with them for three weeks, just me and my son, Giovanni, who was not quite three.

Originally, my husband was supposed to accompany us, but his green card court date was postponed at the last minute, so he couldn't come with us. I had two options: I could cancel, or I could just take Giovanni on my own. I chose to make the trip.

My sister-in-law picked me up from the airport. When we got to my mother-in-law's house, I realized that she was just as nervous to meet me as I was to meet her. That realization helped calm me down. So, there she was, a petite, wrinkled, old lady, and I'm over five feet nine inches tall. I'm not sure why, but we immediately hit it off. I just sensed a kindred spirit and the feeling seemed mutual. But, Giovanni wasn't very comfortable with his grandmother or aunt in this new environment—hardly surprising. He had just met them for the first time, and was hungry and tired.

Most of us live in a small family situation, with one or two adults and one or more children living in a household, independent from our extended family. But we want to stay in touch with those we love, and we want them to know and love our children, even if they don't see each other every day.

I have traveled back and forth between Dublin and Seattle almost twenty times since my oldest son, who is now twelve, was born. The net result of this effort is that my children will wander into my mom's kitchen as if they were there yesterday. They even know where she hides her treats.

Lisa L. has traveled many times within the U.S. with her four-year-old son, Jake, mostly visiting family in Florida and

He was very upset, wanted his daddy and wanted to go home! Things got better over the next few days, but he was still clinging to me. Even when I took a quick trip to the bathroom, it left him in tears. Finally, an unusual event gave him a chance to discover Grandma was OK after all.

Halfway through the trip, I had an allergic reaction to an insect bite on my foot. Late at night, my foot, ankle, and calf started swelling. Since I was essentially on my own with Giovanni, I wanted to get it under control immediately. I needed to get to a pharmacy to get some antihistamine—and quickly. Giovanni had been having trouble getting to sleep since we had arrived, and even though it was late at night, he was still awake, over-tired, and crying. I had to leave him with his grandmother while my sister-in-law took me to find a twenty-four-hour pharmacy. He screamed as I left. When I got back, it was midnight, and he was playing soccer in the living room with his grandmother, using her religious statues as goalposts. It was an unforgetta-ble evening.

Georgia. She sums up the reason for these trips nicely: "Jake just likes to go to the hardware store with his grandpa."

Short trips to spend time with your parents or your siblings are sometimes the first introduction you will have to being a traveling parent. Special times with close family members, at holidays or on vacation, are gifts to your children, which they will never forget. It's true that such trips need careful planning. But—whether you get together with just your sister somewhere nearby or travel to a far-flung place with a collection of aunts, uncles, cousins, and grandparents—there is no doubt that these trips are memorable and invaluable to children. They allow kids to strengthen bonds with family members whom they may not have had a chance to get to know otherwise. And they're good for you, too! At the end of a year, when you think back on the significant moments, you won't think about your daily routine. Instead, you will treasure the times when you stepped away.

Forming Cultural Identity • MD

According to the 2000 U.S. census, almost one-fifth of all children live in a household where one or more of the parents were not born in the U.S. *Culture* is a remote concept for even school-age children to comprehend. But they do understand—and probably enjoy—that you make Swedish pancakes because your grandmother did, and through this, they learn that they are "part Swedish."

In all of our families, there are ways we interact with each other and choices we make about religion, food, entertainment, and dress, which implicitly identify us as having a particular cultural background.

I rushed to a specialty grocery store one afternoon to pick up some cereal. As I was returning to my car, I ran into a friend who commented, "Well, we're really not doing very well at making you into an American," while gesturing at the boxes of Weetabix (a breakfast product that is very popular in Ireland), which my kids love. We laughed. As I retold this story to a Chinese-American friend, she remarked that over the years there had been some interesting reactions in her household when her children's friends had slept over and had been served rice porridge for breakfast.

These habits are part of us, and we automatically pass them on to our children. But as children grow, enter school, and socialize with friends from different backgrounds, they begin to question why we do things the way we do at home. This is healthy. It's good for them to understand who they are and what it means to come from a given cultural or ethnic group. Travel can be a tool you can use to teach your children to understand and appreciate their own culture and also to understand, accept, and appreciate other cultures.

The younger the child, the less she will comprehend the differences between cultures. When we visited Ireland when my boys were very young, they didn't notice that anything was different than in Seattle—except perhaps that they were surrounded by an unusual number of relatives and that people had "funny" accents.

Elementary school-aged children, who understand more about countries and distances, will compare the place you are visiting to their homes and may even judge that place against standards they are accustomed to in the U.S. Connie, who is second-generation Chinese-American, visited China with her three children, Alex (twelve), Calvin (ten), and Grace (eight). What surprised her most about their reactions to China, she says, was the way the kids focused heavily on environmental conditions. In the Pacific Northwest, where she lives, clean air, clean water, and recycling are so much part of the local ethos that even little kids celebrate Earth Day and learn to "reduce, reuse, recycle." Her children brought this worldview with them to China and were more interested in learning what the Chinese were going to do about pollution than they were about anything else.

And yet, even with my own children's complaints about how "not like Seattle" it is, I will keep visiting Ireland with them, teaching them words of Gaelic, and sharing the history and culture of that country. They are ardently American; yet, they are proud to be citizens of both the U.S. and Ireland. Each time we visit Ireland, they learn a little more about it. My older son has been there so many times, I can see that he's got a healthy mixture of both cultures—a fact of which he's blissfully unaware. I've made the effort to travel with him and open the door for him to treat another country as home, too. When he is older and really wants to understand his family's cultural heritage, he'll be able to do so with ease.

Developing Greater Independence • MD/LF

A child's self-sufficiency is a wonderful, painful, frightening thing for any parent. In *Helping a Toddler Ease into Independence* on the website AskDrSears (www.askdrsears.com), the article states, "Parents may feel they are walking a fine line between being over-restrictive and being negligent." This is especially true when you travel. The risks may be higher, but they can also be more rewarding as your child becomes more autonomous.

Active toddlers are starting to become independent beings, and travel is a great opportunity to encourage that behavior. However, a young child's small size means it's easier to lose sight of her in airports, train stations, and bus terminals. Encouraging self-reliance, while keeping a close eye out for her, is paramount. Most kids want to carry their own bulging backpacks or cute pull-along bags as they dash around the airport like seasoned travelers. Ultimately, you know your child's capabilities and limits best. Allow her to spread her own wings, and remember that positive reinforcement works just as well on the road as it does at home.

On a years-ago trip to Portugal, I sat back with the sun shining on me, enjoying my husband's company and watching my six-year-old wander through the stores around the piazza. I kept watch of his progression through the stalls and felt my heart stop each time I couldn't see him for a moment. But then he'd saunter back into view, wave, and continue on his tour.

Travel introduces your children to new places, people, and food. This builds their skills for dealing with the unfamiliar and helps them to become more independent. A child who is an introvert may take longer to bridge the cultural gap in a playground in Europe. And an extroverted child could amaze you by making new friends without knowing a word of the local language. However, both will surely draw upon these experiences to handle new situations once you return home.

Many children challenge themselves when they travel—when you take them out of their familiar environment, you open an opportunity for them to push themselves.

Toniná, a pre-Columbian archaeological site tucked into Mexico's state of Chiapas, has immense pyramids built by the Maya. Lysa S.'s son, Luke, was nearly three years old when he stood at the base of one of the pyramid's steep stone steps. Each tread came up to his chest. "He's never going to be able to climb this," Lysa told her husband. They decided to take turns staying with Luke.

Luke, however, had made up his own mind. "No! I really want to go!" he insisted. Struggling up and over each tier of rough-hewn stone steps, little Luke made it all the way to the top. "He had a look of sheer pride and accomplishment on his face," Lysa says. "It was amazing. I was blown away that his desire to be a part of that experience enabled him to complete a physical feat that many adults couldn't manage."

When you travel with your children, you are guiding them through new, possibly challenging experiences. Subconsciously, you're also expecting them to enjoy these. Take a step back and make sure you're not setting goals that are too high. Know that in time, her maturity and independence will catch up with your dreams. You will both benefit from your having set reasonable expectations early and having maintained them over time.

Once your child enters her teens, it's even more important to allow her some autonomy while traveling. As a fourteen-year-old friend of my daughter said recently, when I suggested that I walk the kids to the hotel swimming pool a block away: "Hey, we're teens. We don't like having our style cramped."

Oh, right! Many of us are so accustomed to doing things for our kids that once they enter adolescence, it's sometimes hard to keep in mind that they really are more capable. However, this doesn't mean we as parents can let go of the reins. We just need to allow them ever-widening circles of independence as they stretch their capabilities.

There's nothing more satisfying to me as a parent than watching my daughter gain the independence she'll need, small step by step, to someday live on her own—which is the aim of parenting in the teen years.

Expanding Horizons • LF

We all want our children to grow up to be knowledgeable, well-rounded individuals who are comfortable in various social groups and settings. There's no better way to achieve this than to pack the kids up and take them along to explore the world together, starting as young as possible. There is no substitute for learning about another country, or even just another city or ecosystem, by going there and experiencing it.

The child who has had the opportunity to scan distant hills with binoculars and see a herd of wild horses grazing with their foals in the wilds of the Great Basin, as my daughter did on one trip, will have that image emblazoned in her memory, and she will be the richer for it.

Since travel takes children into worlds that can be quite distant from their daily lives, the experiences are more intense, and they often prove to be formative in a child's life. That glimpse of wild horses could lead a kid to write short stories, take up drawing, or perhaps start a campaign to save wild horses.

Children are still forming their identities and their perceptions of the world. The youngster who has the opportunity to travel with her parents will incorporate what she observes into her worldview. It's particularly important for those of us who live in more homogenous cultures to consider how to expose our off-spring to other ways of life. Books are a good starting point, but there's nothing like travel to help a child really understand what it's like somewhere outside of her typical daily existence.

Jenny B. and her husband took their four children, ages three to fifteen, to Hong Kong and Vietnam. "The trip has had last-ing effects on our family. My husband and I feel confident that we could take the kids just about anywhere," she says. "Our children are now enamored with many aspects of Asian cul-ture, from the food to art to traditional dress. Most impor-tantly, this trip made my children travelers. It made them curious about the world and gave them the desire to see it."

Embracing the Natural World • LF

A generation ago, after-school time was spent outdoors—playing in the street, playing in the yard, maybe sledding in colder weather. Today, however, this is rarely the case. We all know that it's important for kids to spend time outdoors, but it's not as easily done in this day when most families are over-burdened, and few live near green spaces. Adding to this trend

Liz D.'s Story

Within the space of two years I got a divorce, returned to work full time, and moved to a new location; my eight-year-old daughter, Nell, started at a new school; and my mom passed away. This all took a toll on Nell, who became less confident and more of a worrier. I felt that she and I needed to remember our free spirits, and I wanted an adventure.

I rented a car in Las Vegas and made a campground reservation at the North Rim of the Grand Canyon. At every junction, we opened our travel book and talked about what we wanted to do and where we wanted to go. We were two hippie chicks with nothing more than a tent, a guidebook, and a map.

I didn't take a close look at our campground reservation, and when we got to the South Rim of the Grand Canyon, we realized that our campsite was on the North Rim, about six hours away. It was already dinnertime, and I knew it would be impossible to drive all the way to the North Rim in the dark. If something doesn't work out going to the right, you go to the left. We

are electronics, which eat up ever more of our kids' time. Kids ages eight to eighteen spend an average of forty-four hours each week in front of a TV, video game, or computer screen.

Children who spend regular time in the outdoors are less stressed and better able to cope with life's complexities. Family trips to natural settings can be an ideal way for both kids and parents to relax, and for kids to learn about the interconnecting web of life found in nature. There's no substitute for seeing how young trees are nurtured by decaying logs in a rain forest or for watching antelope bound alongside the car. No stack of books is going to give our kids a sense of excitement at finding their first fossil or discovering that ocean waves roll into shore explained our situation to a park ranger, and he told us about a nearby family campground. He said it's always full, but we might as well check anyway. We were totally lucky. We had to wait a while, but we were able to get a campsite there, within walking distance of a store and visitors' center. It turned out to be the perfect place for us.

Later on, we decided to go hiking down Bright Angel Trail, the same trail the donkey trains use (and on which the donkeys leave their deposits). Halfway down, we were hit with monsoon-like rains, thunder, and lightning. We immediately turned around, and there was dung flying everywhere, and the rain was pouring so heavily we could barely see in front of us. By the time we got to the top, we were drenched through, and my phone had shorted out.

One of the things we talked about that night is how it's all about knowing you can confront anything in life, and dig deep and find your strength, and get through it, and then laugh about it and learn from it.

in regularly measured sets. We as parents can gain tremendous satisfaction from the sparkle in our children's eyes.

Kim C. says that her nine-year-old daughter, Brynn Adelia, likes to talk about her feelings and finds it easiest to do so when in a natural setting. "Brynn feels really comfortable whenever we're out in nature, and she has a tendency to open up about whatever is on her mind. She's very much into magical thinking and believes the tree fairies are there supporting her."

It's essential that our children gain an appreciation for the last green spaces left. After all, someday our kids will be the decision makers. There's no better place to start than with the experiences to be had while visiting Italy's Dolomite Mountains, the redwoods of Northern California, or maybe Vietnam's extraordinary Ha Long Bay.

Seeking Emotional Healing • LF

Much as we wish it were otherwise, life has its downs as well as its ups. Sometimes traveling with our kids is a way for us to nurture ourselves and our children following emotional trauma. While on a trip, living side-by-side with our children on a daily basis and working together toward shared goals can give us the strength we need to keep on going or to find a route through the impasses in our lives. Travel can provide our children with new ideas for dealing with issues, as well. And being able to spend so much time together as a family gives them a sense of security.

Adding Joy to Our Lives • LF

Traveling with our kids isn't just for their sakes. As adults, our responsibilities sometimes weigh heavily as life gets a lot more complicated. It's easy to lose our way in the joy department amid the flurry of homework and frantic dashes to school, orthodontia appointments, and extracurricular activities. The antidote: taking time out from daily life to go somewhere interesting and try out new experiences. It's especially valuable to do that with our children—for their sakes and ours.

Even if it requires some work to manifest, spending time with our children away from daily routines can be transformative. When traveling with our children, we have the opportunity for richer experiences as we see, sometimes for the first time, the quirky little details that we would probably not notice ourselves. If we slow down and try to see the world through their eyes, we can find the kid inside ourselves that we've forgotten for a long time.

When you go on a trip with your children, breathe deeply, kick off your shoes, and plunge wholeheartedly into adventures. You may find yourself grinning so broadly that your cheeks hurt. And what better legacy to give your children than to see you taking part enthusiastically in all of life's adventures?

2.

IDEA GENERATOR: EASY DOES IT!

TRAVELING *with our children offers delights that can't be had in our daily lives. A trip can be the beginning of a journey of discovery for our kids, illuminating for them what they most love. It can offer them a sense of accomplishment. And it can add a new level of enjoyment to family life even beyond the trip. Just follow your dreams to craft an excursion that's especially meaningful for you and your children!*

Weekend Getaways • LF

You can pack a lot into a small amount of time. My husband and I are specialists in planning short trips, which are necessary during the school year or for those times when it's hard to get away from work. It's amazing what you can do if you set your mind to it and utilize weekends. In one whirlwind, four-day trip (leaving Friday and returning Monday), we explored five of the Smithsonian museums in Washington, DC. We also visited Pennsylvania's Amish country, buying fresh apple cider from a ruddy-cheeked boy who was wearing overalls and a straw hat. On a weekend-only jaunt (leaving after school on Friday and returning Sunday night), we hiked and swam in a remote Northern California canyon, plucked wild grapes while on a bike ride through a shady park, and visited a fabulous farmers' market. Our daughter, Kirsten, still talks about the rich experiences we had on these trips.

The demands of the workplace are forcing many of us to choose shorter vacations. More than 50 million Americans don't use all of their allotted vacation days. The traditional one- or two-week vacation is no longer a given; many families are replacing it with long-weekend getaways.

Shorter trips are easier to plan, and they're cheaper, as well. Taking even a little time off is really important for you and your children—it's an important investment in your children's bank of experiences; it's rewarding to enjoy adventures as a family; and it gives everyone a break from the daily routine.

Fortunately, school calendars, with days off for teacher conferences or training, often provide opportunities for three-day getaways. These workdays are nearly always scheduled on a Friday or a Monday. If you plan to leave on your trip immediately after school lets out, you can have a three-night stay and three full days of adventure with your kids.

Sometimes the best timing for a short trip doesn't coincide with a school's day off. I have taken my daughter out of school a day or two early, if the trip is farther away or highly educational. I'm not the only one. One in five parents allows their kids to miss some time to travel.

Taking an extra day or two off will work only if your children are young enough not to have loads of homework. By the time children are in high school, the demands are much bigger, so it's best to schedule weekend family getaways before then. You'll need to coordinate with your child's teachers to get homework assignments before you leave, so he can keep up with his homework assignments. My daughter just brings her homework along; there's always plenty of time in transit for her to work on math, reading, or writing while on such trips.

City Breaks • MD

I live in Seattle, but my favorite city on the west coast of the U.S. is San Francisco. Perhaps because San Francisco is where my husband and I spent our first few weeks in this country when we moved here from Ireland. And, it's become a favorite place for us to go as a family for a break from dreary Northwest winters. We've ridden the cable cars with our boys, visited the Ghirardelli Chocolate Ice Cream and Chocolate Shop, and taken many photos of the famous Golden Gate Bridge. San Francisco is a short (two hour) flight from Seattle, so we can have a quick getaway without having to spend too much time traveling. There are plenty of options for accommodations and many neighborhoods to explore, each with its own unique personality.

Cities are destinations for business and tourism. They can be loud, smelly, and expensive; yet, they are colorful and full of lively hustle and bustle. For people who travel frequently on business, an extra couple of days at the start or end of a work trip can provide an opportunity to see more of the host city than just the inside of a hotel or an office building, offering a fun way to build a break with family. When my older son, Cillian, was about a year old, my husband attended a conference at Walt Disney World in Florida. Visiting Disney World seemed like too good an opportunity to miss, so my son and I flew to Orlando to meet my husband for the weekend. It was a short but enjoyable trip.

If you're traveling internationally for vacation, you will likely fly into a major hub. Rather than rushing straight to your resort, spending a day or two exploring the metropolis can be an invigorating way to start your holiday.

Many guidebook series publish city-specific guides, but city-sponsored websites are also a great resource. An Internet search on "[city] visitor information" is a good way to find these. Look for a website hosted by the government, a visitors' bureau, or a chamber of commerce. NYC & Company (www.nycgo.com), Only In San Francisco (www.onlyinsanfrancisco.com), and Washington.org (www.washington.org) are great examples of this for New York City, San Francisco, and Washington, DC, respectively.

I've found that with city breaks, I don't always have time to research things to see and do before we go; yet, I still want to ensure that we're getting the most out of our visit. Tourist offices, which carry a concentrated amount of information, can be a good first stop. These centers are found at most airports, or you can locate one listed in your guidebook. Hotels usually have tourist maps available at the front desk. Older children love to scour these maps and plan the next day's activities, while younger children can sit with a parent and enjoy the colorful graphics as you point out the fun things you hope to see or do.

Before you plan too much, remember that walking around cities with young children can be challenging. Their little legs have to work harder than yours to cover the same distance, and kids can run out of steam easily. Hop-on, hop-off buses are a great way to explore a city with children. See the section on guided excursions in Chapter 13, "While You're There," for some information on this type of tour.

If you and your family like more independence than you feel a private bus tour might afford, public transit can add to the sense of adventure. Kids love examining subway maps and will eagerly help you navigate the system. In some cities, such as San Francisco, public transit may be a tourist attraction in itself. In this case, most children find the cable cars fascinating. Look for multi-day passes, family rates, and child fares—handy ways to keep your expenses down.

Playgrounds are not usually included in tourist literature but can make or break a day for anyone traveling with a child under five years old. If your tourist map doesn't show parks or playgrounds, check your guidebook, ask at the tourist office, or inquire at your hotel. Within the U.S., you can use the KaBOOM! Playspace Finder (http://playspacefinder.kaboom.org) to find source sites.

Hot Tip! Most cities are packed with attractions and activities. The abundance of choices can lead to challenges in planning how you will spend your days. Remember, it's OK to split up. One parent may want to visit galleries or go on a ghost walk, while another takes the kids to a hands-on science museum or to a concert in the park.

2. IDEA GENERATOR: EASY DOES IT

Theme Parks • LF

"Mom, she heard me! My wish will come true," Kirsten said. Leaning over a wishing well in Mickey's Toontown in Disneyland, Kirsten, nine at the time, had whispered her dream. A disembodied voice echoing off the walls of the well promised that it would come true. Kirsten's eyes shone as brightly as I'd ever seen them, and I felt touched to witness this sweet sign of childhood innocence.

I'm charmed by the fact that, even in this fast-paced digital age, children are still mesmerized by the allure of Disneyland or its sister parks, Walt Disney World in Florida, Disneyland Resort in Paris, and Hong Kong Disneyland. Today, Disney's offerings are just a few in a crowded field of theme parks around the world that cater to eager children.

With all the trappings of childhood, from storybook princesses to rides based on animated movie themes, it would seem that theme parks are just for kids. Yet there are many attractions that appeal to the kid in every adult, with high-speed, high-tech roller coasters; sensory-filled interactive experiences; and gee-whiz technology.

Hot Tip! The book *PassPorter Disneyland Resort and Southern California Attractions: The Unique Travel Guide, Planner, Organizer, Journal, and Keepsake* is just as it's billed—a fabulous tool. Its website is www.passporter.com.

When planning a visit to a theme park, it's best to start by thinking about the ages of your children. Toddlers and pre-schoolers can be easily overwhelmed by the crowds and long lines, as well as by the sheer kaleidoscopic energy of the sights and sounds. Some theme parks cater specifically to younger children, with gentler rides and activities that elementary-age children particularly enjoy.

Jill H., who has six kids, says that it's a good idea to consider your children's personalities too. "Some kids don't like to go on big rides," she says. "Make sure to accommodate each child, but don't make anyone who is afraid or uncomfortable go on rides. At Disneyland, some of our kids were terrified and didn't want to go on the bigger rides, but they enjoyed the gentler ones, like *Dumbo* and *it's a small world*. You need to be willing to split the kids into groups so that all of them can enjoy themselves."

If you're planning a trip abroad, why not stop into a theme park? Theme Park Insider (www.themeparkinsider.com) is dream-inducing eye candy, with its descriptions, ratings, and reviews of top-rated parks around the world.

Some overseas ones offer a glimpse into their country's culture. Tivoli Gardens in Denmark, for example, has rides straight out of Hans Christian Andersen fairy tales, such as *Den Flyvende Kuffert* (The Flying Trunk), with its journey past scenes from stories by the famous children's author.

Roller Coasters • LF — If your children are roller coaster fans, you might enjoy learning more on the interactive Roller Coaster DataBase (www.rcdb.com). This website lists the newest rides, record-breaking ones, and numerous other statistics.

Water Parks • LF — Kids are drawn to water, and a visit to a splash park on a hot, sunny day is one of the most kid-pleasing activities ever. Waterparks.com (www.waterparks.com) calls itself the "official guide to waterparks around the world." This site allows you to search their database by country. It also includes great tips for visiting water parks, such as the fact that by wearing swim shoes, you can go from one feature to the next without having to take shoes off and put them on again.

Hot Tip! Spend time checking out the official theme park websites, but also take a look at the numerous informal ones and message boards that may paint a more complete picture. Theme Park Critic (www.themeparkcritic.com) is just one of numerous such sites, which you can find through an online search for a park name and the phrase "message board."

With theme parks, you don't have to plan ahead very much; all you have to do is reserve a car, flight, and lodging, and the rest all falls into place. With so many options at theme parks, you'll almost certainly run into the challenge of how to fit into your schedule everything that your family wants to do.

Cruise Vacations • LF

Cruises offer quality family time without having to plan all the details of the trip yourself. And, today's cruise ships often have more amenities and opportunities for fun than the standard resort, with pool complexes, rock-climbing walls, big-screen movie theaters, and game arcades, in addition to children's clubs with scores of daily activities. Add to that the excitement of visiting ports of call. There is so much on offer each day, the hardest part of cruising with a family is deciding which activities to do! While some cruise lines specialize in what are essentially floating parties, others focus on family or adventure travel.

The website Cruise Critic (www.cruisecritic.com), a fabulous resource, notes which cruise lines, in its experts' opinions, are the most toddler-friendly. Their top-pick list includes Carnival Cruise Lines, Cunard Line, Disney Cruise Line, Norwegian Cruise Line, and Royal Caribbean.

Saving Money on a Cruise · LF

Cruises are easy to budget: One up-front fee covers lodging, meals, transportation, and entertainment, as well as children's programs. If you can be flexible about your dates, you may save money; on a cruise line's website, try inputting several different times of year, as the prices will vary, depending on the season.

Budget-mindful travelers should consider getting a room with a limited view. On an Alaska cruise, a lifeboat blocked most of our window, but if we stood on the bed, the vista was just as magnificent as it was for everyone else. Some cruise lines offer parents a cost break on the third and fourth berth for children ages two to eighteen, and a few cruise lines allow those two and under to travel for free.

Cruise lines accommodate children in specialized children's programs, which gives the parents a chance for some down time. Some lines also provide babysitting services, typically for an additional fee. Check with the cruise line you're considering for specifics.

For additional savings, you can book your shore excursions independently of the cruise lines. Once in port, you'll find scores of tour operators eager to whisk you off to the same places, and they'll charge you twenty-five to fifty percent less than the ships will. After seeing the sights, it's tempting to dine at a local restaurant, but if you eat most of your meals on board, you can save substantially on your budget.

Most cruise ships can easily accommodate a family of four in a single stateroom, and some, such as Disney Cruise Line and Royal Caribbean, now have staterooms that sleep up to six.

Before you make the decision to sail with an infant, be sure to check the cruise lines' policies. Some will not allow infants, and others have a minimum age of six or twelve months. Ask whether the vessels have cribs or Pack 'n Plays available. You'll want to confirm availability before you sail. Check also to see if the line has bouncy seats, in-cabin high chairs, or umbrella strollers. Staterooms don't typically have DVD players, so if your family routine includes your child watching a favorite movie, you'll need to pack along a portable one.

Educational Trips • LF

I want my child to be excited about learning, and there's no better way to learn about something than through hands-on, personal experience. That's why so many of us choose to take our children on educational vacations, whether the subject is history, culture, or the natural world.

Lisa M. plans such trips for her eight-year-old daughter and ten-year-old son that are based on history. "We do a lot with living history. In Puerto Rico we toured a plantation, where we learned about coffee beans and ground our own corn. We also learned about slavery there," Lisa says.

The opportunity to have our children learn about the world through their own senses leads many of us to spend at least part of our vacation time visiting museums, historical sites and national parks.

Museums • LF — Museums offer fabulous learning opportunities for kids, especially if they're experiential-style facilities. There is such a plethora of museums throughout the world that you'll certainly be able to find ones that speak to your children's special interests. Obviously, children's museums and science museums have a lot to offer youngsters, but pretty much any museum can have aspects that will delight kids.

Laura S.'s Story

When Annika was four, her grandma and I accompanied her as she swam alongside dolphins on a day excursion during a cruise out of Cozumel. Later, Annika got to feed the dolphins. She still talks about it now, four years later. If there's any mention of dolphins, her ears perk up!

We've been on several cruises, and most cruise lines do a good job of taking care of kids. They have fabulous kids' clubs, with all kinds of activities, sports, and arts and crafts. You get a pager in case your children have any needs or issues. Then you as a parent can have a vacation, too. If you're by the pool or somewhere else on the ship, you're just a pager away from your kids saying: "Mom, can I come back? I want to go into the big pool."

As with any cruise experience, you only have to unpack once; you can choose whether or not to do shore excursions; and the food is great, with several restaurants you rotate through, so you're not going to the same eatery day after day. The kids' club takes care of dinnertime, too, if you want. We always ate with our kids, but if there was a special pizza afternoon or ice cream-treat time, our kids did that.

On one cruise, there was an adults-only restaurant onboard, with wonderful cuisine. Having a date with your spouse is a huge deal. That's what vacations are all about—to recharge and reconnect.

2. IDEA GENERATOR: EASY DOES IT

Hot Tip! If you have a membership in your local science center or children's museum, check to see if they have reciprocal arrangements with similar institutions in other cities. Many of these relationships offer reduced entrance fees.

It's important to take into account the age and temperament of your children when planning a trip to a museum. What might be fascinating to a ten-year-old could be boring to a teenager, or too restrictive for a toddler or young child.

For young children, consider a visit to just one exhibit, such as the Rosetta Stone at the British Museum in London or the Tutankhamun exhibit at the Egyptian Museum in Cairo. As with everything child-related, if you haven't spent a lot of time in museums at home, don't suddenly expect your child to be happy with full days of viewing relics. A little at a time will build his curiosity.

Jeanne D. says, "I am a big believer that even young children should be regulars at great museums and sights, and my daughter enjoys them, as they have always been part of her life." Through smart planning and pacing, Jeanne and her husband once visited three museums in a day in Paris with their six year old. "We visited midweek, off-season, and timed the visit to each museum when they would be the least busy. One we visited early in the morning, the next at lunchtime, and the third late in the day," she said. "Between museums we stopped at playgrounds and had snacks and a leisurely lunch."

Hot Tip! To keep younger children engaged in a museum, ask them to search for a particular object or theme. If visiting an art museum, you might ask them to see how many works they can find with horses, dogs, or some other element.

In my experience, the "golden age," when a child is most ready to gain from museum visits is—loosely—around ages eight to thirteen. However, every kid is different, so if you're thinking of an educational trip, consider your children's attention spans, hobbies, and interests first. If you have any doubt at all, it's a good idea to make the learning part of the trip light—a visit to just one museum or historic site a day, instead of a longer day with multiple stops.

Hot Tip! Audio tours for the kids keep them engaged and help them feel independent. They also allow you a few moments to learn about and enjoy the sites, too.

If an art museum is on your family's agenda, check out a book before the visit that focuses on an aspect of the collection you'll be seeing. There are wonderful art-appreciation picture books for young children, and for older kids there are great picture-filled biographies or even chapter books that draw them in to the artist's world.

Jenny N., a home-schooling mom, has compiled a really good art-appreciation book list on her blog, Little Acorns Treehouse (www.littleacornscds.blogspot.com), with links to the products on Amazon. Just search for "art appreciation" on her website. For art museums worldwide, see listings at Artcyclopedia (www.artcyclopedia.com) and select "art museums worldwide."

One of the most rockin' websites for museums worldwide goes by the unstuffy name of MuseumStuff (www.museumstuff.com). Here you can search by type of museum (e.g., art, science, history), country, and even by primary topic, such as science-related museums specializing in dinosaurs. For children's museums throughout the world, check out the Association of Children's Museums (www.childrensmuseums.org).

Hot Tip! Check out Museums in the USA (www.museumca.org/usa) for domestic travel ideas.

2. IDEA GENERATOR: EASY DOES IT

National Parks • LF — National parks around the world offer once-in-a-lifetime sights and experiences. Visits to the fifty-eight national parks around the United States or countless national parks abroad offer our children experiences in nature that can't be found between the pages of a book or in a museum display. National parks offer relaxation, space for our kids to exercise their legs and their imaginations, and learning opportunities about life cycles and habitats. Plus, each national park is amazingly unique, with interesting flora, fauna, and landscapes.

Taking our kids to natural wonders can make a big impact on them. "Our kids were speechless at the Grand Canyon," Laura S. says. We could see their awe. We didn't need to hear words. Just watching them standing there and absorbing the immensity of the setting, rather than rushing through the experience, was something out of the ordinary."

There are scores of opportunities to experience wildlife viewing in national parks. Children are fascinated by animals, and there's nowhere on the planet with the opportunity to see so many species at the same time as in the northern Serengeti in Kenya. During the migration, elephants, gazelles, lions, and zebras wash in waves across the plains of the Maasai Mara National Reserve.

Birders keep ongoing "life lists" of all the birds they've seen in a lifetime. Why not create a life list of national parks you've visited with your children? Ask about children's programs when you check in to a park. In the United States, many parks offer a Junior Ranger program, for additional learning opportunities. Coloring books, activity sheets, and self-guided "treasure hunt" activities are commonplace. Once a child has completed the activities, he scores a Junior Ranger badge.

Laura S. travels to lots of national parks around the U.S. with her husband and three young children. "The park programs are great for teaching respect for the environment and for learning about the surroundings. We slow down to look at trees and learn how to take care of nature. Each of our boys has about eighty Junior Ranger badges right now, and our eight-year-old daughter has close to thirty," Laura says. "It's a fun family activity. There are tons of projects you can choose from in packets designed for each individual park."

Even a couple hours can make a lasting impression. If you have more time, schedule a hike into lesser-visited areas, so your children can have the thrill of discovery. Many national parks have campgrounds, allowing you to spend one or more nights for a richer experience. Some even have yurts or cabins, making it unnecessary for you to take along a tent.

Hot Tip! Kids are naturally more interested in what they can see with their own eyes. To involve your children in the choice of national parks to visit, buy a good pictorial book on national parks.

To look for national parks in North America, visit the websites for the National Park Service (www.nps.gov) or Parks Canada (www.pc.gc.ca).

Elsewhere, check out the country's main tourism website for a list of parks. To whet your appetite, have a look at "The International A-List: 15 Spectacular World Parks," by Alissa Mears, at Gorp (gorp.away.com), then search for "world parks."

UNESCO World Heritage Sites • LF — When I'm planning a family trip abroad, one of the first resources I check is the list of United Nations Educational, Scientific, and Cultural

Stacia C.'s Story

Since we live in the Pacific Northwest, our kids know intellectually that there is snow out there somewhere in the summer. But when we arrived at Logan Pass in Glacier National Park in Montana, the reality was way more exciting.

When we parked the RV, they all got out to test if they would really be comfortable outside in shorts and a T-shirt—that was the first surprise. The second came while looking out the picture windows of the visitors' center. Were they really seeing a few snowboarders, skiers, and people with sleds hiking up the hill? Sure enough, it was summer, but that didn't stop the "winter" fun.

The kids immediately decided to see how far they could hike in the summer snow, which quickly turned into their tossing snowballs at each other. It was so fun to watch the kids; they were so silly. And they kept laughing at the fact they were playing in the snow on the Fourth of July.

Organization (UNESCO) World Heritage sites (www.unesco.org), to see what fascinating places we can fit into our plans. These destinations are considered to have great cultural, historical, or natural significance. The "superstar" sites are imaginative and inspirational places to visit with your kids.

There are more than 850 UNESCO World Heritage sites throughout the world, from manmade structures such as Teotihuacán—with its temples of the sun and moon, near Mexico City—to natural treasures such as the Belize Barrier Reef Reserve System. Exposing our children to such great world resources helps them acquire a greater interest in our planet.

At the Ubirr art site in Australia's Kakadu National Park, rock carvings tell long-ago stories of the Aboriginal People who camped in rock shelters in the area. Early artists carved their tales of hunting mastery into the area's rocks—depicting opossums, wallabies, and other animals that are still hunted for food today. At places like this, you and your children can almost feel the presence of the ancient inhabitants of these beautiful spaces.

Guided Tours • MD

Consider a multi-day package, if you prefer a full-service vacation, where someone else arranges the meals and accommodations and not only provides you with a day plan, but also arranges any transportation and escorts needed. Guided tours also make many once-in-a-lifetime trips possible to places only accessible with a guide. These include going on safari in Tanzania or visiting the Galápagos Islands. A tour company has the local knowledge required to organize transportation, accommodation, and guides—details that are difficult to arrange independently in some destinations.

Tour companies quote a single, per-person price for multi-day trips. Examine the components carefully, taking note of any hotels or restaurants mentioned. Typically, flights to and from your destination are not included. Look for reviews of the hotels and restaurants mentioned in the tour information on TripAdvisor (www.tripadvisor.com) before you book. Ask the tour operator about the qualifications of the guides, so you can be sure you'll be getting the most out of your experience.

The day plan is the most important part of the tour information for children. Days packed full of activities, particularly more adult ones, such as guided tours of historical sites, are difficult for younger children. Look for a tour company that recognizes that family groups need to be able to opt out and that provides alternate options—even if that's just to play by the hotel pool.

Operators such as Thomson Family Adventures (www.familyadventures.com) include kid-centered activities in their tours, such as matching your child with a pen pal in the destination country before you go and arranging a meeting while you're there.

There are also many options for taking advantage of guided tours within independent trips. When we visited Rome recently, we intended to tour the Colosseum on our own, judging that Brendan, at eight, was too young to pay attention to a detailed historical spiel. But when we arrived, the entrance line was really long, and we discovered that by joining a tour group—just starting—we could avoid the queue for a small premium on the entrance fee. Brendan did have a hard time staying focused on all of the information the guide shared, but Cillian, age twelve, loved the tour.

Tours don't have to be serious. Retired DUKWs (WWII amphibious vehicles) are now used for passenger tours in many cities in the U.S. and Europe, including Washington, DC; Boston; Miami; Seattle; and London. The trucks themselves lend an air of fun to the tour, which most groups play up with duck-themed paraphernalia, such as the duckbill-shaped noisemakers given to every participant.

Beaches • MD

Your ideal family getaway may include a week of blissful relaxation in the sun, while back at home, the days are short and feet of snow are piling up in your driveway. At some point, every family needs to just take a break, after all. And why not unplug from work and school by heading off to paradise to reconnect, have fun, and enjoy each other's company?

You can easily book your own beach vacation by renting a home or arranging for hotel accommodations, and then independently planning activities your family might enjoy. This will allow you to be as close to (or as far away from) shops, stores, and sights as you like. Alternately, you might consider an all-inclusive package, where meals are prepared and activities are scheduled on-site. All-inclusives are often located away from tourist areas in their own enclave. The greatest benefit is that they provide most everything your children will need in order to take full advantage of the water, including boogie boards, tubes, towels, and private pools for lounging. This means less packing for you!

If you're traveling during high season, you may need to book well in advance—as much as six months or more. Hotels and resorts can easily sell out in popular beach destinations, such as those in Mexico and Costa Rica. Expect costs for flights and accommodations to be highest during this time.

Many properties located in hotspots are timeshares, in which a person or family "owns" a week or more to be used at their discretion. If you find it difficult to secure accommodation at a resort or hotel, you might try booking a timeshare listed by someone who is unable to use their property that year. Try searching on Vacation Timeshare and Rentals (www.vacationtimesharerentals. com) for worldwide options.

3.

IDEA GENERATOR: ADVENTURE

I F *you're passionate about adventurous pursuits—such as mountain climbing, scuba diving, or biking—your enthusiasm is sure to rub off on your child. And, if you don't already have the skills, learning one of these activities while you're on the road can be exhilarating for all involved. Whether you're following your current passions or pursuing new ones, there's no question that adventures take the relationship with your child to new heights of fun and friendship.*

Take a Hike • LF

Hiking is a wonderful way to expose your kids to the beauty and diversity of nature, and it also allows you and yours to get some exercise. You'll get a much better sense of what a place is all about when you get up close to wildlife, and look for different types of trees and plants on a trek. You can walk for an hour on an urban footpath or for days on trails that take you far from cities and roads.

The key consideration with children is the ease of the hike. If your kids are beginners, you'll want to look for short routes with little to no elevation gain. You can do quick excursions with your child when she is as young as preschool age. Signposted interpretative loops are a great place to start.

It's easiest to keep your children's interest if there are a number of diversions along the route. I started taking my daughter on day hikes when she was five; I looked for fun features like streams, waterfalls, or lakes—basically, anything having to do with water is exciting for kids. Every kind of landscape has features well worth the visit, though, from lava-cast trees in a volcanic region to oasis-ringed springs in a desert.

To plan a family hike, check out online sources such as Local Hikes (www.localhikes.com), which features outings near major urban centers throughout the U.S., or Trails.com (www.trails.com). You do have to pay a small fee to join this site, but it's worth it for the interactive information about more than 43,000 routes in North America. Trails.com offers trail guides, maps, real-time weather, and driving directions.

Nearly anywhere you look on the globe, there are hiking opportunities. Europe's extensive routes carry travelers across diverse landscapes and countries, where the language spoken shifts with the miles. In Spain, the well-worn Camino de Santiago de Compostela is a pilgrimage path that weaves through numerous scenic villages. England offers gentle hikes through pastoral landscapes populated by sheep. The resident animals in Switzerland are cows, which you'll encounter as you take an exhilarating ride up a ski lift, then hike downhill to the valley floor.

Tropical hikes are a big hit with kids, as you'll see bugs, animals, and oversized foliage that inspire young imaginations. In Belize you can wander through jungle to treetop colonies of howler monkeys that roar as loudly as lions. In Hawaii, push through tropical vegetation on the Na Pali Coast of Kauai, with spectacular ocean views. Hikes in Thailand include butterfly- and bird-watching, as well as visits to fascinating geological formations and ancient ruins.

New Zealand hikes put together elements from many different landscapes, all in one trek. Trails here can include everything from gnarly mountains and active volcanoes (especially fascinating for kids!) to sandy beaches. Locals call hiking *tramping*, and it's a favorite national activity.

Hot Tip! There are specialized guidebooks that focus on kid-pleasing landscape features such as waterfalls or hot springs. The Mountaineers produce an especially fine series, "Best Hikes with Children" (www.mountaineersbooks.org).

When you're determining where to hike, take into account whether the region or country has a stable political situation. Don't take your children into a place where there may be civil unrest. Check out the U.S. Department of State's Consular Information Program (www.travel.state.gov/travel), as well as online forums or blogs (see Chapter 6, "Pre-trip Planning" for information on these), to gain a sense of the safety of a country.

3: IDEA GENERATOR: ADVENTURE

Barbara T.'s Story

We were in the northeastern part of Switzerland, in the Appenzell region. It's very rugged and above the tree line. My husband and I are rock climbers and love this terrain. The trails can be very steep and exposed, so there are ropes and steel cables there for added safety. We put a short rope on our eight-year-old daughter, Miriam, to keep her really safe, and so that she would feel secure. (Earlier, she had felt intimidated by the exposure of the Wanderweg hiking trail.)

As soon as she was on the rope, Miriam pulled herself up the rock wall, stopping to eat wild onions growing in the cracks. She had pulled up and over one ridge after another. There were dozens of ibex in one spot that were really close. She had this incredible sense of accomplishment, and we were so proud.

That night we got a whole alpine hut to ourselves. The alpine huts are always built where there's the best view, so when we woke up in the morning and had breakfast, we could see down the entire valley, east and west. It was absolutely exhilarating. With hut-to-hut hiking, Switzerland is really a playground for kids!

Hot Tip! If your family loves to hike, check out hut-to-hut hiking and camping, available in Austria and Switzerland, in North America (in the mountains of British Columbia, Colorado, and New England), and even in Patagonia, Argentina. To learn more about this style of travel, do an Internet search for hut-to-hut hiking in the country or region that most interests you.

The Lake District of England is one of Laura S.'s favorite places to take her kids hiking. "The Lake District is all about hiking," she says. "England has public pathways that are phenomenal. They're well marked. We greet everybody we pass; the kids are natural ambassadors. When the hiking trail dips down into a village, we give our kids spending money and have them buy their own souvenir or ice cream, so they have the experience of dealing with the shopkeeper."

For adventurous families, backpacking is a rite of passage. By pushing into a remote location and using it as a base camp, you'll escape the crowds of casual day hikers and can get into some astonishingly beautiful places. If you're interested in putting together this kind of trip, be sure to increase the kids' hiking experience gradually, beginning with short, interesting day trips. Allow your child to set the pace, make plenty of snack and water stops, and build in rewards to keep her going.

Hot Tip! To keep a little one moving on a hike, have one adult walk ahead and hide a small trinket, such as a Hot Wheels car, alongside the path for your child to find.

Camping Out • LF

Camping allows us to step outside of the mainstream of life and have quiet spaces to just be. No manmade toy can compete with kids using their imaginations while playing with natural objects such as pinecones, leaves, and stones. Even teens can get a lot out of finding special rocks in a river-side camp or whittling downed branches into "spears."

Tenting also offers us opportunities to teach our kids about fire safety, the proper use of a knife, water purification, and a host of other topics that will serve them throughout life.

Sleeping under the stars is good for us as parents, too! Freed from the restraints of everyday life, it's easy to let our playful side out. In all of the camping excursions with my daughter,

Kirsten, we revel in the beauty around us, go exploring and try to identify plants, look for signs of animals, and deal with the occasional challenge. Once, I forgot to pack the fuel canister for our camp stove, but as a result, we met nice campsite neighbors who, oddly enough, had brought along three stoves!

Just be sure to get your kids out into nature as young as possible. Barbara says: "If kids aren't used to camping, they can be intimidated by the power of the mountains and the weather. At nighttime the wind might be howling in the trees. It might take several camping trips for kids to lose their fear of the intensity of the outdoors, so be sure to start young."

Hot Tip! It's a good idea to reserve a campsite in a national park far in advance, preferably six months to a year, as spots fill up fast.

If you're sold on the idea, but you haven't tented since you were a kid, where do you start? To dip your toe into the waters, it's easiest to start with car camping rather than backpacking, since you won't have to shoulder heavy packs with all of your gear. Also you can carry more creature comforts than you could on foot. Better yet, you can more easily move along if the weather takes a turn for the worse.

State and provincial camping guidebooks are an invaluable resource, offering detailed listings for regional, state (or provincial), and national campgrounds throughout North America. To book a campsite in Canada, visit the Parks Canada website; for camping in the United States, visit the National Park Service website or Recreation.gov (www.recreation.gov).

It can be expensive to travel abroad; by staying in campgrounds, you can keep your lodging expenses low. Nearly every country has its own website filled with campground information.

Research carefully, however. Some nations have very different ideas about back-to-nature fun. Italians, for example, favor thumping discos at many of their sites!

Hot Tip! Before plunging into a major camping expedition, do a practice campout at a local site, to work out the bugs and ensure that you'll be well prepared.

There are typically lots of kids for your children to play with at campgrounds. While these areas are usually quite safe, it's best not to take chances. Unless your child is old enough to be responsible for herself, say around the tween years, be sure to tag along with her and her new friends. You never know when the group of kids may return to their campsites, and you won't want your child to be left unaccompanied. If a fellow camper offers to watch your child along with his, trust your instincts and decline the offer if the situation doesn't seem right.

If you stay at a campground with hosts, there's an added measure of security, as it's their job to help out when needed. Sometimes hosts will go above and beyond to lend assistance, as Liz and her daughter, Nell, found on their Southwest road trip.

"Every campsite along the way was full, but we drove into one anyway, and the campground hosts, a retired couple, were sitting at their trailer," Liz says. "I told them: 'We know you're full. It's just the two of us, though. We're tired, and we'll pay whatever. We just need a small spot.'" They invited mother and daughter to pitch their tent at their site, and within hours Nell was calling them Auntie Norma and Uncle Bill. "That night they made a huge campfire and called friends from other campsites over to meet us—and the next morning they made a huge breakfast and included us! It's amazing how the world opens up to you when you're in need," Liz recalls.

Hot Tip! Teens like to have their own private spaces, so check to see if your child would like for you to pack an extra tent just for her.

One of the most convenient camping options for families—especially ones with small children—is to stay at a campground that offers huts, yurts, or small cabins. These offer more conveniences than just bunk beds and a roof over your head. Some even come equipped with running water, a refrigerator, and a microwave. These types of facilities are especially valuable for families who fly to a camping destination, as you can leave the tent and sleeping pads at home.

Stacia C. took her children on a road trip to national parks in the western U.S. As often as possible, they stayed in KOA (Kampgrounds of America) facilities, which have camping cabins. Most also have a swimming pool, laundry facilities, and free Internet access. "The camping cabins at KOA were dandy," Stacia says, "and each campground was like a little community, with fun things for the kids to do. At Devil's Tower National Monument in Wyoming, the campground management rigged up a big-screen TV and showed *Close Encounters of the Third Kind*. The kids loved it!"

For a listing of campgrounds with yurts in Canada, the United States, Mexico, Costa Rica, and Panama, see Pacific Yurts, Inc. (www.yurts.com).

Water Sports • MD

A photo of a toddler playing in the sand on a blue-sky summer day is a quintessential memento from any family vacation in the sun. As kids get older, beach fun expands to include every-thing from volleyball or Frisbee to snorkeling, boogie board-ing, sea kayaking, surfing, and scuba diving. Encouraging your child to try out a new activity builds confidence and indepen-dence. Doing something new and daring together is a fabulous bonding opportunity.

Confidence in the water is very important. If you're planning a beach vacation and your child isn't a strong, confident swim-mer, consider investing in some lessons for a few months be-fore you go.

Snorkeling • MD — Snorkeling is a great parent-and-child activity. A kid as young as five can pull on a snorkel, mask, and flippers and hold your hand as you kick over a reef near the shore. You can snorkel in many locations in the U.S., in-cluding Hawaii, Florida, Virginia, the Carolinas, Texas, and the Great Lakes (brrr). Top worldwide locations include Mexico's Caribbean coast and Baja, California; Australia; Belize; many Caribbean islands; and Thailand.

Retail stores that sell scuba-diving equipment usually carry some kids' gear for snorkeling. If there isn't a dive shop in your neighborhood, check out Divers Supply (www.divers-supply.com) or Dive Booty (www.divebooty.com). Products by Oceanways, ScubaMax, and U.S. Divers—popular manu-facturers of snorkeling and scuba equipment for adults and children—are available on these websites. Equipment rental is also an option. Research ahead of time to find an outfit-ter and verify that it stocks equipment for children. Rental equipment can be poorly maintained, and a leaky mask or flippers that don't fit well will hamper your child's snorkel-ing fun. Make sure you examine the equipment before you leave the store. Test the mask by holding it to your face with

3. IDEA GENERATOR: ADVENTURE

the strap hanging loose. You should be able to keep it in place by inhaling slowly.

For first-timers, it may take a while for your child get used to using a mask and snorkel. If you've purchased your own equipment, practice at a local pool before you go on vacation. If you've rented equipment, test drive it in shallow water or the resort pool before going out into the ocean. Make all the adjustments necessary while you stand in the pool or on the shore.

For an unfogged view, spit into your mask, then smear the liquid over the plastic lens. Quickly dip it in the ocean to cut the yuck factor!

When you snorkel with a younger child, hold hands at all times. It's safer, and you're providing most of the power so she won't get tired so easily. It will also allow you both to watch fish for a longer period of time.

If wind or rain blows up, you can get into difficulty quickly. In tropical areas, midafternoon rain and windstorms are common. Pay attention to the time and the weather on the horizon when you're getting into the water. Make sure someone on the shore knows where you plan to swim and when you expect to return. Take frequent breaks from the underwater show to check the weather conditions. If you do get into difficulty, keep calm and swim toward shore.

Scuba Diving • MD — *Scuba* stands for "self-contained underwater breathing apparatus." You may think of it as primarily an adult activity, but there are programs that teach children as young as eight years old how to use scuba equipment. Dive shacks are prolific at most beach resorts worldwide. If the ocean in that area is divable, some enterprising soul will have opened a shop to rent equipment, provide facilities for trained divers, offer classes for newbies, and lead excursions.

When my older son, Cillian, then aged ten, took his first dive in the ocean, he was so slight that his air tank dwarfed him as he tried to climb into the boat. Thankfully, when he was in the water, buoyancy took over, and the tank floated at his back (attached to his buoyancy control device). We were staying on the Yucatán Peninsula in Mexico, and our dive sites were between the coast and the island of Cozumel. Even though the reefs were showing some ill effects from the ravaging by Hurricane Wilma the previous year, there were still abundant fish, turtles, and sharks. My son still describes it as one of his greatest experiences.

There are five main scuba diving instruction organizations:

- PADI: Professional Association of Diving Instructors (Worldwide), www.padi.com

- SSI: Scuba Schools International (North America and Southeast Asia), www.divessi.com

- NAUI: National Association of Underwater Instructors (North America), www.naui.org

- BSAC: British Sub Aqua Club (U.K. and Europe), www.bsac.com

- CMAS: Confédération Mondiale des Activités Subaquatiques (Europe), www.cmas.org

Each of these organizations teaches similar material and techniques, though they each maintain their own training standards and certification requirements. However, an open-water diver certification card (C-card) issued by one agency is generally accepted by the others. Most dive operators require that you show your C-card before they rent equipment to you. PADI, the largest agency, has a presence at most dive destinations worldwide, and offers courses for children.

3. IDEA GENERATOR: ADVENTURE

In many beach towns and resorts worldwide, short, introductory courses are offered by one or more of these agencies. These include one or two days of learning how to use the equipment in a pool or shallow beach area, and then simple tests with the equipment under water.

These exams are to make sure you are competent and confident with the gear. The final step is to participate in an open-water dive. The descent will be limited in time and depth, and upon completion you will not be a fully certified diver. For children ten and older, this kind of course is a great introduction to scuba. And, it's a fairly inexpensive way to try out the sport.

PADI offers two different discovery courses for eight-to-ten-year-olds: Bubblemaker and Seal Team. The courses are pool-based, introducing your child to scuba equipment and letting her try it out for herself, with some fun and games thrown in. She won't yet be able to participate in any open-water diving, but it's still a fun way to learn about what the adults are doing in a hands-on way.

If you and your child (twelve +) want to dive for longer periods and at greater depths, you must be a certified open-water diver. You can either plan to spend the first three to five days of your vacation completing a full course, or you can undertake the coursework prior to your trip and do the water tests when you get there ("known as a tropical referral"). Most of the agencies support the latter approach by providing course material online or on DVD for your family to study prior to your vacation. However, switching instructors can disrupt the learning process, and two-step certifications usually are more expensive

Surfing • MD — Surfing is called the "Sport of Kings" because, in Hawaii, it was the royalty who were the champions. It is extremely popular in warmer coastal areas like Hawaii,

California, and Australia, but there are surfers even on the chilly Washington and New Jersey coasts—not to mention the west coast of Ireland. No doubt, it's much easier to introduce your child to surfing in warm weather and water.

Most surfing schools run two-hour lessons. The price usually includes a surfboard rental, a leash, shoes, and a rash guard. Class begins on the beach, where you learn some surfing vocabulary and practice working with your board. Those experts we see on TV make it look so easy, but it can be tricky to pop up and balance on a nine-foot longboard even on the sand. Next, your instructor will take you into the water, where you get to try out your new skills by catching waves. Surfing is tremendous fun, but it is highly unlikely that you'll manage more than a minute or two upright on your board after just one lesson. With younger children, it's a good idea to set these expectations up front so they are not disappointed.

Since you spend so much time lying on your board waiting to catch a wave, you need to be particularly careful about sunburn. The rash guard—a thin shirt of spandex, nylon, or polyester—will protect your upper body, but if you're not wearing a good waterproof sunscreen and long shorts, you could end up with an unpleasant reminder of your surfing lesson. (See Chapter 12, "Health and Safety," for information on sun-protective clothing and products.)

Surfing America (www.surfingamerica.org) is the national governing body for the sport in the U.S. They provide a list of member schools on their website.

Surf camps are popular in most developed coastal areas. These are typically weeklong programs that your child can attend as a day or overnight student. For younger age groups (six through ten), the focus will be on learning about the beach, the sea, marine life, and boogie boarding. Boogie boards are shorter than surfboards, rectangular in shape, and made from hydro-dynamic foam. These are easier for beginners and young children to manipulate. The ocean safety component—learning how to identify different types of currents—is a good foundation for any open-water sport. Camps for older children focus on gaining a deeper knowledge of the sport, and improving skill and performance. In some areas, you can find courses that parents and children can take together. That is definitely a recipe for an exhilarating few days with your kids.

Boating • LF — Since youngsters love being in water so much, a boating vacation is a crowd pleaser. The beauty is that your vessel can carry you to gorgeous places that are off the tourism path, where you can experience the natural world. There's something magical about viewing whales and porpoises as they leap alongside your boat, or splashing in sparkly green phosphorescence at night, far from the lights of the city.

The kid who has set the course of a sailboat or helped paddle in a double kayak is the kid who can think of herself as competent and a lover of adventure, ultimately building confidence.

Hot Tip! Keep a close eye on the weather forecast for your destination prior to your arrival. If there is any possibility of a storm during your excursion (if a small-craft warning is predicted), it's vital to cancel your boating plans and choose another activity.

Sailing • LF — Sailing is one of the most popular ways to enjoy a vacation on the water. While learning can be a fabulous family experience, you don't have to crack the books to enjoy a skimming the waves. Numerous sailboat charters offer trips along waterways around the world. These companies typically offer boats with a skipper (the most expensive option, but good if you aren't interested in learning to sail beforehand), or bareboat rentals. With the latter, you can just cast off and go wherever you want; you don't have to share your boat with a stranger. Bareboat charters save money, but you must provide documentation that you have successfully completed a sailing course.

If you're lucky enough to live near the water, you may even consider taking lessons as a family, then putting your new skills to use on an excursion. There are numerous websites dedicated to sailboat charters; for starters, check out Charter World (www.charterworld.com).

Houseboating • LF — Houseboating is a bit like traveling in an RV, since you have the chance to explore interesting places, yet your conveyance is also your home. This offers quality family time for swimming, fishing, and sightseeing. The activity's perfect for reunions and parties, as houseboats frequently sleep eight or more people. One of the most kid-friendly elements is being able to jump into the water right off the deck!

Lake Powell, on the Colorado River, is a classic U.S. houseboating locale. Deep blue waters here lap at the base of brilliant orange cliffs. At night, boaters can choose to sleep on a beach under the stars or be lulled on the waters of the Glen Canyon National Recreation Area. Shuswap Lake, in British Columbia, is one of the best options for houseboating in Canada. The lake has 620 miles of shoreline with twenty-five marine parks—and the average water temperature is a pleasant 72° F during the summer.

Check out Houseboating.org (www.houseboating.org) for rental listings throughout the United States; Gordon's Guide (www.gordonsguide.com) also covers Canada. All About Houseboats (www.all-about-houseboats.com) lists companies around the world, including countries such as Africa and India.

The European cousin of houseboating is barging or canal boating. More than 250 years ago, an extensive system of waterways was built to transport goods throughout England, France, Germany, and the Netherlands. Upstaged by highways, these canals now mainly delight recreational boaters.

Barges floating down the Rhine River take in the spectacular medieval castles, vineyards, and pastoral landscapes. In England, narrowboats drift through canals or rivers, occasionally passing through self-operated locks or even soaring high in the air on ancient aqueducts. One of the most exciting ones to traverse is the Pontcysyllte, which carries barges high over the River Dee Valley in northeast Wales. At more than 1,000 feet long and 126 feet high, it's the longest and highest aqueduct in Britain.

Narrowboats are long and skinny (typically six feet wide) that were designed to fit into narrow locks or aqueducts. Some canal boats can hold up to twelve people. Most self-catering models contain cook stoves, refrigerators, showers, and pump-out toilets. Pilots stand in the stern, navigating with a tiller usually, rather than a wheel. Easy to grasp, this skill only grows tricky when you're entering a lock two inches wider than the boat— or approaching a manual lift-bridge. There the driver idles back, while the crew scampers down the bank and hangs off the bridge's "handles," using their bodies as counterweights. Narrowboaters traitionally moor beside countryside pubs for relaxing lunches after all this excitement.

If you take a guided tour, you unpack only once, and all meals are prepared for you. The boats travel at approximately three miles per hour—about the same pace as walking—so you can explore alongside, then return to the boat. This is perfect for families, giving kids a chance to burn off some energy, yet "home" is mere steps away. See Boating Holidays (www.boatingholidays.com) for listings of European barge tours.

Kimm S. and her husband and young daughter went on a canal-boat tour of the Netherlands, from Amsterdam to Rotterdam. Each day while the barge was making its way to its destination town, Kimm and her family would bike twenty-five to forty miles alongside the canal, then rejoin the vessel at its evening stop. If they grew weary partway through the day, they would just catch a train back to the boat. "We biked through beautiful countryside, with windmills, lots of farm fields, and small towns with great cafes. The entire route was on dedicated bike paths, so we didn't have to deal with traffic," Kimm says. "The food was incredibly good, and our cabin was comfortable. It was a really fun way to sightsee and be active."

Rafting • LF — On a float trip down the Yakima River in Washington, we drifted down quiet stretches with sagebrush-dotted hillsides, where colorful goldfinches darted and a deer paused to watch us. We yelled, "yahoo!" as riffles bucked the craft up and down. At a low bluff, locals were jumping off into a current that was running fast through a deep, green pool. We tied up and joined the fun. Our daughter's friend Aqua jumped in as we cheered. "You know when you chew mint gum, and you get that burst of freshness? I got that tingly feeling through my whole body!" he said.

Rafting can range from slow-moving float trips that offer plenty of chances to get out and explore the landscape, to heart-thumping whitewater experiences. Before you commit, consider the ages and temperaments of your children, then start slowly with a relaxing float trip.

Be sure to ask lots of questions about the quality of the experience before you book. One key piece of information is the tour's difficulty ranking on the international river classification system, which ranges from Class I (easy) to Class VI (extreme and exploratory). The California Whitewater Rafting Association (CWRA, www.c-w-r.com) does a good job of explaining the variables. Key on "classifications" to find the charts.

CWRA has a list of the best rafting rivers in California, Oregon, and several others states; for other locations, do an online search for your destination. For worldwide rafting opportunities, check out Gordon's Guide to Whitewater Rafting (www.whitewateradvertures.com), which features rafting companies in places as diverse as Morocco, Siberia, and Fiji.

Always check out the safety record of a rafting company. You can start by inquiring how long the company has been in business, then ask how they train guides and how long your specific leader has been running the river. Finally, do a visual inspection of the rafts and gear. If you sense alarm bells at any point, choose not to participate. And, of course, if all is well, be sure you and your kids wear life vests for the entire excursion, no matter how hot or uncomfortable they may be.

Kayaking • LF — Sea kayaking vacations offer numerous family teamwork opportunities, and give kids a chance to challenge themselves. Additionally, the locales, such as the Baja Peninsula, New Zealand, or the rain-forested islands of British Columbia, are often spectacular. In a sea kayak, your child can spend days outdoors experiencing the gentle rolling of waves along a shoreline, as she gets close to droopy-limbed, purple sea stars or the majestic fin of an orca slicing through the water. And when it's time to climb out of the boat, the beach becomes a playground.

Sea, or touring, kayaks are made for the open waters of lakes, bays, and oceans. They are narrow, long boats with a covered deck, and kayakers use a double-bladed paddle. Touring kayaks are maneuverable, fairly fast, and have good cargo capacity for stowing camping gear for overnight or lengthier excursions.

Double kayaks are more stable and easier for parent-child paddling teams. In a double, young kids can have a lot of fun splashing you on a hot day or sitting back and watching the scenery unfold while you do the work. Yet when you need to undertake a crossing or get somewhere on a schedule, kid-power will help you get going. There are even triple kayaks available, for two parents and a child.

While you don't need to know how to kayak in order to participate in a guided trip, you'll get a lot more out of the excursion if you and your children enroll in a course prior to your journey. You'll learn important safety techniques; it will save you and your children from sore shoulders; and your kids will likely be more invested in the enterprise. If you plan to go on a several-day excursion, it's very important to take lessons, so you can be well prepared when on the water.

Hot Tip! Unless you and your children have learned kayak-exiting techniques (in case of capsizing), do not use a spray skirt to cover the cockpit and keep paddle drips off yourselves. This way you can easily exit the craft in an emergency.

You'll find countless kayaking tour operators listed online. *Canoe & Kayak* magazine (www.canoekayak.com) can help highlight the best outfitters, along with Gorp (www.gorp.com) and National Geographic Adventure (www.adventure.nationalgeographic.com).

Hot Tip! If you are planning a self-guided kayaking or canoeing trip with your family, you'll need to acquire a map of boat put-in and take-out spots from a paddling tour operator or rental shop. Ask if nautical charts and time tables are recommended.

Canoeing • LF — Canoeing is frequently the entry to boating, as it's fairly easy to find rental facilities on lakes, and these boats are relatively stable, making it easy to take even babies and toddlers along. Canoes work best on lakes and slow-moving rivers. You can easily fit up to three family members and lots of gear into a vessel, making these craft ideal for camping.

You can't expect to travel far in a canoe the way you could in a kayak, since they're slower and less agile. Yet they don't require specialized knowledge, if you wish to head out for an overnight trip. Still, read up on safety precautions and talk to an outfitter about additional measures prior to setting out for any boating trip, even if it's just for an hour.

Canoeing vacations allow you to access more remote, quiet areas; in many rivers or lakes, there are special sections or parks set aside for non-motorized boats. You'll be able to slip past onshore wildlife nearly undetected, so be sure to pack binoculars for this type of trip.

There are myriad options for canoeing: a strenuous expedition portaging among a string of lakes, a placid float trip down a river, guided or self-guided tours. You can canoe in Finland's extensive lake system, in Canada's Boundary Waters, or maybe in Florida's Everglades. It's best to start by figuring out what geographic area you would like to canoe in, then using a search engine to locate outfitters.

Tammy H.'s Story

We were out in the kayaks, getting up close to sea lions when we came upon a tug pulling a string of hundreds of logs. Seeing things you wouldn't see from shore is part of the fun of kayaking. In harbors we met an entirely different culture of people who live on boats for the summer. It was fun to pull up to a dock with a little café on the end of it, and to climb out and go eat.

We made sure to teach our kids the basics. Where we live, there are a lot of kids' kayaking classes. Before setting out on a longer trip, we did day trips in our two doubles. Building up the kids' confidence as they learn is important.

We stay close to shore as much as we can. Sometimes, the kids are intimidated by situations we face on the water. Our kids would look at a long crossing and bubbling water, and say, "I don't think we should cross." I'd say, "We'll give it a try, and if it doesn't seem right, we'll skirt back around." If you put them in a situation that's too scary, they won't go again. Even if you, as an adult, could do it, why would you want to put your kids through it?

I haven't let them be in the stern yet to steer, but I'm looking forward to that challenge for them. When they learn the process, they're more connected to an activity.

Horsing Around • LF

A dust cloud whirled up from the heels of Denny, my daughter's horse-for-a-week, as she nudged her heels against his flanks, aiming him at a series of vertical poles. She pulled back on the reins, and he skidded to a near stop, then deftly dodged left around a pole, and immediately right around the next, then left again. Wheeling at the end of the slalom course, he repeated his steps, then ran full out to the start line. A cheer rose up from the temporary cowpokes perched on the top rail of the paddock.

Spending one-on-one time with a horse is the dream of numerous children who grew up reading *The Black Stallion* and *Misty of Chincoteague*. My pre-teen daughter was the impetus for this adventure. Like many girls, she had been collecting pony figures, books, and posters since she could first say the word *horse*.

Guest ranches—ranging from rustic to luxurious—abound in the Western U.S., Mexico, and Canada. There, the days are filled with active outdoor pursuits, and evenings often feature theme nights such as barbeques or moonlit wagon rides. In addition, many ranches are geared toward children, offering experiences ranging from horseback games to story time with an authentic cowboy.

Hot Tip! Take your horse-loving child on a themed vacation, planning the route to take advantage of stables in a given region that offer trail rides.

Before making reservations, consider your family's riding experience and the ages of your children. Some dude ranches have a daily children's program that keeps the younger kids happy wading in creeks or playing in teepees, while older ones are off on horseback. Tweens or teens may rebel at the thought of being part of a plodding, dusty procession on a designated route each day, so look for a dude ranch that offers individual rides. Some offer excursions such as river float trips, fishing, or hiking. A couple of long days in the saddle could quickly cure your children of the romance of horseback riding, and they'll long for other alternatives.

When booking, consider the size of the ranch. They range from small enterprises, where you feel like part of an extended family, to immense operations with crowds waiting to saddle up each day. The smaller outfits typically offer a more authentic experience.

Riding horses is a dusty affair, and you'll need several changes of clothing. Be sure to pack plenty of jeans, long-sleeved shirts, and English riding boots or cowboy boots (along with knee-high, padded socks). You'll need footwear with heels, so your boots don't slip through the stirrups. Some ranches stock boots for their guests; at others you'll need to take your own, so check prior to heading out. At most horseback-riding facilities, helmets are mandatory for children. They're usually available to rent or buy onsite, but again, make sure. Also pack safety straps for sunglasses—Croakies is a popular brand—so gear doesn't fall off in a fast-moving situation.

Hot Tip! Pack a bandanna for each family member. Other than jumping in and wading in the water, there's nothing that beats tying a cool, wet cloth around your neck when you stop at a creek during a hot, sweaty ride.

Hit the Slopes • MD

One of my very favorite sights is the warm, healthy glow on the face of a child after a day on the slopes. That, and the treat of the winter sun shining through a cloud-break at the mountain-top, is worth the expense of a lift pass. My family enjoys ski vacations, even though it may take wheedling, cajoling, and unprecedented levels of organization for us to get out the door in the morning. At day's end, our boys invariably fall into bed happy and tired, no matter where we're staying.

There are ski resorts all over the world—even an indoor slope in Dubai!—but not all are equal in terms of terrain or amenities. For a successful family ski vacation, the quality of the facilities can be more important than the quality of snow. Family-oriented resorts provide ski schools with programs for children as young as eighteen months, discounted passes for children under sixteen, areas zoned for "family skiing," and terrain parks intended for kids.

Snowboarding is another option, especially popular with tweens and teens. The initial learning curve is less steep than skiing's. So this sport can serve as a great introduction to the slopes.

Planning-wise, first choose the region you want to visit, for example, the Alps, the Rockies, the northeastern U.S., or maybe even Korea. You will probably find multiple resorts in that region. The Lake Tahoe area of California and Nevada, for instance, has fifteen different ski resorts!

Hot Tip! Look for activities that are not dependent on snow, like indoor swimming pools, bowling alleys, or movie theaters, so you can have a fun vacation even if the weather isn't cooperating.

Booking engines like Expedia (www.expedia.com) and Orbitz (www.orbitz.com) have a "ski trip" section—usually under the tabs "Activities" or "Packages"—where you can book special ski-vacation bundles. Travel companies such as Ski.com (www.ski.com) focus exclusively on ski trips. The larger resorts have their own websites that include travel planning and reservation options.

For skiing, warmth tops everything else. If your child is too cold, she (and you) will be miserable. Dress her in multiple layers: long underwear, a fleece or wool second layer, and an outer layer of padded, waterproof skiwear. Land's End (www. landsend.com) and REI (www.rei.com) stock affordable options. Gloves or mittens are critical, and ski helmets imperative. At sporting goods and resort stores, look for specialty products like HotHands to keep little fingers and toes warm.

Keep extra HotHands in your pockets for later use. They can save the day if the wind is a little too cold or the lift lines a little too long for your little snow warrior.

If you have enrolled your child in ski school, keep her personality in mind and consider a back-up childcare plan if necessary.

Hot Tip! Look for ski resorts where children ski free with a paying adult or lift tickets for those under twelve are reduced in price.

Cross-Country Skiing • LF — For a child who's initially reluctant to try downhill skiing, cross-country can help her gain confidence. Also know as "Nordic," this style is a wonderful family-togetherness experience, since you can ski alongside your child on groomed tracks (stepping aside to let others pass, of course). The sport doesn't have the learning curve of downhill, and no lessons are needed. At its simplest, it's an exhilarating, gliding walk through wintry landscapes, where you can look for animal tracks in the snow and cheer each other on as you slide down small slopes. Even preschoolers can be successful if you choose a beginner-level trail.

As with downhill skiing, it might be best to rent skis, boots, and poles for your children. Buying can be cost prohibitive, unless you're avid skiers, as kids will grow out of the equipment every year. The clothing for a cross-country expedition is

Things to Keep in Mind When Choosing a Ski Resort • MD

1. Childcare facilities. Not all resorts have nurseries for infants. Even where such facilities are available, advance reservations are usually required, since availability is limited.

2. Ski schools. Most mountains have some form of ski school. Look for one that advertises lessons as "Kids' Clubs" or "Kids' Programs." For younger children, seek out small group sizes and half-day lesson options paired with a suitable childcare program.

3. Resort layout. For ease and comfort, choose a resort where all the off-mountain facilities are clustered in a village-type location at the peak's base. Select accommodations that have convenient access to services. Get a copy of a resort map either from the resort website or by calling guest services in advance.

4. Terrain. Just like resort maps, mountain or terrain maps are also usually available online or from guest services. A good one will provide information on the size of the resort, the amount of skiable area, the number of lifts, and the number of runs that are available of each type, coded as easy (green), medium (blue), and difficult (black).

quite different from that worn in downhill skiing, however. A down parka or snowsuit would be way too hot; think, instead, of breathable layers, such as long underwear, a fleece, and a waterproof shell, top and bottom. Similarly, pack a lighter hat and gloves or mittens, so that your child doesn't overheat. Do, however, bring warmer clothing in daypacks for rest breaks.

Outdoor stores carry foam pads to serve as seats in the snow during pauses. Be sure to carry along one for each family

5. Accommodation. Most ski resorts provide a variety of accommodation types, from hotel rooms to condos and houses. Check a resort map before you book, so that you know how accessible your accommodations are from the facilities.

6. Pricing. Skiing is expensive. You can pay up to ninety dollars for a daily lift ticket at some of the major U.S. resorts. Ticket prices will vary across resorts within a region and over time during a ski season. The changes in rates are often based on holidays and school closures. Christmas is most expensive for both lift tickets and accommodations. Rental prices, however, do not usually vary during a season.

7. Additional activities. Consider whether the resort has other activities, such as cross-country skiing, snow tubing, snowmobiling, sleigh rides, and snowshoeing.

8. Equipment rental. If your kids are new to skiing, consider renting equipment until you're sure the sport is for them. To save money, look for a retailer in your neighborhood, which should have cheaper rates than at the resort. However, if you are flying, keep in mind that your airline may charge additional fees for odd-sized baggage.

member. There won't be any slope-side cafes when you're cross-country skiing, so pack a lunch, snacks, and plenty to drink.

Hot Tip! To ensure that cross-country trails remain just as enjoyable for the next skiers, you'll need to remind your children that natural areas need to stay natural: No "decorating the snow" by carving their names into it or shaking the snow off bushes with their poles.

There are many destinations to get you and your kids kicking and gliding through snow-cloaked forests. For tips on family cross-country expeditions and links to ski areas around the world, visit Cross-Country Ski World (www.xcskiworld.com).

Biking • LF

Biking is a wonderful alternative to viewing the countryside through the windows of a car, bus, or train. It's a great way for children and parents to get some exercise while traveling, to enjoy valuable outdoors time, and to experience the sights and scents of a place close-up. Cycling's also a welcome breather after tramping through city streets for hours. Kids just need to move. And bike riding brings a grin to nearly any child's face.

European culture has historically embraced bicycling in earnest; there are numerous gorgeous regions that are easy to explore via pedal power, and complete networks of cycle paths. Among the countries with off-road paths are Belgium, Denmark, and the Netherlands, which are ideal for riding, with their charming small towns.

Even countries that don't have dedicated bike routes have regions that are ideal for family bike trips. Many of these areas are just under the radar of most tourists, so you'll likely have a more enriching experience, as well. In the United States, the West Coast and the Northeast are bike-friendly. France, Italy, Ireland, and New Zealand are also well known as popular cycling destinations.

Some major cities have dedicated bike lanes, too. Check out your destination online to see if it's easy to cycle there. "Our kids aren't good at walking in big cities," Sarah C. says. "If we have bikes, we can cover way more terrain. Renting bikes is always easier for us, especially in a town like Munich, which has

Best Places for Biking • LF

To get a taste of some of the places that work well for biking, check out:

- Worldwide: Trento Bike (www.trentobike.org)
- Northern Europe: Cycletourer (www.cycletourer.co.uk)
- Austria: Cycle Tours in Austria (www.radtouren.at)
- Germany: Bicycle Germany (www.bicyclegermany.com)
- Switzerland: Cycling in Switzerland (www.cycling-in-switzerland.ch)
- New Zealand: Cycle New Zealand (www.cyclenewzealand.com)
- North America: Adventure Cycling Association (www.adventurecycling.org)

big, broad boulevards. The sidewalks are really wide, and they have a bike lane on the sidewalk so you can ride off the road. Everybody rides old clunkers with baskets—you see nuns on bikes, businessmen on bikes. On a bike our kids feel more independent, and we get to see lots more."

No matter what the ages and ability levels of your family are, there is a bike option that will work for you. Not every rental company will be geared toward options for children, so research to find the right outfitter. It's important to plan ahead and contact a rental shop before you embark, to be sure it has what you need.

In some central European countries, train stations rent out bicycles. Sometimes you can even pick up a bike at one station and drop it off at another. These services rent out only standard

3 · IDEA GENERATOR: ADVENTURE

69

models, so your children would need to be large enough to ride an adult-sized bike.

If you have very young children (eight months to four years), a bike trailer is the way to go. These are easy to pull behind your cycle; they're waterproof in case of rain; they're exceptionally comfortable for the passengers; and they offer a sense of security and home-away-from-home for your little ones. There's also plenty of space for extra clothing, water and snacks, a tire pump, and any other items you may need.

For preschoolers or a child who isn't quite ready for biking solo, a Trail-A-Bike is a great invention. This clever device is a single wheel, with seat and handlebars, which attaches via a tow bar to the rear of your frame. A Trail-A-Bike works great for kids who want to actively participate in biking but who do not yet have all the skills to ride at a regular pace. You benefit from your child's pedal power, and the whole contraption is surprisingly stable and easy for you to pull.

The Trail-Gator is another option. It's a tow bar that allows you to attach your child's bike to the back of yours. Trail-Gators are terrific for touring, and once you get to your night's destination, you can unhitch your child's bike so she can use it on her own.

When planning a family bike-riding expedition of any length, you'll need to strike a balance between your children's capabilities and your expectations. This is a time to be realistic, taking into account your child's physical and emotional states along with her bike-riding ability. It's best to plan for contingencies, so that you have options for turning back or shortening a ride if anything goes awry.

Safety has to be your top concern. All bike riders (including parents) should wear properly fitted and adjusted helmets.

Test this by trying to tip the helmet back. If it easily slides off, it needs to be tightened—but also be sure it's comfortable. Check over any rental bikes to be sure the brakes are functioning properly and the tires are fully inflated and have plenty of tread on them. Review with your children the rules of the road, and ride with the youngsters between two adults, if possible. If it's just you and your children, have them ride ahead of you, with the oldest in the lead.

Jill H. and her husband have six kids, and biking runs in their blood. They have biked in twenty-five countries and almost every Western state. "There is a lot of planning to be done before leaving home, starting with phone calls to the bike shops in the area where you plan to ride. You need to be sure you know what the terrain is; you need to be sure you have the right equipment for that terrain; and you need to get guidebooks and plan routes according to the difficulty of the area," she explains. "If you're not prepared, you can waste half your morning, and it can ruin the experience for your kids, so it's really important to do advance planning.

"People who are used to only biking around their hometown may have no idea what it's like to bike on thick, muddy clay or in areas with thorns, where you need tire sealant in your tires. On one trip, we flatted out seven times because we weren't prepared," she says. Simply by checking in with local bike shops, you can get the local expertise needed to help prepare for the terrain and conditions.

If you'll be embarking on an overnight or days-long excursion, you can carry all your camping gear in panniers attached to your bike. Check ahead to see if you can rent panniers or if you'll need to take your own with you.

For families who would prefer more hands-on help, bike-tour operators around the world do all of the route planning and provide everything needed, including the cycles, food, and lodging. Tours are especially helpful for families with young children, who may not have the stamina to keep up on a full day's bike ride. They typically offer a support and gear (SAG) wagon that drives the route with the luggage and picks up stragglers—children or parents who become fatigued and would like a lift to the evening's destination. While more expensive than do-it-yourself tours, these offer comfort and convenience, which are bound to make your trip more of a vacation.

Adventure Travel • LF

Whether or not you were brought up journeying off the beaten path, it's never too late to jump into the excitement of adventure travel with your children. By their very nature, most kids thrive on active outdoor adventures. Trips that include bike riding, kayaking, rafting, canoeing, horse or llama packing, or zip-line fun are sure to be kid pleasers. If you include at least some active outdoor element in your travel plans, you can feel satisfied that you're exposing your children to the confidence that comes from an adventurous undertaking.

You'll quickly discover that "adventure travel" has no set definition; it can range from a multi-day safari to an afternoon dog-sled outing. The good news is that a little action goes a long way with kids! You can just sign up for a day trip wherever you're traveling, to enjoy a bit of the wild side.

Hot Tip! With adventure travel, start with an activity at which you know your children can succeed. If your goal is to get your kids out on a multi-day backpacking excursion, for instance, begin with a short hike.

When Joanne D. and her son, Bryce, were traveling through northern Laos, they found that the bigger cities all had guided tours of waterfalls or caves available. They chose a cave adventure. "We sat on an inner tube in a river and pulled ourselves along by a rope," Joanne recalls. "We ducked through a mossy opening, then we hooked our feet underneath the tubes to stay together. We were wearing headlamps that illuminated amazing limestone formations inside the cave. It was utterly cool, and Bryce loved it!"

Hot Tip! Trust your instincts, and don't be hesitant to ask lots of questions when arranging adventure travel. Ensure that your children will be safe and that all their needs will be met on an excursion.

If money isn't an obstacle, adventure-travel companies offer daydream-worthy trips to the farthest corners of our planet. Several that cater to families are Mountain Travel Sobek (www.mtsobek.com), a pioneer in family adventure travel; G.A.P. Adventures (www.gapadventures.com), specializing in low-impact, sustainable, small-group trips worldwide; and Adventure Travel (www.adventure.travel), with an immense list of expeditions.

As complicated and demanding as it can be to arrange for and go on active trips with your children, the frustrations and challenges will dissipate when you see their excitement. And in my book, nothing tops having a child who gains boldness and confidence in something they didn't think they could do. Today, my daughter's favorite T-shirt says: "Row, row, row your boat, gently down a raging, bone-crushing, life-threatening, class-V stream, merrily, merrily, merrily, merrily, life is but a dream." I couldn't be prouder.

3. IDEA GENERATOR: ADVENTURE

Lisa M.'s Story

In Ecuador, my kids got a real thrill zip-lining through a cloud forest. It was a mile hike to get to the zip-line—a long hike for them, but it whetted their appetite for more. We climbed to the top of a tower and got harnessed in, then we zoomed through the lush cloud forest high above a creek. It was a little buggy and hot, but so worth it.

After, it was so hot, we did a one-hour float down the Mindo River to cool everyone off. Our kids are used to whitewater rafting, so they held on tight when the guide yelled, "*seguro* (secure)!"

We stayed at Sachatamia Lodge, on an ecological reserve, which had hummingbird feeders all over, with identification guides. My son, especially, is into birds, so he had a great time identifying the various species—all of them were so beautiful.

Later on our trip, we learned at an education center about the area's endangered Andean condors. And we visited a butterfly garden. There was so much wildlife for them to see. When we stayed at Hacienda San Agustin de Callo in Lasso, our kids got to feed the llamas in the courtyard every night. And they just loved the dogs at all of the haciendas.

On Safari • LF

Safaris seem custom-made for kids, with the drama of searching for big game and opportunities to see the raw power of nature up close and personal. They are fabulous as long as your children are old enough to handle long days in a vehicle with potentially few animal sightings. Also, they need to stay quiet when asked—which is to say that safaris are best suited for tweens and teens.

On a safari with her three children, ages eleven, fifteen, and seventeen, Lisa K. says that her boys especially enjoyed the "blood and gore" elements. "At one place, a big baboon had caught a dik-dik—a small, almost cat-sized antelope—and it was eating it, ripping off its legs and throwing them over its head," Lisa says. "They loved it!" They also watched a cheetah bringing down a gazelle, and then the vultures started circling in—one, five, twenty-five, thirty—until a huge flock had swooped down and chased the cheetah off.

Even Lisa's seventeen-year-old daughter, who initially couldn't imagine being stuck with her family in a jeep for two weeks, had an amazing time. "We had some pretty hilarious moments," Lisa says. "Once, I was in an outhouse in a very rustic campsite, while my daughter, Gillian, waited outside for me. Then I heard Gillian gasp. I opened the door to find an African elephant right beside the outhouse, staring her in the face."

Hot Tip! Look for a safari company that keeps the vehicle time to a minimum and that has alternate activities, such as walks, biking, or canoeing, to break up all the game viewing.

Safaris go beyond animal counts to cultural exchange opportunities. Lisa and her husband opted for guided daily hikes with their children, to get some exercise and work off the kids' steam. On one hike, the family trekked to Tanzania's Ngorongoro Crater, which is famous for its wildlife. On the way up, they came across colorfully garbed Maasai children tending their herds of cows, and the locals walked with Lisa's family for an hour as they passed waterfalls and other points of interest.

3. IDEA GENERATOR: ADVENTURE

Extended Journeys • MD

When I started planning our round-the-world trip, my children (then aged eight and twelve) were a little shocked. We explained that we would take them out of school for a year, pack everything up, and go. They were initially resistant to the idea of being on the road (well, being away from friends) for an extended period. I involved them in the planning process from the beginning and referred to the trip regularly during normal daily conversation.

Within a short time, my boys started talking about "when we go" and "when we visit." It was very exciting to see them integrate the concept of being nomads into their reality so quickly. They had plenty of time to get comfortable with the idea of traveling for an extended period of time—and to voice all their worries and concerns—well before we bought tickets to leave Seattle.

An extended trip, whether it's a round-the-world journey or simply a long excursion, is an incredible experience. Planning such a trip is exciting and exhausting at the same time—there are so many details to consider. Kids introduce two additional considerations: how to handle schooling, and the importance of the pace. But, extended travel also offers families a deeper, richer experience than short, two-week vacations. Children can grow and learn while being exposed to sights and sounds that broaden their imaginations and their understanding of the world in which we live. Your family can also have a ton of fun.

Hot Tip! Start your trip planning by reading about other people's round-the-world experiences. Six In The World (www.sixintheworld.com), Nomadic Matt (www.nomadicmatt.com), and Daniel Glick's book, *Monkey Dancing*, are good sources for families planning an extended trip.

The Practicalities • MD — The duration of your trip will drive your budget and your route. Restrictions in your life may provide a timeline; consider how long you can take as a leave of absence from work or the period between ending one job and starting another. Once you decide on the ideal length of your trip, you can then consider budgeting.

For an extended trip, money management becomes exponentially more important than for a shorter journey. You'll want to make sure your budget includes transportation, food, accommodations, entertainment, gear, home-related expenses, insurance, and medical expenses. (See Chapter 6 "Pre-trip Planning," for ideas on wrangling your bills.)

Hot Tip! Many books and websites dedicated to extended travel provide examples of daily costs, usually by country.

Extended trips require strict budgeting. Frugality is important both before your trip (as you save to make it a reality) and during the trip (to manage costs while you're on the road). Karen H. says, "to keep costs down, we stayed in guest houses with just one bedroom and a bathroom." Jeanne D. recommends choosing accommodations that allow you to "walk or take inexpensive mass transit during your visit." To keep food costs low, she also suggests learning to live "like a local, cooking much of your own food bought fresh at local markets."

Transportation is the biggest travel expense and, as such, deserves plenty of research in advance. Using frequent-flier miles can keep these costs down. And, a combination of purchasing longer flights ahead of time and using planes, trains, or buses for shorter hops, which you can arrange along the way, is the most cost-effective.

Round-the-world airfares (where you book all of your flights in advance) can seem like the best value for the money, but you need to read all the fine print, particularly relating to the direction of travel, the number of stops possible, and the carriers on which you can travel.

Determining what to do with your home, mortgage, cars, and any other financial commitments is a highly individual decision. Consider renting out your house to help pay your mortgage while you are traveling, or partaking in a house swap (see Chapter 9, "Home Away From Home," for more information).

Hot Tip! Don't pre-determine the amount of time you spend in any one place. As you travel, some destinations will exceed your expectations, while others will disappoint. There should be enough flexibility in your overall plan to accommodate this.

School • MD — When I thought about taking my children out of school for a year, I assumed they would be held back and enter their next grade level when we returned, fifteen months later. My children had other ideas. "What about school?" was one of the first questions they asked when we originally told them about our plans. Both cited being able to re-enter school with the same peer group as an important condition to participating in the adventure. In order to accomplish this, they agreed to be homeschooled while traveling. I began researching how we could achieve the goal of keeping them at their grade level while we were on the road.

Teaching two children on the road is a daunting thought, if, like me, you've never homeschooled before. Start by breaking down the schoolwork into subjects, including reading, writing, math, science, and so on. With this methodical approach, the tasks seem easier. Travel already helps your children learn about the history, geography, and language of each place you visit. The other topics may require some ingenuity and a little more elbow grease.

Having your child write a travel blog or even just postcards and e-mails to friends and family goes a long way toward meeting writing requirements for school. For math and science, you'll have to stick to the school's curriculum. However, thanks to the growing population of homeschooling parents, there are plenty of workbooks and other such teaching materials available at bookstores all over North America.

Hot Tip! A willing grandparent or friend can mail necessary school materials in batches to a hotel or post office box in a far-flung city, so you don't have to lug everything along for your entire trip.

For older children, those in middle and high school, there are online study options. These include distance-learning programs offered by the Center for Talented Youth (CTY) at Johns Hopkins University. The program covers science, math, and language arts. You'll want to check with your child's school in advance, but students can often earn credits that are recognized by their base schools.

For an extended trip, think about how you will pace your trip. Children crave routine and structure—neither of which is easy in transit. Consider adopting the Slow Travel (www.slowtrav. com) style: staying a week or month in one place and exploring that area completely. Remaining within the same country for a while—even if you are moving around in that country— can be beneficial. With a balanced mix of busy sightseeing, and time to stay still and relax, you will have an incredible, life-changing experience with your children.

3. IDEA GENERATOR: ADVENTURE

4.

CHALLENGES AND SOLUTIONS

TRAVELING *with children has great re-wards, but can also be challenging. You'll make mistakes on your first trip or three, but once you figure out a travel rhythm for your family, it will seem no more difficult than teaching your child to ride a bike.*

Traveling While Pregnant • MD

Ramona S. traveled to Japan toward the end of the second trimester of her second pregnancy, while her three-year-old daughter, ReElle, spent two weeks with her grandparents. Ramona describes how her friends reacted: "They thought I was crazy to travel to another country while so far into my pregnancy. But, it was a great experience for all of us. I got to enjoy two weeks of travel with my husband before our second child arrived, and ReElle got to have a wonderful time with her grandparents."

Many women travel for business or pleasure while pregnant. If you are generally in good health, have no known issues that may cause complications, and your doctor has approved your plans, there's no reason why you shouldn't take that trip.

To make your journey a huge success, you should be conservative in judging your physical capabilities. If you haven't biked or hiked before, now is not a good time to start. If you're planning an adventurous trip, consider all that you might encounter. A backpack may be too heavy to carry when balancing a baby bump, a cramped bus or train can be nauseating, and you really do need your sleep—for you and the baby.

For flights, try to book an aisle seat to make the many potty breaks you'll need a little easier. Use frequent-flier miles to upgrade, so you can have additional legroom. Keep in mind, however, that pregnant women are not permitted to sit in emergency exit rows.

Whether you are already pregnant or there's a possibility you may be pregnant by vacation time, it's worth keeping the following considerations in mind when choosing a destination and activities for your vacation.

To make pregnant travel successful, keep the following in mind: • MD

- Morning sickness is usually at its worst in the first trimester.

- Risk of miscarriage is highest in the first trimester.

- It's likely you will be tired throughout your pregnancy, but you will be more weary in the last trimester.

- You are at greater risk for deep-vein thrombosis (DVT) while pregnant. (See Chapter 12, "Health and Safety," for steps to prevent this from occurring.)

- Risk of pre-term labor and other late-stage complications are highest in the last trimester. In fact, airlines discourage (or outright prevent) travel by women during the final weeks of pregnancy. If you are heavily pregnant (in your third trimester or you're pregnant with multiples), you may be asked for a medical certificate declaring that you have been examined by a doctor and are fit to travel. Check with your airline for specific rules and requirements, as policies vary from airline to airline, especially outside North America.

Timing Your Trip • MD — Travel is easiest and safest during the middle trimester. During this time, you can usually do everything you would do if you weren't pregnant, except maybe some riskier sports, such as scuba diving and downhill skiing. You may be more tired than usual, but that means you have an excuse to plan more lazy days to enjoy the company of your spouse, partner, or other children. And there are plenty of alternate activities that can make up for the things you can't do. For example, you can see almost as much marine life at a good snorkel spot as you would in full scuba gear.

Pregnancy, Travel, and Your Small Child • MD — If you are pregnant and traveling with a young child, you'll need to plan activities carefully. I ventured to Melbourne, Australia, with my husband and three-year-old son when I was in the first trimester of my second pregnancy. A pregnant mom and a jet-lagged preschooler do not mix well. Pregnancy (in addition to jet lag) makes you tired, but you cannot ignore the small child who depends on you to look after him. On the positive side, traveling with a small child forces you to take things more slowly, and that will probably suit you just fine.

Diet • MD — In addition to good prenatal care, the easiest way to ensure a healthy pregnancy is to eat healthy foods, including plenty of fruits and vegetables, get lots of exercise, and remember your multivitamins and folic acid supplements.

Unfortunately, getting beneficial foods can be difficult while traveling. It helps to know some healthy recommendations before you go. The popular book, *What to Expect When You're Expecting,* by Heidi Murkoff and Sharon Mazel, and the website What to Expect (www.whattoexpect.com) provide lots of information on eating well while pregnant. Alternatively, the American College of Obstetricians and Gynecologists (ACOG) offers the pamphlet *Nutrition During Pregnancy* on their website (www.acog.org/publications/patient_education).

Hot Tip! Bring enough prenatal vitamins with you for the whole trip. Your body has already become accustomed to that brand, and a different one may cause you to experience an upset stomach.

Medical and Health Issues • MD — Complications in pregnancy are not predictable, but if a problem does occur, it may limit any travel plans you have. For example, to prevent pre-term labor, bed rest is commonly prescribed for the health of both the mother and the baby. If you book a trip during the time you'll be pregnant, purchase cancellation insurance. (See Chapter 12, "Health and Safety," for more information.)

Before departure, find out what your insurance offers for pre-natal care, labor, delivery, and neonatal care while you're away. It's common for health insurance providers to limit coverage for labor and delivery away from your home area after thirty-seven weeks' gestation.

Also consider the medical facilities where you're going. If you are traveling in North America, this can be as simple as asking your doctor to recommend an obstetrician at your destination, so that you can have a number to call in case of an emergency. Abroad, consider in advance how to handle an emergency should it arise, if you are away from western-style medical facilities. (See Chapter 12, "Health and Safety," for ideas on contacting doctors while traveling.)

For a trip to a less-developed country, visit your prenatal-care provider before you leave to discuss any special measures you should take. Consult your provider well in advance, in case he makes suggestions that have an impact on your plans. See the website of the Centers for Disease Control and Prevention (CDC) (www.cdc.gov) to learn what shots are recommended and safe for pregnant women. Live viral vaccinations—such as typhoid, measles, mumps, and rubella—are not recom-mended if you are pregnant or planning to get pregnant, be-cause of potential risks to the developing fetus.

Frequent urination is a common side effect of pregnancy, because your newly expanding uterus is bumping into your bladder, and your body is adjusting to these changes. If you have concerns about the cleanliness of the facilities, pack some disposable toilet seat covers—if you can't find these locally, try Drugstore.com (www.drugstore.com)—and plenty of alcohol-based hand sanitizer to protect yourself from unwanted infections.

Preeclampsia (toxemia) and gestational diabetes are two of the most common pregnancy complications. Both usually develop during the second trimester, and both require medical assistance to ensure that the mother and baby stay healthy. Check with your doctor before traveling if you think you may be at risk for one of these conditions. He may request that you come in for an additional checkup or may simply provide you with information on how to detect these conditions.

The possibility of miscarriage exists anywhere, as one in four pregnancies end with the loss of the fetus. A miscarriage may require surgery. If you don't get the required medical care promptly and in a safe, clean environment, you may risk your future fertility. In the last trimester, the highest risks relate to the possibility of premature labor and complications with the fetus, and delivery. Educate yourself about these potential issues, discuss them with your doctor, and have a plan for how you would handle the situation, should it arise while you're traveling.

Malaria in pregnancy is dangerous to the mother and the unborn baby. Therefore it's wise to avoid countries where the disease is common. While anti-malarial medication is available for pregnant women, not all forms are safe to take while gestating, and the CDC cautions against their use during pregnancy. If you are planning to try to get pregnant, you should wait until after your course of malaria prophylaxis before doing so.

Medications and Prescriptions • MD — I avoided over-the-counter medications during both of my pregnancies. However, if you're traveling, you may choose to rely on these to quickly recover and get the most out of your journey. Always consult your doctor prior to taking anything, because the medication that creates issues for one pregnant woman may not adversely affect another.

The ACOG includes guidelines for medications and pregnant women in their pamphlet, *Tobacco, Alcohol, Drugs and Pregnancy*. Acetaminophen (Tylenol) is OK to take, but ibuprofen (Motrin and Advil) and naproxen (Aleve) are usually not recommended. Over-the-counter allergy medications (antihistamines) are generally considered safe, but starting a course of allergy shots is not. There are different opinions on the safety of decongestants (pseudoephedrine), due to their risk of elevating blood pressure. Dramamine should be avoided, because it may induce uterine contractions. It's worth repeating: Check with your doctor if you are unsure of the safety of any medication.

Note, too, that names may differ from country to country, so either pack your own brand or know the generic names of the drugs' ingredients, so that you can be sure of purchasing the appropriate remedy.

Hot Tip! Ginger is a natural remedy for nausea. If you have a propensity to motion sickness, pack some tea, candy, or cookies containing this spicy root to help settle your stomach. Or try using acupressure wristbands, which can be found at TravelBand (www.travelband.com). Dry crackers, such as saltines, and sucking on peppermint candies can also help settle an upset tummy, as will keeping something in your stomach at all times.

Traveling with Infants and Toddlers • MD

It takes work to travel with really young children. But this should not prevent you from leaving on a jet plane. I live in Seattle, while most of my extended family lives in the U.K. and Ireland. So I have traveled with both my children since they were infants. My first trip as a new parent was to take my six-month-old firstborn home to Dublin to meet his grandparents. Since then, our family has wandered many times to Europe and South and Central America, plus countless trips within North America. My two boys are accomplished travelers because they began early.

Infants are totally portable. Their daily rhythm of eat-poop-sleep differs very little whether you're at home or on the road. Even jet lag is rarely an issue for an infant feeding at (somewhat) regular intervals. He will still expect to eat every four to six hours, regardless of the time zone. Mariah V. described the impact of traveling from the U.S. to Nepal with her son, Walter, when he was five months old. "It wasn't so bad. He was so small, he was still sleeping most of the time anyway."

Hot Tip! Allow a day to get over jet lag for each hour of time difference between your home and your destination. For example, if there is a three-hour time difference, expect it to take three days before your little ones (and you!) are over the effects of zone hopping.

There's no way around it. Traveling with toddlers is more challenging. These bundles of energy are not as easy as infants to pick up and carry along. While it's good that they are more likely to have settled into a sleeping pattern that includes short naps during the day and less waking during the night, this fact can make jet lag an issue. Even with the added challenge, it's magical to travel with children at this age, and they bring out the best in people around them. "The people we met in Spain loved children. They patted our baby's head, touched her, squeezed her cheeks," Alejandra T. says, who traveled with her daughter, Natasha, when she was just over a year old.

Breastfeeding • MD — If you're breastfeeding, looking after your own diet and nutrition will ensure that the baby is eating well. Research in advance whether or not nursing in public is culturally acceptable at your destination. La Leche League is an international mother-to-mother support organization for breastfeeders. The La Leche League International website (www.llli.org) is a good resource, providing local contact information for the group's leaders in many countries worldwide. Use a nursing bra and loose-fitting clothing to allow you to feed your baby on demand without inadvertently offending anyone. Alternatively, many mothers worldwide skip the specialized clothing and just use a blanket thrown over their shoulders for privacy when feeding a baby in public.

Alejandra cautions, "keep in mind that in different countries, people have different attitudes toward small children and breastfeeding." She also suggests remembering the effect breastfeeding in different time zones could have on your own body. "This is how my daughter ended up being weaned. My body was out of sync with the time at the destination. When my body was ready to nurse, she wasn't hungry and vice versa." Be prepared for this and perhaps take a hand pump for expressing milk, so that you don't run into mastitis issues. Also this provides milk when your baby is hungry.

Bottles, cleanliness, and sterilization will be the biggest formula challenges while you're traveling. There are three options: wash bottles by hand, carry a sterilization unit, or use disposable bottle liners. I opted for the old-fashioned, wash-by-hand method, since it reduced the amount of "baby stuff" I had to tote with me. The cost was small, requiring only that I had access to boiling water (for washing) and that I carried a bottle brush. For travels in any country where tap water is considered safe to drink, sterilization of bottles and nipples is not necessary.

Because disposable bottle liners are made of plastic, they are not very eco-friendly, but they are very handy for traveling. If you choose to carry these, pack more than enough for your whole trip, and remember to bring a small, sealable container in which you can wash and store nipples and pacifiers.

Formula Tips • MD — Baby formula is available worldwide, but you may have difficulty finding the familiar type. The more popular brands are often available in pre-packaged, single-serving packets of powder, and these are excellent for traveling. Specialty products like lactose-free and soy formulas can be found in health food stores and some grocery stores in the developed world. It's a personal choice as to whether you pack enough formula for your entire trip; just cart enough for the first few days and purchase additional amounts as needed. Companies like JetSetBabies (www.jetsetbabies.com) and Babies Travel Lite (www.babiestravellite.com) can also ship products to your destinations.

I nursed each of my children until they were six months old. Thereafter, I used a soy-based formula to avoid milk allergies. Even though soy formula was a specialty product, I had no trouble finding a similar blend in health-food stores when I traveled, and my babies didn't seem to notice any difference.

Alejandra consulted with her pediatrician before her travels to Spain. She knew that baby formula would be available in local grocery stores, but most likely would be a different type (or contain different ingredients within the same brand) than the one she was using in the U.S. The doctor recommended taking some formula with her and mixing the two brands together over a few days, starting with seventy percent of the familiar formula and working down to one hundred percent of the new formula.

Hot Tip! Pack some formula, as well as bottles and spare nipples, into your carry-on bag, just in case your suitcase arrives at your destination days after you do. This will save you from late-night, panicky formula-shopping!

Solid Food for Toddlers • MD — For toddlers and older infants who are eating some solid foods, bring along a sippy cup, a bowl, and a spoon—and plenty of bibs. If you're still at the single-grain cereal stage, pack what you'll need during the trip (into zip-top bags) to take with you. Baby food varies just as much as formula. At this stage, when you're still introducing foods and watching out for allergic reactions, it's best to play it safe. Similarly, blended baby food is generally available in grocery stores in major cities worldwide, but the contents will vary from what your child eats at home. Traveling is a good time to use a hand-cranked food mill to grind up food for baby—at least you can then be sure what he's eating.

Diapering and Potty Care • MD — Diapers and traveling do not go well together. If you use cloth diapers, you have to think ahead about carrying and washing soiled ones and about how to dry them (sometimes a bigger problem). If you use disposables, they will swell your suitcase and, since you'll likely run out, you'll have to buy extras locally—if you can find them. When planning your travels, double everything you normally carry in your diaper bag, including wipes, diapers, rash cream, and plastic bags (for soiled diapers). If you're flying, depending on the Transportation Security Administration (TSA)'s latest requirements, creams and gels may have to be in containers that are three ounces or less in carry-on luggage. If you normally rely on wipes, pack a washcloth as a backup.

Disposable diapers are usually available in major cities worldwide. For example, Procter & Gamble sells its popular Pampers brand in over eighty countries. Even so, the challenge may be finding a source. If you can't locate a grocery store (or the one you've discovered doesn't have any in stock), pharmacies usually carry a small supply. Do not assume local brands will be of the same quality as those you use at home. The first time you try a new sort abroad, buy more than you think you'll need. If it's a less-absorbent diaper, more frequent changes will be required to prevent rashes.

Pippa C. is from South Africa, but lives in the U.S. with her husband and two sons, Grant (two) and Trevor (four). She has traveled home at least annually with her children since Trevor was born, frequently on her own. Even in this developing nation, Pippa says, "Diapers are easily available in major urban centers."

Laundering will be your greatest challenge with cloth diapers. If you're staying in one place for a number of days, you'll be able to use your hotel's or a local laundering service. However, things get tricky for those on the move. You'll need to rely on diaper liners, which are, thankfully, often biodegradable and disposable. They will hold solids inside the liner to prevent soiling of the cloth, and the entire bundle can be disposed of when you change the diaper. This is a bonus when you need to carry soiled diapers for laundering later. You'll also want to take some trusted powder detergent so you can wash the diapers on the road.

If your toddler has been recently potty-trained, expect more accidents than usual when you're traveling—and pack accordingly. When Debbi T. was planning to spend a month in Vietnam with her recently potty-trained three-year-old, she was concerned that accidents might be an issue. "Rather than taking up valuable luggage space with Pull-Ups Training Pants, I used the Internet to determine what products were available at our destination."

Sleeping • MD — If your infant or toddler normally naps during the day, you might find it helpful to relax any home rules about dozing only in a quiet, darkened room. These constraints will limit your sightseeing time. Better to set your expectations that napping will take place wherever and whenever, and that you'll need to plan ahead to re-institute the normal regime after your trip.

Hot Tip! Write down the time and duration of naps your child takes as well as any nighttime wakefulness. You will then have a record of cumulative sleep and can be more confident that your child is adjusting to the new time zone.

The type and duration of your trip will strongly influence whether you bring equipment from home, rent from your accommodation, or do without. Strollers, car seats, and backpacks all become valid spots for daytime naps. If you're traveling to a sunny destination, a shade for your stroller or backpack might be a worthwhile investment. For single-destination trips, cribs like the Graco Pack 'n Play portable playard (www.gracobaby.com) can be invaluable. Most hotel chains have bassinets that are available for rent. Book these in advance.

If you don't bring special equipment, slumbering together can make travel easier. The mini Arm's Reach co-sleeper (www.armsreach.com) is a good choice. Or, like Pippa, you could use luggage as an infant bed. "We have an extra-large suitcase that was perfect for this."

Plan your sightseeing with naptimes in mind, and choose quieter sights for those times when you expect your child to be sleeping. And above all, be ready to adjust your itinerary on the fly. If an on-the-go nap is just not working, you may have to return to your hotel, condo, or guesthouse.

Regardless of the type of accommodation and sleeping arrangements, you will need to think ahead about safety concerns in an unfamiliar room. (See Chapter 11, "Pack It Up," for a list of items that you may find useful.)

Toddler Time • MD — When my boys were toddlers, they were either racing around at top speed or fast asleep. Toddlers are remarkable to travel with because everything is interesting. But mood swings and temper tantrums are a hallmark of this phase too. Frustration, insecurity, and thwarted independence cause most of these "terrible two" behaviors. The key is to manage these behaviors actively while traveling. Talk to your child about your trip before you go, when you are in transit, and when you get there. The more he knows, the more likely he is to be excited about the adventure, rather than scared of leaving the familiarity of home. Be prepared to walk a safe distance behind a kid who wants to explore. This is healthy independence and is so much easier than battling with your child to get him to sit still.

When you travel with a toddler, the world really does open its door to you. Your little guy will be puttering along a street, stopping every two to five minutes to investigate something. Meanwhile, the people around will pause, smile, and be friendly to you both. It's the most amazing thing. While in Nepal, Mariah noticed that everyone loves little kids. "Everyone wants to hold your baby and touch your baby." She was moved by the affection, but at the same time, she had to be careful about strangers touching Walter's mouth, hands, or face. She knew there was a danger of his ingesting local germs and bacteria—against which her breast-milk could not protect him—that could cause him to become ill. Your child will likely put his fingers in his mouth often. Avoid these germs by washing frequently and using a hand sanitizer.

Alejandra suggests that travelers with small children be vigilant. "We all relax on vacation. Just because people are kind and welcoming to you and your child does not mean you should be any less careful about safety than you would be at home."

Jet lag is difficult on toddlers. They're too young to understand the effects of crossing time zones and not old enough to amuse themselves if they have trouble sleeping. The only thing to do is reset their body clocks as quickly as possible—even if that means skipping naps during the first day or two. Pippa summarizes it best: "I've learned to just wake them up and not let them sleep during the day. The first two to three days are hell. If I let them sleep in the day, they stay awake all night."

Traveling with School-Age Children • MD

Traveling gets easier when children are in elementary school, ages six to twelve. They're old enough to carry their own luggage (mostly), you don't need to bring extra equipment for them (as with babies and toddlers), they don't need naps, and diapering and potty-care are things of the past. I find it exciting to take my school-age children somewhere new and to expose them to exotic languages and cultures. And they, in turn, have responded extremely well to these experiences.

Even though it's easier traveling with children this age, be prepared for some resistance beforehand. Tweens may balk at plans that interfere with school, sports, or social activities. My older son, Cillian, who is now twelve, has a collection of grievances around the activities missed because of travel. Someday maybe he'll forgive us for imposing on him so cruelly. The good news is that once we're on the road, these things tend to fall into the background as involvement in the trip itself takes over.

Kids this age are old enough to be involved in early discussions about the journey. Even Cillian can't resist poring over a map or checking out a website when invited to do so. But it's hard to keep a six- or seven-year-old focused for long enough to talk about all the exciting experiences awaiting him in a country he has never visited and may know little about. I've found that surreptitiously involving the country and culture in our everyday life—with movies, food, books, and general conversation—helps teach my children and excite them about the trip.

Karen H. has done some really incredible excursions with her boys, Aamon (ten) and Bodhi (eight). In 2005, they spent two months in southern India and had a fabulous time. "The key to that trip," Karen says, "was that I didn't have anything planned and gave the boys vague options for each step of the trip, allowing them to choose what they wanted to do. There was only one place I really wanted to visit; the rest was up to them." This kind of involvement in direct decision-making is a great way to keep elementary school-aged children involved.

Hot Tip! Mealtime conversations are an excellent opportunity to slip in tidbits of information about the places you plan to visit.

As adults, we read guidebooks to help plot a trip. To get your child involved, you can't really hand him your *Lonely Planet* or *Time Out* guide and expect him to take the initiative from there. The Travel for Kids website (www.travelforkids.com) includes listings of books about places and people, organized by country. For independent readers, the book series that have worked a charm for my kids have been Scholastic's *Horrible Histories* and Mary Pope Osborne's *Magic Tree House* from Random House. Dorling Kindersley's *Eyewitness* and *Top 10* travel guides follow a similar format and are very accessible to older children; both of these series cover destinations worldwide. If your child is excited and interested in your trip, it's likely he'll help choose some sights to visit before you get there.

In all the trips I have taken with my children, I have found that exporting some habits from home goes a long way toward making them feel comfortable and therefore relaxed in their new surroundings. That means we usually start our vacation by finding a coffee shop. (Hey, we are from Seattle, after all.) This becomes our place to start the day for as long as we're in that neighborhood. My boys will settle in, examine the different pastries and drinks available, compare them to domestic ones, and try to negotiate a treat from me or from their dad (just like at home).

Many parenting experts have praised the value of structure and routine for providing children with a sense of security and helping them develop self-discipline. This is also important when traveling, as is providing some way for them to feel like they have some control over what they can do and see. I find that having some planning time, either at the start of the trip, or perhaps daily, is important. An older child is not likely to throw a tantrum, but if they are insecure and confused, they can (and will) refuse to engage or show interest.

When our family travels, everyone gets a say in what we do on any given day, and compromises are brokered accordingly. With multiple children, desires will differ, but simple strategies like having a daily leader can help address this. At times it may be better to split up: say, for one parent to take the kids and the other to visit an art gallery. No hard-and-fast rule says you must stay together constantly. And, unplanned time is just as important with elementary-school children as it is with younger ages. It's OK to hang out by the pool or wander through a village with no set destination or agenda. Sometimes days like this lead to the experiences that your child will treasure forever.

I relax rules around treats (I will never understand the power of a simple ice cream cone) when we're on vacation. It allows me some bargaining power to lobby for museums and archeological sites that they might otherwise veto.

And for times when negotiating doesn't work, Karen says, "Flexibility really is the key to traveling with children." She cautions not to pack the days too full and to leave time for children to "enjoy what's happening around them now." And Marie W., who has traveled with her six children throughout the U.S., agrees, "The biggest challenge [to having a successful trip] is just making sure that no one is pushed beyond what they're able to bear."

Traveling with Teens • LF

Once your child enters his teens, it's even more important to allow him some independence while traveling. As a fourteen-year-old friend of my daughter said recently when I suggested that I walk the "kids" to the hotel swimming pool a block away, "Hey, we're teens. We don't like having our style cramped!"

Oh, right! Many of us are so accustomed to doing things for our kids that once they enter adolescence, it's sometimes hard to remember that they really are more capable. However, this doesn't mean we as parents can let go of the reins. We just need to allow them ever-widening circles of independence as they stretch their capabilities. Some young teens are eager to assert their autonomy from the get-go, while others might need a gentle nudge out of the nest to give their new wings a try.

Teens need to feel that they aren't trapped with their parents all of the time; this is especially true when traveling. You can help by asking for their input into trip plans, so that you're sure of visiting a few places they're personally interested in. Allow them their moody days and don't take offense over little issues. And give them the chance to be on their own in places that are safe, such as museums, parks, or streets in safe neighborhoods.

Hot Tip! Ask a concierge or desk clerk at your accommodation where the local teens gather and if it's safe for your teenager to spend time there.

Like members of a club, teens like to hang out together. If you're staying in the same spot for a week or more, consider signing your teen up for a course where they'll have the chance to meet locals. My fourteen-year-old daughter loves to sing and is a member of the Seattle Girls' Choir. When planning a trip to Sweden, I suggested to Kirsten that she might enjoy taking a youth choir class that was part of a festival we were attending. On the opening day, Kirsten stood at the side of a room filled with kids all chatting in Swedish. Her nerve failed her, and she was edging toward the door when the administrator announced the "special guest" all the way from the United States and asked Kirsten to join the other teens of the same age.

By the time I picked her up, her look of anxiety had given way to a look of confidence. She said: "Mom, you came too early! I'm having fun with my new friends!" By week's end, she was ecstatic about performing in a concert with a prestigious visiting adult choir from Stockholm.

There's nothing more satisfying to me as a parent than watching my daughter gain the independence she'll need, small step by step, to someday live on her own—which is the aim of parenting in the teen years. Travel brings numerous opportunities for our teens to stretch their capabilities.

With a teen's need for individuation and increasing time spent with friends, it may seem that he is no longer interested in spending time with family. Don't let this discourage you from going on trips with him, however. While he may initially balk at the idea, once along for the ride, he may just surprise you with his enthusiasm for exploring. The confluence of increasing maturity and eagerness to prove that he's capable can make a teen an ideal traveling companion.

We were in the grand hall of Kronborg Castle in Denmark (immortalized as Elsinore Castle in Shakespeare's *Hamlet*), when Kirsten called to me. "Mom! That actor dude in the video just forgot one of Shakespeare's lines!" my daughter gleefully informed me. Eyes sparkling, Kirsten burst into a dramatic recital of the piece, including the missing passage.

Just when you think you know a lot about your teenager, he will surprise you with his knowledge and passion for a subject. Kirsten's personal interest in all things Shakespeare, newly gained after a middle-school Shakespeare class, made what might have been a standard castle visit into a fascinating learning experience for both of us.

For my daughter the draw was the Bard. For your child it may be a rock concert, World War II airplanes, or rock climbing. Is your daughter an animal lover? Is your son really into his garage band? Whatever your teens are involved with, the best travel experiences may incorporate some of their interests.

For Dizy B., the magnet for her thirteen-year-old son was big-wave surfing at Playa Zicatela in Puerto Escondido, on the Pacific Coast of Mexico. "Christopher is an extreme athlete; he does motocross and lives to surf. It was really a surfing safari adventure for him."

It's best to select lodging within close walking distance of several interesting tourist sites. This allows your teen to take some time on his own to explore the neighborhood. Just be sure he has pocket change, a business card with the hotel's name and address on it, and a cell phone. If you're traveling abroad, provide him with an international cell phone into which you've programmed your cell phone's number, as well as the number of the hotel and the local equivalent of 911.

We might be pleasantly surprised by our children's behavior when they experience both the challenges and opportunities that come through travel, especially independent travel.

Kylene Q.'s teenage son worked and sweated alongside her and other volunteers while building a Habitat for Humanity house in Ecuador. She says, "You see a side of your kids you don't see at home, because they're participating as equals with adults. I felt that he was more of a peer at that point."

While you're likely to see some shining strengths in your teen, you're also likely to experience the occasional black-hole day.

After all, teens are moving through an emotional minefield as they negotiate hormonal surges and all of the pressures of schoolwork and social life, as well as trying (at least some of the time) to meet their parents' and society's expectations.

It's common and natural for a teen to be wary of the idea of spending a lot of one-on-one time with his parents. The reason for this, in two words, is "comfort zone." Think about it. What's the favored state of the standard-issue teen? Cozied into the nest of his room, surfing the Net with a friend, his favorite snack within arm's reach? Perhaps conjoined to his iPod and cell phone? The teen years are all about fitting in with peers, and teens these days do this through electronics. The prospect of family bonding, disconnected from his friends, may be uncomfortable at first.

Some parents ban electronics while traveling, to encourage more family time. Personally, I've found that allowing gadgets is a great motivating factor and eliminates conflict. There's a lot of middle ground on this issue, as Stacia C. found on a "Wild West" RV trip with her teenage daughter and tween son.

"We allowed our kids to take cell phones, do texting, and check their e-mails. We didn't allow this in communal or social situations, but our kids could have some time after dinner to plug back into their lives. Our daughter set up a blog before we left, and during the day she would take pictures, and then she'd update her blog each night. For our kids to be able to jump online and share a buffalo coming down the road with their friends was a really special experience. It would have been a punishment to say no texting, no calling, no e-mailing. While we didn't grow up with those things, it's a part of their world. We simply chose to set clear tech boundaries for the trip."

Many families find that allowing a teen to bring a friend on a trip is a win-win situation, as you get a break and your child can enjoy the companionship of a special buddy. You'll likely even find that your teen is much more cooperative and agreeable with a pal along. (For more information on traveling with a friend of your child, see Chapter 5, "Friends and Family.")

Dating • LF — Teens are hard-wired to notice other teens of the opposite sex (or the same sex, as the case may be). The telltale sign of this is the neck swivel. While younger teens will most likely merely appreciate the "scenery," you may find that an older teen will express an interest in getting together with a girl he encounters on a trip. When is it wise or safe to allow this?

Pay close attention to your instincts. Is your teen responsible? Ask to meet the young person. If a boy seems a bit too mature for your teenage girl, you probably wouldn't allow the date at home; why take a risk when you're traveling?

Context is everything. Paula B. puts it simply: "Use judgment. Is your child talking about coming back at eleven p.m. or talking about playing on the beach at three p.m.? You'll meet kids who are respectful, and you'll meet kids who aren't. If your kids are prone to run into problems outside of travel, they'll run into problems while traveling."

If you do decide that it's OK for your teen to get together with a local girl or boy, follow the same rules you would at home: Inquire where they will be going (and make sure it's to a public place); set a reasonable curfew; and be sure your teen takes along a cell phone, to call you in case of an emergency. For your additional comfort, you might consider a "training wheels" date, by going to the same places he will with his new friend. If it's out for pizza in Italy, why not get a table across

Tips for Traveling with a Teen • LF

Here are some strategies that can help make traveling with your teen easier.

Exercise—Teenagers have an abundance of energy. Plan ahead for plenty of active outdoor recreation.

Choices—To help your teen feel invested in a trip, let him make some choices, such as where to eat or when to call it quits for the day.

Sleep—If a teen feels that there's little personal space, he'll seek emotional distance. Even a loft or an alcove with a day bed in it can provide a welcome buffer for a teen to feel a sense of control over his surroundings.

Time Off—Teens have different biorhythms than adults; they often have a hard time dozing off and need to sleep in to compensate. If you can allow your teen enough rest, you'll be rewarded with his brighter constitution and eager attitude. By alternating early-start and late-start days, everyone can get some of what they most need. If you're eager to get going and your teen is still snoozing, leave him a note and get out for a brisk walk in the neighborhood.

Downtime—It's hard for teens to feel glued to their parents during a trip. Allow your teen the time and opportunity to meet peers wherever you travel. (For ideas on this topic, see the section on meeting the locals in Chapter 5, "Friends and Family.")

the room from him? If it's to a local carnival, why not go there yourself and check in with him regularly?

It's best to forge the tradition of family travel when your children still enjoy spending time with you. Laura S. says: "Our kids are growing up. Soon it will be summer jobs, and then they're gone. So we're trying to cram in as many family vacations as we can while they're with us and want to spend time with us."

The Reluctant Child • LF

For most children, travel is an adventure waiting to happen. They are eager participants in the planning stages and are enthusiastic companions. Yet some kids aren't keen; they're simply more comfortable at home, and they just don't see the reason to go anyplace else. A homebody may repel all suggestions, lag behind when everyone else is climbing into the car, and make it clear that he would rather be back at the ranch.

For some children, however, travel goes beyond the inconvenience and dissatisfaction of having to sleep in a different bed to outright anxiety. While some kids outgrow this phase once post-toddlerhood, for others it is just a part of their personality: Change is hard for them. As a parent you already know which category your child fits into.

On their Southwest road trip, it seemed to Liz D. that her daughter, Nell, was dealing with lots of issues, so she asked her, "What do you worry about?" It was as if floodgates had been opened. "Mom, I worry that our wet shoes won't dry, and we won't have shoes. I'm afraid that a wind will blow our tent away, and we won't have a place to sleep. Or my bear will get blown away, and I won't have it anymore."

"I asked her, 'What do you think we could do if there was a bad rainstorm right now—if it was very windy, and we didn't think our tent was secure?' We discussed our options, from tying down the tent to getting into the car and finding a hotel. It was the start of some very powerful conversations," Liz

105

says, "with the theme: If you don't like your circumstances, you have the power to create different circumstances."

Liz was able to turn a difficult trip into a positive for her child, because she paid attention to her needs. It's a good idea before traveling with a reluctant child to get him to buy in on trip plans. Forcing a fearful kid to go on a family trip will accomplish a temporary aim, but it will most likely increase his reluctance in the future and will not create a bonding experience. It would more likely create a nightmarish trip for the rest of the family.

Speaking from an evolutionary standpoint, there were important reasons for children to be reluctant about traveling. Those who stayed closer to home, and were cautious and alert undoubtedly survived in greater numbers. Yet today we want to explore the world with our children, and we want them to have fun. If you have a child who frequently exhibits anxious behavior, please know that you don't have to limit your trips to visits with relatives or nearby attractions.

Reluctance often equates to fear of the unknown. Choose a quiet time, perhaps while driving in the car or when tucking your child into bed, to gently question him about what he thinks the trip will be like. You may be able to find out about any misperceptions and address them.

It's very important with children who are not eager starters to introduce them to the idea of travel in a gentle way (see Chapter 7, "Learning Before You Go"). Involving your child in the planning will help. But sometimes just the very idea of leaving home is stressful for a child. This is especially true of those who are overwhelmed by sensory stimulation. One of the best books I've read about this is *The Highly Sensitive Child: Helping Our Children Thrive When the World Overwhelms Them*, by Elaine Aron.

Aron, a clinical and research psychologist, notes that this is a personality trait shared by fifteen to twenty percent of the population. Aron finds highly sensitive children (and adults) to be empathetic, smart, intuitive, careful, and conscientious. Yet they are easily overwhelmed by stimulation and require parental supervision to help them learn to stay within their optimal level of arousal and prevent stress-related illnesses. Sometimes extracurricular activities need to be reduced for these children. Aron says that you can think of a sensitive person as having a certain quota of energy for dealing with stimulation, and when you pass that point, you'll have trouble.

Sensitive children need, when possible, to be kept away from loud noises (such as amplified concerts), bright lights, and crowds. Instead, choose quieter spaces at the periphery of tourist centers, and plan to allow plenty of down time for your child to step off the trip treadmill to enjoy peaceful activities. You will undoubtedly find that doing so increases the whole family's enjoyment.

My highly sensitive child wanted to attend a musical at Universal Studios in California. I was concerned because I knew that loud noises are physically painful for her, and at most public events these days, they have the loudspeaker system turned up so high that it can cause ringing in the ears afterward. I purchased earplugs for her in advance, and she sat through the entire performance with a big smile on her face; the earplugs blocked just enough sound to make it enjoyable for her, and she actually heard every word.

Once you have accumulated a few good travel experiences to call upon, be sure to remind your child of the good times he had on the trip, to build the case for future travel. Each time it will get easier. Most of the time, as children grow older, they become more accustomed to new experiences and gradually lose their reluctance.

Elaine Aron's Travel Tips for Highly Sensitive Kids

1. A sensitive child will be more aware of others, which means that when too much is going on, he will be overwhelmed. The parents' job is to be a buffer. Don't be part of the problem by being rushed or distressed yourself.

2. Do not try to downplay a child's fears. Sensitive kids are better off if you talk about their anxieties in a straightforward way and discuss how to cope with them.

3. Your child should be well rested before taking a trip.

4. Be especially careful not to allow junk food while traveling. The nervous system needs many different nutrients to operate well, and if your child is low on calcium, potassium, magnesium, or some other essential, things won't go as well.

5. During a flight, have your child listen to something familiar—a book on tape or music on an iPod.

6. On car trips, take frequent breaks. Also, be sure not to add to any pressure your child might already be feeling by urging him to look at the scenery.

7. Sensitive children often know how to soothe and comfort themselves in order to modulate their level of arousal, so

Children with Special Needs • MD

A special-needs child may find more joy in travel than you could ever anticipate, and the experience can be a tremendous bonding experience for everyone. Whether your kid has a physical, psychological, or developmental challenge, you will be your child's best (and perhaps only) advocate while away from home.

You'll want to first familiarize yourself with your child's rights under both the Americans with Disabilities Act (ADA) and the Air Carrier Access Act (ACAA). The ADA extends civil rights don't interfere by trying to entertain your child more than the child needs.

8. It's so easy to confuse a child who is overstimulated and has withdrawn to regroup with a child who is shy and afraid. If someone says, "Your child is shy," just answer, "No, he's not shy, he's just taking it easy."

9. It's very important not to force sensitive kids to play with other kids or talk to strangers if they resist it. They are probably trying to avoid the overstimulation that occurs for them in these situations. If you're introducing the family to others—even to extended family members whom you are visiting—your child needs to feel that you're on his side. If your child can't look people in the eye or greet them, you need to say, "It's been a long day. Everything is new for him. Shall we save getting to know each other for tomorrow?"

10. If your child says no, he has to know that he has your support. But do leave options, or if there is no option, ask if you can strike a compromise. "You do need to talk to your cousins, but not now. How about in an hour?" or "Should we make it very brief?"

protections to people with disabilities within the United States. It includes specific rules for the construction and alteration of public transportation facilities, including train stations, bus stations, ferry terminals, and airports. Aircraft, airlines, and air travel, while not covered by the ADA, are covered by the ACAA. These rules prohibit discrimination on the basis of a disability with regard to air travel and require carriers to accommodate the needs of passengers with disabilities. There are similar regulations in other countries, particularly in Western Europe, but these rights are not standard worldwide.

Flying with a child who is in a wheelchair or other mobility or support equipment presents a parent with a unique set of challenges, including checking in, navigating security checkpoints, getting on and off the plane, and managing toileting needs in-flight. The Federal Aviation Administration (FAA) oversees rights for disabled passengers as outlined in the ADA. Their website (www.faa.gov) is an excellent resource.

My oldest son has attention deficit hyperactivity disorder (ADHD) and takes medication to help him with this condition. Traveling is challenging since he is most agreeable in the familiar environment of home. I find the following steps help my kid to be more cooperative when traveling, but they apply to most children in general:

1. Prepare your child ahead of time. Talk to him about where you are going, when you are leaving, and any details that may need special attention, such as going through security checkpoints.

2. Try to adopt as much of your home routine as possible at your destination. If bedtime follows a certain pattern normally, for example, try to maintain that while on vacation.

3. Pack items that are familiar from home, including clothes, toys, and accessories.

Hot Tip! Use the Internet to research wheelchair accessibility for museums and other attractions you wish to visit.

Though it can be more challenging if you are traveling over long distances, keeping track of medication schedules is extremely important. Kim M. travels with two children who have special needs and has developed her own method. "Keep a list of medications that your child is taking and a schedule of what is taken when. Plan ahead if you will be changing time zones, so that you can manage the transition in daily routines that this will cause."

Carry copies of prescriptions and the contact details for your doctor and your insurance company. Many travelers scan these and email copies to a web-based account, like Hotmail, Gmail, or Yahoo. Also, leave duplicates with a family member or trusted friend who's familiar with your child's condition. You will depend on this person if there is an emergency and you need to coordinate care between your child's doctor and one at your destination.

All medications should be kept in their original packaging for traveling. This will help you prove that the prescriptions are yours or your child's, if you're questioned by authorities.

Hot Tip! When you travel internationally with your child, learn how to describe your child's disability in the local language. Even writing these phrases down in a notebook is helpful, if you're not up to the pronunciation. Or, consider using visual aids such drawings to help describe the issue. Kwikpoint (www.kwikpoint.com) publishes cards and booklets with pictures of items such as a doctor and body parts (so you can point out what hurts).

You are not required to notify the airline that you will require support for a disabled passenger, but your travel experience may be easier if you do so. Call the customer service department in advance, so they can note your child's needs on your passenger record. That way, any requests are in the system before the day of flight. Check in as early as possible to give you and your child additional time for security screening. This will

Kim M.'s Story

My two-year-old son, Stephen, had been falling down a lot. I took him to the pediatrician in our hometown for some tests for balance and equilibrium issues, but he could find nothing wrong. I felt like I was being dismissed as a hypochondriac.

After this doctor's visit, I had decided to travel to Colorado with all three of my kids (their dad was on deployment to the Middle East) to visit relatives. During this time, Stephen was still falling down and started crying a lot at random times. I was worried and called my insurance company to find out if I could take him to a local doctor. To my dismay, I discovered they would only cover an emergency room visit.

It was a difficult time. I wasn't sure if my baby was truly sick or if I was being overanxious. I decided to trust my instincts, called around to find out which nearby hospital had the most children's experts on hand, and took him to the ER. I explained what was happening, that I was traveling and concerned enough to bring him in. They agreed to see him and were also concerned, calling in a pediatric neurologist. She ordered an immediate MRI that revealed there was a tumor inside his spinal cord.

There was a lot of information coming at me from many directions, and being away from home during it all really added to the stress. It took me far too long to realize the value and helpfulness

also give the airline additional time to ensure that any necessary equipment is available at the gate for boarding.

Before you travel, become familiar with your child's health insurance policies with regard to getting care away from home, and have a contingency plan in case there is an emergency.

Security agents treat passengers in wheelchairs just as they would any other, and all security checks must be satisfied. Kim of a hospital's social worker. They are often a wealth of information and can provide practical support. Social workers also know of all local charities and facilities available to families who find themselves in a difficult situation like this.

We ended up staying in Denver for weeks while Stephen recovered from the spinal surgery he needed, before he was prescribed a course of chemotherapy and we were released. Only one parent is usually allowed to stay overnight with their child in a hospital, and siblings are not, which requires lodging for the others near the hospital. This, along with paying for every meal can quickly rack up a pretty expensive bill, especially when it extends travel plans. In the U.S. one can often find a Ronald McDonald House or similar clean, comfortable, charity-run property available at an extremely low rate and located very near a hospital.

Another thing I learned from all of this was that it's okay to ask for help, even from strangers. When not a stitch of clothing from the suitcase was clean any longer, it was a nurse who exclaimed, "Oh, you poor thing, we should've told you there are laundry facilities that families of in-patient children can use." These facilities are offered at no charge, which is essential when you are living out of a suitcase. This need, as well as many other practical needs, can be met, but often only when you are assertive enough to ask a busy hospital worker.

says, "Every time we've flown, the TSA agent has requested that my child, who is in a wheelchair, walk through the screening gate—usually because she thought that he was in a stroller rather than a wheelchair." You can expect to be directed to a side screening area where your child and his wheelchair will be screened with a wand. His shoes will have to be removed, and any special equipment attached to the wheelchair will also have to be removed for inspection.

Any aircraft with more than thirty seats must have aisle seats with removable armrests, to facilitate transferring passengers from an on-board wheelchair to the aisle seat. If a plane has more than one aisle (as most wide-body aircraft do), it must have at least one wheelchair-accessible lavatory. Furthermore, any aircraft (narrow or wide-body) with an accessible lavatory must have an operable on-board wheelchair. Airlines are not permitted to charge additional fees to provide facilities, equipment, or services to a disabled passenger.

When your trip involves multiple flights with layovers, familiarize yourself with the terminal layouts in advance. You can find a map of the facility on the airport's website, and some airlines provide maps on their websites and in-flight magazines, as well. Advocate for your child by communicating your needs to the check-in agent, the staff at the boarding gate, and the onboard crew. Sometimes this brings out the best in people, as told by Kim: "Once, when in flight, the pilot discovered that there was a disabled child on board. Not only did he invite my son, Stephen, to the cockpit to have his picture taken, he also escorted our whole family to our connecting flight."

5.

FRIENDS AND FAMILY

ENJOYING *travel adventures with friends and family shares the burden and doubles the fun. It builds in a bit more flexibility so everyone can do what she likes and have relaxing times, too. Travel can also bring the excitement of new friends in faraway places. Here are some ways you can add a dash of friendship and family to your trip.*

Family Gatherings • MD

I have a treasured photo of my older son walking down a street in Portugal with his grandfather. They are arm in arm like the best of buddies, although they see each other perhaps once a year. Another photo from the same trip is of a gaggle of smiling children with ice cream dripping down their fingers as they sit in the sunshine. Yet my brood lives in the U.S., and their first cousins are spread around the British Isles and in Portugal.

The children bonded quickly, although they hadn't spent time together in the previous two years—a significant length of time for elementary- and preschool-aged children. The adults enjoyed seeing the kids getting to know one another better, and we agreed to gather more frequently in the coming years to strengthen these budding friendships.

You may choose to visit a destination near where your family lives, or you may agree to congregate in an area that is new for all. Whether these reunions include a small number of people or a larger group, organizing the trip may not be easy, but it will absolutely be worthwhile.

Traveling to spend time with family at their home is the most common type of travel we do with our children, because most North Americans do not live in the same city or state as their parents or siblings. These trips may be the only way for your children to build a relationship with extended family. You have the added benefit of spending time with the people that you love, and your children create lifelong memories of time spent with aunts, uncles, cousins, and grandparents.

As a new parent, the idea of traveling with a young child may be overwhelming. However, choosing a familiar route and location (such as the kids' grandparents' home) will help get your feet wet. You already know how to get there and will have help in managing logistics (and the kids) when you arrive.

If everyone in your family is open to traveling, you may choose to vacation in one location together. Had you asked me early on whether I would consider vacationing with my parents-in-law and my husband's extended family, I would have balked at the idea. With a limited amount of money and time each year, my priority was to spend break time with my husband and children. But, we have now taken two successful vacations with extended family, and we enjoyed them so much that we are planning more.

If you decide to venture off with extended family—whether it's to Disneyland, Martha's Vineyard, or Italy—consider the following:

1. Determine the intent of your trip before deciding where you'll go. Gather input from all family members, so you all know what you'd like to get out of the journey.

2. Decide how you'll make your decisions. My siblings and I usually plan our trips through e-mail, but a combination of phone, Skype, and e-mail can work well when everyone is scattered around the country or world.

3. Decide on a specific destination. Consider visiting a theme park, exploring a national park, gathering at a resort town, or making an adventure in the area where you grew up.

4. Designate one person for researching accommodations that will suit everyone's taste and budget. This person needs to respect financial and location suggestions set by the group and should help book reservations.

5. Reserve accommodations close to each other. It's not always feasible for everyone to share one rental property or hotel,

and this may be a good thing. To avoid conflicts in parenting styles, book separate rooms in the same hotel or condos in the same development. Even single-family homes near each other work well. Children will love the fact that cousins are right next door, and you will still have somewhere to go for quiet time (or time-outs), if necessary.

6. Plan for different interests, needs, and energy levels. Pick out some things you will do together as a group, such as dinner every evening, and then be flexible at other times.

Where to Go • MD — If you live in North America, and you're not traveling specifically to see family where they live, there are many choices for spots where you can all meet. Top destinations include theme parks such as Disneyland, Walt Disney World, Six Flags, Universal Studios, SeaWorld, and Legoland. Places of historical interest such as Colonial Williamsburg are also popular, as are areas of scenic beauty. Theme parks and cruises are good choices, since they easily cater to the accommodation and entertainment needs of multi-generational groups. My preference is a resort area (coastal, mountain, or lake) with a diverse selection of accommodation and various day and evening activities. Read the trip ideas described in Chapters 2 and 3, "Idea Generator," for information on planning a trip to theme parks, national parks, and cruises.

If you prefer to travel internationally, your costs will probably be higher, and the differences in language, culture, and food may create stress for some members of your family. The earlier you can agree on a destination the better, as this will give everyone plenty of time to research.

The location of your accommodations will help determine how you'll manage logistics. What works well for me is a place away from large tourist centers, but from which you can arrange sightseeing day trips. You'll need enough space for your family to spread out and relax, and this is tougher to find within large urban areas. And, you may pay less for accommodation outside major cities, making the trip affordable for everyone.

Intergenerational Travel • LF

Bringing your parents along when you go on a vacation with your children can ease trip burdens and save money. For Barbara T., traveling with her parents and young daughter was also fun, relaxing, and deeply meaningful. "We did a lot more laughing," she says. "You know how your relationship is with your parents at home? It was so great to do something with them outside of that environment. Taking them into an extremely different environment was fantastic."

The largest group of seniors in our nation's history, the baby boomers, will soon be retiring. Many have paid off their mortgages and have fewer responsibilities, and they're still in good health. Seniors are choosing to hit the road with their children and grandchildren in unprecedented numbers, making intergenerational travel one of the fastest-growing trends in the travel industry.

A three-generation trip allows a bit of freedom from continual childcare. It gives your children a chance to spend quality time with Grandma or Grandpa, and it gives your parents special memories of times spent with their child and grandchildren. If you're lucky enough to have healthy, eager-to-travel parents and your extended-family dynamics are loving and supportive, give intergenerational travel a try—it can be a life-changing experience!

5. FRIENDS AND FAMILY

119

Barbara G.'s Story

I live in Seattle with my husband and children, Ben (twelve) and Daniel (nine). I grew up in the Midwest, where most of my family still lives; although, we are lucky to have extended family in the Seattle area. One summer, everyone came into town for a cousin's bar mitzvah, so we decided to use the opportunity to spend a few days together. I took on the responsibility for organizing a short trip and decided on Whidbey Island, where there are plenty of great places to enjoy the Pacific Northwest. There is a direct ferry just north of Seattle, and there's also a land route, so you're not totally dependent on the ferries.

I used the Internet to find a rental house big enough for all of us. There were sixteen people in our group, including eight adults and eight children. Basically, I looked for a place with enough bedrooms and bathrooms—assuming that younger children would sleep in the same room as their parents, and older children could use sleeper sofas or shared rooms. We had wanted a house on the beach, but by the time I was looking (in April for August), the houses that were big enough and located on the beach were already booked. The house we rented was about a ten-minute walk to the beach and neighborhood pool. The walk was good for getting the excess sand off before returning to the house. There

Planning is crucial to be sure everyone's needs and wishes are heard. Ask all family members to identify the top places they'd like to visit or experiences they'd like to have, and then be sure that the trip accomplishes some of each person's aims. It's important not to overburden grandparents. While some may be perfectly happy to spend full days taking care of their grandchildren, while parents are free to explore; many more will want an equal opportunity for free time to see the sights.

were enough bedrooms for everyone and a basement apartment that the grandparents were able to use. That was nice because it gave them some quiet space away from the kids.

My family is a hang-out crowd. We can drink coffee and talk all day and drink wine and talk all night, so I didn't have to plan many activities or entertainment, even for the children—they played with each other. With that many kids, they mix and match as they play and never really get sick of each other. We walked on the beach and went hiking and whale watching. We took turns watching the kids, and some of the adults kayaked. We brought some games and toys from home to play with. It was really fun.

The only real planning I did was for dinners. Everyone picked a meal they wanted to make and e-mailed the recipes to me. I went to Costco before everyone arrived, so we had most of what we needed. That said, we made several trips for more milk or whatever little things people wanted. Since we were only fifteen minutes from town, a quick trip to the store was easy to do and provided a chance for those who wanted to get away for a while. We split the costs for food and accommodation equally among the four families. We all had a wonderful time, and everyone is looking forward to the next trip!

Everyone must be realistic in this early planning phase and put everything on the table. Our parents may not want to talk about any physical limitations, yet this is the time to discuss how strenuous the trip will be and what a typical day might be like. Keep in mind that seniors won't typically appreciate a fast-paced trip with little downtime. If your children are young, you're likely to go at a slower pace anyway, which would suit many grandparents.

Hot Tip! Having a home base from which to explore is easiest for everyone on a three-generation vacation.

This is the time to discuss parenting issues, as well. It's common for the oldest generation to indulge their grandkids on occasion, but you'll want their buy-in on several non-negotiable topics such as bedtimes or how you deal with behavioral issues. Ultimately, the parents should have the final say in any discussions involving discipline.

Hot Tip! Renting a home—whether a cottage, condo, or villa—works well for extended families who are traveling together, and it's often less expensive, as costs are shared. Look for a rental in an area with a wide range of options, to suit the age differences.

There are numerous travel programs for intergenerational travel. Elderhostel (www.elderhostel.org), for those ages fifty-five and up, features excursions to some fascinating places for seniors and their kin. The trips are oriented toward learning about other cultures and locations, making them ideal for traveling families. Trips range from exploring Mayan ruins in Honduras to a cultural visit to Venice.

One of the easiest ways to travel with parents and grandparents is to go on a cruise. With a wide variety of activities and amenities—including swimming and spa facilities and maybe even an onboard golf course or climbing wall—there's something for everyone. The buffet-style food service guarantees that everyone can eat what she likes. Cruise ships are so immense that you can easily find your own special nook for relaxing away from family members, should you need a break. And if you negotiate, you can spend the evening dancing while your parents do kid duty.

Laura S. has a wise mother. She declared: "You're not getting any of my money when I die. We're going to spend the inheritance now! We're going to take trips." Since that famous declaration, Laura and her children have enjoyed a number of incredible trips with her mother, adding to the whole family's bank of rich memories.

Traveling with Another Family • LF

Touring with another family and their kids can be double the fun. Stacia C. went on a lengthy RV trip with her partner and children, along with friends and their kids. "Having two families and having friends their ages to hang out with was nice for our kids, and it kept the parents' stress levels down," she explains. "It was fun to plot the route together. The kids could talk about the upcoming trip throughout the year and get excited with the other family as they planned evening games and activities for the trip," she says. "And it was comforting knowing that we would have both adult and youth friends at each destination. The enthusiasm of traveling with another family really helped make the trip special."

Let's face it. Our kids are different when they're with their buddies. Friends mean sheer energetic entertainment for them. That positive spirit pays off. Two families traveling together often results in kids who are happier, and more involved and cooperative. And why wouldn't they be? From their perspective, it's a mobile party! It's a lot of fun for us parents, as well, since we can split tasks and childcare and relax with our friends.

Traveling with others is especially helpful for single parents. When I was a single mom and my daughter was young, we occasionally traveled with another family. On these trips, I felt as though my daughter, an only child, had the opportunity to

Lysa S.'s Story

Traveling with another family that has kids of a similar age is always wonderful. We camp in the Clearwater National Forest and the Selway-Bitterroot Wilderness in Idaho. We go deep into the woods to places where campers are expected to pack out what they pack in. It's very rustic. There are no creature comforts and no ready-made entertainment other than the woods and the river.

It's always such a joy to go with our friends, because all the kids build forts, go fishing, collect rocks down by the riverbank, and cook s'mores over a campfire. Our kids get to share a wilderness experience with their friends, and they keep each other completely entertained. We just round them up when it's time to eat or when we're all going on a hike together. It gives us adult time with friends and leaves us more relaxed.

gain a small bit of understanding of what it might be like to have a sibling. I enjoyed the chance to step aside and watch her interact with friends in the intimate setting of shared housing. By traveling with another family, I was also more confident about going on adventure trips. Having other adults along made the planning and logistics much easier, and it increased the margin of safety when setting out on a cross-country ski trip or pushing a raft into a fast-flowing river.

Activity-oriented vacations are especially good for sharing. If you can arrange lodging at a recreational area with a lot of different options, everyone doesn't even have to do the same activity at the same time. This flexibility can create space for each person to do whatever she most enjoys, and it gives the opportunity for trading tales of adventure in the evenings.

Sharing travel with another family is also great for saving money. As just one example, when we (three of us, today) visit our favorite resort with another family, we are able to rent a really nice vacation home for around one hundred dollars per family per night, if we visit in an off-peak season. Traveling as a threesome, we wouldn't be able to afford the same home.

Dealing with Differences • LF — Despite all of the pluses to spending vacation time with another family, there are bound to be differences of opinion, ranging from the inconsequential—whether to cook dinner yourselves or to go out—to deal-breaking, significant differences in child-rearing styles. It's wise to consider which family would mesh the best with yours before broaching the topic of joint travel. Take into account how well the children and the adults get along together; whether the families have similar lifestyles and values; whether your child-rearing styles are compatible; whether any of the children have developmental, physical, or behavioral issues that would make a joint trip challenging; and whether the other family has a positive energy that would add to the fun.

If you don't already have a longstanding relationship with the family you're considering (perhaps your kids are school friends), or you haven't seen the friends in a long time (maybe they're old college buddies who live across the country), the time to get to know them is before the trip! If distance precludes a casual getting-acquainted dinner, you'll need to discuss all of your trip expectations and kid ground rules via e-mail or phone, so there are no friendship-breaking surprises when you do get together.

Once you've decided on the right travel companions, pre-trip planning is in order. For lodging, it's best to plan for private

5. FRIENDS AND FAMILY

spaces for each family. No matter how compatible you are, there will be times when you'll appreciate a chance to unwind by yourselves. Condos, rental houses, or apartments—with central living spaces surrounded by bedrooms—are perfect for shared family trips.

Your accommodation is usually the largest shared expense. You'll need to figure out how to divvy up costs equitably, based on the number of people, beds, and bedrooms. In terms of finances, costs while eating out can be easy: ask the waitperson to divide the bill. For grocery shopping, make sure that everyone knows to keep the receipts; later, one of the adults can calculate the total cost and work out who owes whom.

One of the greatest benefits of co-traveling is sharing childcare. Plan for each set of parents to have a "date night" while the others have a pizza-and-movie or games night with the kidlets. And, be sure no one person is stuck with the majority of grocery shopping, cooking, or driving.

During your pre-trip planning, you'll also need to discuss how to handle any issues that arise with the children, so that everyone knows about and agrees on family rules in advance, and there are no surprises. It's best to agree on the same guidelines for all the kids, so there's no sense of favoritism or envy. You may find that you'll need to relax your usual regulations when traveling with another family. Key points to discuss include bedtimes, snacks, and how you would like the children to spend their time.

After making your plan, talk to your children about any changes to their routine. One scenario might be to tell them: "We don't usually eat after dinnertime, but Brianna and Jacob are used to having ice cream before bed every night. Since we're going on a trip with them, we'll allow nightly ice cream, but it's just for this trip. When we get home, ice cream will be something that we enjoy now and then, but not every night."

Hot Tip! A three-bedroom rental unit gives each couple their own space, and if the children are similar in age, they can enjoy a sleepover atmosphere by bunking together in a "kids-only" room.

Co-traveling means you can play some group games that you couldn't as a small family. If you're traveling by car, you'll have more space (in the trunk) to take along items such as board games, sports equipment, and crafts kits to keep the kids happy and occupied. Be sure that each child in the group brings a book or two, so she can have some quiet time alone at the end of the day to unwind before sleeping.

Taking a Friend Along • LF

"Can we build a fort?" my daughter's friend pleaded. We had ridden our bikes down a steep bank to a lovely stretch of driftwood-covered beach, with glittering water spread out in front of us. Traveling with just my daughter, we would have had our picnic lunch, enjoyed the scenery, and looked for pretty rocks in the surf. But when she brought an active, outdoors-loving friend along, the dynamics shifted. The excursion turned into a joyful frolic with entertaining diversions that we wouldn't have thought of doing ourselves.

At its best, having an extra child on a trip can turn what would otherwise be a quiet car trip into a laugh-fest. It can offer a breather for parents, who can relax, knowing their child is happy and engaged. And it just makes for a richer experience all around as the joys of discovery are multiplied. Tammy H. took her daughter's friend on a trip to Lummi Island, Washington.

"The dynamics of bringing a friend were so positive," she says. "It turned out to be really fun. You have to choose wisely, though. Especially with teens."

Having an extra child or two along can also be one of the worst ideas you'll ever have. It depends on a number of issues, ranging from advance preparation to compatibility. Until I went on a disastrous family trip with my daughter and one of her pals, the issue of compatibility had never occurred to me. When my daughter asked that a friend come, I didn't consider that one of her friends might have very different interests and values. Yet the long weekend at a lake became very long indeed, as the girl-friend and I had run-ins over everything from getting out of bed in the morning to helping out, from cell-phone usage to participating in activities. If I had done my homework and had gotten to know the girl and her parents, I would have been better prepared, with a parent-approved plan to deal with the girl's obstinacy and challenges to authority. Or I might have asked my daughter to choose a different friend, one who was more compatible with our family.

Taking a friend really makes sense when your child is a tween or teen. Social life is important to children of this age, and being separated from their best buddy for the duration of a trip can feel unbearable to them. Traveling with only their parents can seem too close for comfort for some teens (especially only children), and it's easy to see how adding another child can lift everyone's spirits.

Having an extra kid or two join you is especially great for single moms, as it can turn a sometimes-quiet occasion into a richer, more entertaining experience. However, there's a caveat: If your children are young and there's only one parent—you—to manage the herd, you'll probably want to think hard about taking along more dependants. When children are too young to care for their own needs, there's just a lot of extra work required. That extra responsibility can be challenging, unless the child is a frequent visitor to your home and you have a good rapport with her.

Ideally wait until your children are responsible enough to manage things like packing and carrying their own luggage and helping out with simple chores. Then having an extra child along won't be as big of a burden. Every child matures at a different pace, but you can probably count on kids to be responsible enough to have a friend join you when they're around ten or eleven years old.

Having another body on a trip means additional expenses. While the lodging may not be an issue, as it's often easy to fit one more person into a room, food costs can really add up, especially in a restaurant, and even more so if the kids are teens. Out to eat, offer suggestions for reasonably priced menu items, if you are on a budget.

Should your plans include entertainment—whether to movie or a visit to a fair, waterslide park, or zoo—costs can mount up incredibly fast. Keep in mind that you'll have many more expenses than just admission. At a fair, for instance, you'll undoubtedly pay for meals, rides, snacks, and drinks.

You shouldn't have to shoulder the financial burden of providing a vacation for someone else's offspring; on the other hand, the child's family may not be able to afford such luxuries. So, before giving an automatic yes to your child's request to take a friend, consider the other family's financial situation and decide how to handle the expenses. On some occasions, I've been happy to pay entirely for a child we enjoy whose family couldn't swing the cost of a vacation. Other times I've proposed that the child's folks pay some portion of the additional

5. FRIENDS AND FAMILY

trip costs. Since the lodging cost is typically not an issue, it's usually pretty easy to suggest a contribution toward food or even just spending money.

For the good of both families, be sure to meet with the parents early to discuss finances—before the children are completely invested in the outcome. And once you've arrived at an arrangement, be sure to talk over issues related to health (physical and emotional), food, personal care, and bedtime routines.

On your trip, set clear expectations each day. Children will typically be much more amenable to scheduled activities if they know about them in advance. To be sure that the friend doesn't pose too much of a burden, ask the child to participate in basic daily tasks with your own kid. And don't be afraid to call the child's parents if you need to discuss any behavior. It won't ruin the vacation—rather, it will help make the rest of the vacation even more enjoyable for all concerned.

Meeting the Locals • LF

Traveling to places where the traditions and appearances of the people are different is an invigorating experience for us and our children. This helps open our eyes to the richness of cultures around the world. By learning a few simple ways to meet locals, you can increase your confidence and find people wherever you travel who can greatly expand your knowledge and appreciation of their culture.

Getting to meet and spend some time with a local family can be a lot of fun for children, and it's an excellent opportunity for them to learn how their lives compare and contrast with the lives of those they meet. You don't even need to travel abroad to have an enriching experience; there are numerous different cultures to be found, even when traveling within the United States.

Essential Items to Pack when Traveling with Another Child • LF

- The child's own sunscreen (only for sensitive skin)
- Any medications, including a bee-sting kit or an EpiPen for allergies, if needed
- A copy of the child's health-insurance card
- Emergency contact information
- The child's school ID or passport
- A signed statement from the child's parent(s) or guardian(s), permitting you to take the child on the trip and giving you the authorization to administer or request emergency medical care. If you'll be flying—domestically or internationally—or crossing an international border by any means of transportation, this statement must be notarized.

5. FRIENDS AND FAMILY

It can be really helpful to make the acquaintance of locals who can serve as a sort of safety net, in case anything goes wrong with your plans. Laura F. says: "Our experience has always been that when something goes wrong, you end up interacting with people you wouldn't have otherwise. People invariably want to help, and it ends up being a tremendous experience." On a trip in the southeastern part of the Czech Republic, Laura and her family couldn't find a hotel for the night, and it was already ten p.m. They drove up to some teenagers in a parking lot, and two of them got into a car and indicated that the travelers should follow them. "They directed us to a lovely pension that we never would have found on our own," Laura says. "Being open to whatever arises and not being afraid are important. The worst experiences always make the best stories!"

Before you leave home, ask everyone you know whether they have friends in the places you'll be visiting. You may be surprised at how many people have connections in faraway locales. It's best to write or e-mail these friends-of-friends and establish a correspondence with them at least several weeks before your trip. This is an ideal opportunity to learn about some of the things to see and do in their area that you might not find in guidebooks. If you're lucky, you may find that you share similar interests and may even receive an invitation to visit or to go sightseeing.

Laura says, "I work hard in advance to find potentials for connecting with people." She and her husband went to China with their daughter, Eden, when she was four months old, and they returned when she was six years old. "I did a lot of research, before the second trip, to find schools where Eden could meet kids her age," she explains. "We got to meet a family in Chengdu who have a son, Max, who is Eden's age. He played well with Eden. One afternoon we went with Max's dad to pick him up from school. When we got out of the car, a huge crowd of kids swarmed around us. They all started chanting in English the numbers from one to ten, and then sang their 'days of the week' song. They were so excited to use their English."

By being pen pals, your children may be able to meet peers who live abroad. If a friendship develops over time, you could visit the child's family while you're in the area. (See Chapter 7, "Learning Before You Go," to gain more information.)

By speaking a little of the local language, your opportunities for connections will increase. Before your trip, learn as many phrases as possible. You'll show respect, it will help you get what you need, and the home team will appreciate the effort, no matter how meager your skills. Numerous self-study guides are available; plan to study up for at least two weeks prior to your trip. And be sure to pack a phrasebook. (For more information, see Chapter 7, "Learning Before You Go.")

Exploit your family's hobbies or special interests. Check to see if there are corresponding clubs or organizations at your destination, then contact one or two of the members to let them know you'll be visiting the area with your children and would like to meet another family. Is your child into soccer? Perfect! Soccer—or rather "football"—is popular around the world. With a little online research, you may be able to fit an age-appropriate game into your plans. You could meet local parents and kids, and your child could have the thrill of enjoying his or her favorite sport in a faraway place.

No matter where you travel, if you let down your guard by smiling and being courteous, you can reach across the divide and help others feel more comfortable with you. Fortunately, children are the great equalizer—they're loved in every culture. You'll find that you have instant commonalities with other parents and families. Most people will be happy to offer tips or advice on anything from the transportation system to their favorite restaurant.

The longer you stay somewhere, the easier it is to get to know folks. The kind of traveling that's best for families—savoring one place for several days, going slowly on sights seen in a single day, and lingering when you encounter unexpected delights— is also best for meeting locals. However, even if you have just a short amount of time available, there are ways to meet people.

Around the world, children attend summer camps. Why not sign your kids up for a weeklong program wherever you'll be visiting? They'll have the excitement of encountering peers in that area, and you'll have some much-coveted free time to enjoy sights your children would find boring. You'll probably

5. FRIENDS AND FAMILY

Dizy B.'s Story

Before my thirteen-year-old son Christopher and I left for our trip to Central America, we were shopping for surfboards at a local surf shop. The owner gave us many leads on fun, safe places to surf. He also told us all kinds of good things about a fellow called Alex, who runs a surf hotel and teaches surfing in a little town in El Salvador, so we decided to look him up. It turns out that Alex runs a surf camp for kids from the community. Through surfing, he has been instrumental in keeping the local kids healthy, drug free, and in school.

Christopher was tentative at first when he met the local kids, but he loves surfing. The kids were really encouraging. They would say: "You come! You come!" He finally joined the group of teen-agers, and they surfed together every day. I watched my son con-nect with the kids through a common language of smiles and gestures. Even with the language barrier, they found a connection through *olas grandes* (big waves). By the end of the first week, he was asking, "Mom, can we buy property here?"

Christopher surfed with them the full three weeks we were there, participating in a surf competition, at one point. We felt com-fortable and became very attached to the community. He also learned valuable lessons about the culture and the language.

We've stayed in touch since our trip via e-mail, and I've promised a return visit soon. I would also like to sponsor one of the kids from there to come to the States as an exchange student.

find that camps in other countries offer many of the same ac-tivities as those at home, such as outdoor activities and crafts. Others offer unique opportunities for cultural exchange: Your child could surf in Australia, make crepes in France, or learn origami in Japan.

If you're traveling to a non-English-speaking country during the school year, visit a class that's learning your language. This can be an extremely rewarding experience for your family and may lead to friendships. Many cities abroad have conversational English classes. Some of these programs welcome visits by native speakers, so their students can practice. If your children are old enough to participate in this sort of experience, contact the visitor's bureau to inquire about classes, then touch base with the teacher before your trip.

Some cities have official meet-the-people programs. As just one example, Hong Kong's offers activities such as learning about kung fu from an expert and touring the city's Space Museum—which has one of the largest planetariums in the world—with a local docent.

Hot Tip! Be sure to pack a few souvenirs from home for your new friends. (See Chapter 11, "Pack It Up," for gift suggestions that are easy to transport.)

It's easiest to find organized activities for meeting locals in cities. However, if you get off the beaten path, the residents may be more eager to make your acquaintance. That's why I always include visits to islands, smaller towns, or other such relatively isolated areas when I travel. I've taken this approach for years when traveling with my daughter. We've never failed to run into thoughtful locals, who offer insider tips, and who invite us to join them for a meal or sightseeing. It's truly a joy to find that you're the only tourists in an area. And it doesn't take long before you start feeling like a part of the community.

Spend some time where the natives do. Beaches, pools, parks, playgrounds, plazas, and farmers' markets are among the places where you can interact. Swimming spots and playgrounds are particularly attractive to kids. Children's play is universal—your kids will undoubtedly be attracted to others and will make their acquaintance faster than you can imagine.

Consider staying at locally owned accommodations for at least part of your trip. Small, family-run pensions, bed and breakfasts, or hostels will be much more personal and offer greater odds for interactions than hotel chains. At these types of accommodations, you also have access to hosts who can tell you about their city or region.

Lysa S. appreciates the deeper connection to a region and its people. "We're backpacker-level travelers. It's brought us into contact with down-to-earth people who are interested and happy that we're visiting their area," she explains.

Home stays also offer a built-in way to meet the locals. (See Chapter 9, "Home Away from Home," to learn more about various lodging options.)

At campgrounds abroad, you'll be sure to encounter an interesting mix of people from that nation and travelers from nearby countries, while washing dishes in a community kitchen or swimming in a lake. (For more information on camping, see Chapter 3, "Idea Generator: Adventure.")

Paula B.'s kids have international friends. "When my son was nine, we visited Sri Lanka. We were at the beach when some kids started playing cricket. Zack started to watch them, and the kids came over and asked him to join them. They included him in their game. Five years later, Zack is still in touch."

When it's mealtime, choose the small, tucked-away eatery in a neighborhood over a large, central restaurant, as you'll be more likely to meet the regulars. The rule of thumb is to avoid any place with touts and tourist menus. For transportation, take the local bus. Even if it takes some effort to figure out the schedule and route, the bus can offer opportunities to chat with people as you ask for their help in figuring it all out.

If your children are old enough to volunteer, consider spending at least a part of your trip benefiting a good cause. This is a wonderful way to meet locals, and it teaches compassion at the same time. In general, it's easier to find volunteer opportunities with teens than tiny ones, but it's always worth checking out. Global Buddies, for example, caters to children ages seven to seventeen (www.globalbuddies.net). The program takes families into Ugandan villages and South African townships. (See Chapter 14, "Responsible Travel," for more ideas.)

With a teen, you likely won't even need to make any introductions. Teens the world over are naturally drawn to each other. (See Chapter 4, "Challenges and Solutions," to ensure that your child is safe while she's having fun with new acquaintances.)

When it's time to take to the road, spending time with others adds interesting twists to what might otherwise be a straight road. Whether taking along grandparents or your child's friend, meeting up with family and old friends, or traveling to meet interesting people at your destination, you're bound to have a much richer experience!

6.

PRE-TRIP PLANNING

RESEARCHING *and planning your travels is far more fun than organizing and juggling your daily routine. I enthusiastically look forward to all aspects of trip preparation. Being methodical in my approach ensures that I don't miss any details, and ultimately, we all get to enjoy the fruits of my (planning) labors.*

Scheduling Your Trip • MD

Coordinating your family's daily or weekly schedule can seem like a full-time job. Planning a trip can make this job even more difficult. You'll have to consider the adults' work obligations, as well as school schedules. You will also need to factor in price fluctuations based on the season, the availability of hotels and flights, and festivals and other events at your destination that effect tourism.

It's worthwhile to evaluate how the above considerations might change the cost of your trip. If your schedule is flexible, you might even be able to save some money!

Work Schedules • MD — Ideally, on a family trip all members travel together. However, work can get in the way for one or both parents. If your schedules don't quite jibe, don't write off your plans entirely—remember to compromise and be flexible.

Linda K., author of the blog Travels with Children (www. minnemom.com), is a stay-at-home mother with four children. Her husband is a farmer, which means that she must plan journeys around harvest times. Sometimes, the family takes a "summer" vacation in December, and sometimes her husband simply isn't able to go with them. "I'm not afraid to travel without him. If there are experiences we want the kids to have, I make the plans, go with the kids, and pray for rain so he can join us at the last minute."

When I planned a family trip to Mexico, my husband wasn't able to take ten vacation days from work. I didn't want to travel with the kids such a long distance for a short amount of time, so I booked two legs: a fourteen-day trip for myself and the boys, and a shorter one for my husband, who joined us for the second week. This worked out marvelously.

If you are a single parent or your partner cannot accompany you, yet you'd like some adult help, consider inviting a companion. Traveling with one of your siblings, a grandparent, an aunt, or even a nanny can be a fun way to get the assistance you need.

Should you go solo with your kid, elementary school-age and older children may thrive on the additional responsibilities. These trips can also lead to special bonding that may not occur otherwise.

School Schedules • MD — It's easier to take children out of daycare or preschool than elementary or secondary school, when class attendance is far more important.

For moms with older children, school is a large factor in deciding the best time to travel. Even for short trips to Grandma's in a nearby state, you'll have to consider the educational calendar as you plan the trip. Most districts publish these at the start of the school year. If you have children in different schools (even in the same district), they may have different closure and holiday dates.

Longer breaks, such as summer and winter holidays, tend to be very similar across school districts. The exceptions are year-round schools where the summer vacation will be shorter.

Three- and four-day weekends are like little gifts and are the perfect opportunities to take brief trips.

Hot Tip! Check out the educational cycle at your destination before booking. If schools are in session, you may encounter fewer crowds. Most districts in North America post calendars to their websites. You may also be able to find this information for schools abroad, but it may not be published in English.

To help avoid crowds during summer and winter school vacations, adjust your dates to slightly before or after these peak times (don't travel on Friday afternoon, for example). Even a day or two can make a difference in missing hordes of tourists, and helping you save on flights and accommodations. Unless your child has exams, the final days before a long break can be a great time to take off, although you'll want to be sure not to miss scheduled concerts or parent-teacher conferences.

If your child will miss more than a day or two, work with his teacher to ensure he won't fall behind. Be honest with yourself about your child's academic progress. For someone struggling, every classroom minute will be important. Therefore, weigh the benefits of the travel experience against the effect of taking him out of school.

Budgeting • MD

Once you've determined the timing of your trip, review your household finances to get an idea of how much vacation you can financially afford. If you don't already have a proper budget, creating one will help you identify ways to save for your journey and will also help you when you're on the road.

Hot Tip! You can find budget worksheets on personal finance websites such as Kiplinger (www.kiplinger.com). Creating a travel budget with this tool can be a fun project for you and your kids.

There are many ways you can save money to put toward your vacation and get the kids involved, too. These include preparing lunches (rather than purchasing them), making pizza at home (rather than ordering out), and checking books out of the library (rather than buying them). While these changes probably won't pay for the entire odyssey, they may provide your child with some spending money for the trip.

When I'm budgeting, costs may differ from my expectations by a large margin, and this may force me to make changes to our plans. When researching a trip to Europe, I thought that taking a train between two cities would be less expensive than flying. I discovered, however, that low-cost airlines, such as Ryanair (www.ryanair.com), connect many major cities and that rail is no longer the cheapest option.

The five categories of travel expense to budget for are transportation, accommodation, dining, entertainment (including tickets to attractions), and incidentals (anything you may have left behind or run out of, like shampoo). To begin budgeting, research and document potential costs for each category. Use websites such as Farecast (www.farecast.live.com) to determine the approximate costs of flights within North America and some parts of Europe. Check Vayama (www.vayama.com) for international flights. Hotels.com (www.hotels.com), Hotwire (www.hotwire.com), and online booking engines will give you an idea about pricing for accommodations. Most guidebooks provide cost estimates for dining and attractions, as well as websites like TripSketch (www.tripsketch.com).

Remember that guidebooks are written six months to a year before publication and that rates can easily increase during that time. When budgeting, add ten to twenty percent onto the prices listed, and bear in mind how fluctuating exchange rates might effect your expenses.

Entertainment costs and entrance fees can vary widely in different countries and even within the same city. In London, for example, it costs twelve pounds (about seventeen U.S. dollars) to visit the Tower of London, but the British Museum is free (donations welcome, though). If your budget is tight, opt for attractions with little to no cost, or look for ones that offer family discounts or that waive entrance fees for children. Travelers with a membership to a zoo, children's, or science museum may be able to gain free or discounted tickets to similar attractions elsewhere.

By averaging out your expenses, you can leave room for activities you didn't anticipate; after all, even the best-laid plans need some flexibility. Perhaps you've arrived on the Australian coast when sea turtles scramble onshore to lay eggs. You won't want to miss out on this once-in-a-lifetime opportunity, but you haven't specifically budgeted for it. Go see the midnight magic of the turtles, but forgo another outing later so that you aren't completely blowing your budget.

Sarah C. has visited Europe with her husband and two boys, Timmy (nine) and Sam (thirteen). Friends and family often inquire how they can afford their trips. She says that her family lives and journeys simply. "We don't have cable TV at home, and we travel on the cheap. When we're in another country, we might buy food in a grocery store and sit on a riverbank instead of eating in a restaurant. Traveling this way, we experience more of the culture."

Resources • MD

Now that you have a grasp on your budget, researching your destination will help you and your family take full advantage of your time once you arrive. There are numerous resources to get you started and you may choose to explore a variety of the following.

Guidebooks • MD — Guidebooks are still indispensable, even in the online era. Though publishers may cover similar

Budgeting Tips for Family Travel • MD

1. Look for last-minute offers on websites such as Expedia and Orbitz, and meta-search engines such as Farecast and Kayak, and airline websites.

2. Fly low-cost carriers such as Southwest Airlines (www.southwest.com) and JetBlue (www.jetblue.com).

3. Rent accommodations directly from owners. Vacation Rental by Owner (www.vrbo.com) and Owner Direct (www.ownerdirect.com) are good places to start your search.

4. Book your airfare using frequent-flier miles.

5. Travel during off-peak seasons. Ski resorts, for example, are great places to hike or mountain bike in the summer.

6. Purchase packaged deals that combine flights with accommodations or car rentals. Rates can be much lower when bundled together.

7. Travel during the shoulder seasons (in other words, not during the high or low season at your destination). During these months, airfares between North America and other countries can drop by about thirty percent.

8. Consider house-swapping using an organization such as HomeExchange (www.homeexchange.com).

material, each has a different perspective. Before you invest in a particular volume, browse through your local bookstore or library to determine which best fits your family's style of travel.

I always start by reading guidebooks. I can't make decisions on trip details unless I have some degree of familiarity with the destination. I examine the guide's maps, make lists about kid-friendly attractions, read about a city's neighborhoods, and study the public transportation system. This

6. PRE-TRIP PLANNING

is necessary legwork for a successful journey. Only when I have a good base of information do I start booking.

Hot Tip! Secondhand bookstores often sell slightly used guidebooks. Historical, political, and geographic information generally changes little between editions. However, specific details such as business hours and prices may not be current in older editions.

Many guidebook series highlight kid- and family-friendly sights and activities. Check a book's index for "Families," "Children," or "Specialized Travel Resources."

The Internet • MD — After a relatively short exposure, I now wonder how I ever planned vacations without the Internet. I find myself heavily relying on the information found on websites, blogs, and forums.

Start your search on websites that are created by guidebook publishers. Not only is there a depth of information here, but older children—with their experience in surfing—may be eager to participate in the research. My favorites include Lonely Planet, Frommer's, Let's Go (www.letsgo.com), and Moon (www.moon.com).

Search to find travel websites published by online-only companies and independent travelers. These often include personalized recommendations that can be quite valuable. Be sure to check the date of an article's publication. If there's no time stamp, you can't rely on the information being current. Nor can you count on its accuracy—fact-check everything.

Hot Tip! Subscribe to e-mail lists and newsletters that provide information on special travel offers. For example, I receive weekly notices from Farecast about the latest deals on flights out of Seattle.

Guidebooks at a Glance • MD

- The Dorling Kindersley *Eyewitness* series follows a similar format to other DK books that your child may already be familiar with. These guidebooks are very accessible. The pictures pop off the page, and the text is short and direct, easy for even the most distractible second-grader to read. Go to (www.dk.com) to view the *Eyewitness* series.

- Lonely Planet (www.lonelyplanet.com) stands out for providing detailed information on history, activities, and off-the-beaten-path experiences.

- Rough Guides (www.roughguides.com) started as a series for student travelers, but has expanded to include information for all budgets.

- Frommer's (www.frommers.com) first guide was *Europe on $5 a Day* in 1957. This series continues to focus on budget travel, but with a decidedly middle-class mindset now.

- Fodor's (www.fodors.com) provides information for the discerning traveler with, often, a commensurately large budget.

Forums • MD — Most of the larger travel sites provide a forum (also known as a bulletin or message board) on which travelers may exchange tips. Lonely Planet's Thorn Tree (www.lonelyplanet.com/thorntree) is probably the most well trafficked. Here, you can ask and answer travel-related questions and engage in discussions with other users, often receiving replies to your questions within minutes.

Blogs • MD — Web logs, or blogs, vary from stream-of-consciousness observations to more professional opinions, product evaluations, and recommendations. In the world of travel blogs, a huge number are written by individuals who simply document

6. PRE-TRIP PLANNING

their journeys. Those who post informative or educational blogs often include tips, interesting articles, and travel-related news. Many blogs are a good source of family-travel information. If you're a newbie to this world, blog search engines such as Technorati (www.technorati.com) or Google's Blog Search (www.blogsearch.google.com) can help you find ones pertaining to a specific subject, be it the best beaches in Croatia or tango lessons in Argentina.

Some blogs specifically talk about traveling with kids, including DeliciousBaby (www.deliciousbaby.com), Traveling Mamas (www.travelingmamas.com), Travel Savvy Mom (www.travelsavvymom.com), and WanderMom (www.WanderMom.com), written by yours truly.

Maps • MD — I was deep into planning our summer trip to Europe. Flights had been booked, but nothing else was arranged. I was e-mailing website links to my husband daily, and I had purchased a number of guidebooks. But, I couldn't get my children interested in this scheming. I knew that if they weren't involved now, it would be difficult to engage them in activities on the road. Then I came home one evening with a rail system map that I laid out on the kitchen table. Immediately I had two eager kids poring over it, intrigued by the cities, routes, and the complicated symbols that explained the train system.

Stacia C. kept a wipe-off map of the U.S. on the wall in her kitchen. As they planned their trip through the West, the kids would circle where they wanted to go. "We kept the map up for a year. It created a sense of ownership for our children. The kids were very aware of it and very well versed in what we were going to see. They knew where we were going and where we'd be stopping."

I, too, like to know where I'm going, so I start by studying a map. Now my kids enjoy this as well. Some guidebooks come with handy, pull-out, area maps and detailed city maps. A road map is a must if you're driving, and railway maps are invaluable for making sense of large transit networks.

Maps are not only good for navigating once you're there, but they help in planning as well. Refer to a street map when selecting your accommodations, so that you know how close you'll be to attractions. I've had the same spiral-bound London street map from Geographers' A-Z Map Company (www.a-zmaps.co.uk) for years. Because tube stations are marked, it makes choosing a hotel easy. If my children are tired when we arrive, I can honestly tell them that it's only another block when we come out of the Underground station.

Chain bookstores, specialty travel stores, and online travel retailers stock many international city and region maps. These usually provide information on key tourist sights and activities. Laminated street maps, such as those published by Streetwise Maps (www.streetwisemaps.com), are a worthwhile addition to any daypack, as are large-scale maps from Michelin and HarperCollins.

Magazines • MD — In addition to providing valuable information, travel magazines are eye candy that you can browse through time and again just to enjoy dreaming.

Hot Tip! Many schools and organizations use magazine sales as part of their annual fundraising campaigns. Subscriptions can cost just ten to fifteen dollars per year. You can easily support your child's school, scout troop, or soccer team and receive a monthly treat full of travel tips.

Many include sections on family travel and tips for traveling with children. Some magazines even offer adventure travel suggestions for off-the-beaten-path destinations. The National Geographic Society (www.nationalgeographic.com) publishes country-specific editions, with breathtaking photos and in-depth coverage that are a great introduction to a place and its people. They will grab the attention of young and old alike. *National Geographic Kids* exposes smaller children to the world in an easily understandable way.

Formulating a Trip for All • MD

When I sat down to plan a summer vacation, my mind was filled with fantasies of where we might go. Our trip was anchored by a one-week family get-together in Tuscany in late June, but my husband and I had been accumulating our vacation days and wanted to spend a total of three weeks in Europe. That gave me two glorious weeks to fill. We decided our boys were old enough for us to try urban backpacking, focusing on low-cost travel with a lot of flexibility. I ordered a Thomas Cook rail map of Europe and got down to the business of planning.

Barbara G. knows that it's not always easy to appease everyone. She has taken her children throughout the U.S. and Asia. "It's an art to learn how to travel well as a group, to balance everyone's different interests and objectives." To do so successfully, you must first determine the goals of the trip, whether they include busy days filled with sightseeing or lazy days relaxing and unwinding.

When I plan a trip, such as our family backpacking jaunt through Europe, I use a few simple steps to help me create a journey that everyone will enjoy.

1. Select your accommodations wisely. Stay in the same place for as much of the trip as possible, so that you can easily explore the surrounding area.

2. Research your destination thoroughly, and plan a menu of activities, alternating busy days with relaxing ones.

3. Create a day planner and include all outings and travel times. Look at this with a critical eye and be realistic about your children's tolerances, interests, and activity levels.

4. Factor in when and where childcare might be needed.

Jeanne D. organized a multi-generational two-week trip to Spain. The age range of her group was six to eighty. "Planning is the first step in keeping everyone happy," she says.

It's difficult for both you and your child if you are constantly moving during your adventure. Debbi T. traveled to Vietnam for a month with her three-year-old daughter Jora and wanted to have some stability. "I figured Jora would do better with a stable base, so we set up in one location and then took day and weekend trips during that month." Often, older children find frequent moves less stressful than younger kids, but they will also appreciate staying in the same place for a few consecutive nights.

Consider the ages and personalities of your children when selecting attractions. If you have a quiet, easy-going infant who is fully portable, you may be able to spend a few hours at an art museum. Parks, piazzas, and markets are always a hit with toddlers, preschoolers, and even some younger elementary school-aged children, while museums may be more difficult for these kiddies.

If you still want to include a museum or other activity that your youngster may not enjoy, focus on one element. When

6. PRE-TRIP PLANNING

151

visiting the British Museum in London with my boys, we spent the whole morning at this impressive complex, but only took in the Egyptian rooms and a special exhibit on the New World. We had a great time, and they loved it. But had we stayed longer, I'm sure that they would have become tired and cranky, and would have left the museum with no desire to return.

Even a reluctant traveler can be engaged if you start a dialogue well in advance. I had talked up the Egyptian exhibits so much that my younger son, Brendan, woke everyone up early. He insisted that we get going or we wouldn't be able to see the mummies. This was six months after we originally had discussed the exhibit.

Shelly Rivoli is the author of *Travels with Baby: The Ultimate Guide for Planning Trips with Babies, Toddlers, and Preschool-Age Children*. She has two preschool daughters with whom she has explored the U.S., Asia, and Europe. She says, "Children are never too young to share your excitement before the journey." She suggests focusing on the positive aspects of why you're going on the trip in the first place.

With younger children, tell them about all the kid-friendly activities at your destination. Older kids may already recognize famous landmarks, but it helps to supplement what they know with interesting details. I usually put together a rough itinerary of notes on scrap paper. I then start selling highlights to my children. I write down the details of where we'll be staying, any transportation information I have, and options for fun activities. This trip plan becomes my reference for when we chat and brainstorm.

It can be difficult for children to conceptualize a trip, and they may not engage in discussions in the weeks and months before you travel. This can make it difficult to plan activities, since you do want their input. I stay cheery and persistent and throw out ideas for kid-friendly activities during normal conversation before the trip.

With differing interests among adults and children, compromise is key. In Cyprus, we visited the amphitheater at Kourion. I found it spectacular, but my boys' interest was only held for about two minutes. We negotiated. They got ice cream and, in exchange, they walked the site with me.

When planning the day's activities, determine how much information is adequate to share. An easy-going child may not need to know the day's schedule, while others may need to know exactly what the plans are in order to feel more secure.

Marie W. makes cross-country car trips with her six children. She talks about the difficulty and importance of the transition from everyday life, where the focus is on the individual, to the enforced closeness of traveling together in this way. "Everyone learns that we have to respect each other's individual needs."

Hot Tip! Wandering can be the best way to experience a destination with a child. They may not care if they see the top attractions. By slowing down and exploring at their pace, you allow yourself to see in an entirely new way.

Don't spoil your planning efforts by passing on any stresses to your children. It's easy to be tense during the days prior to your departure, when packing and finalizing last-minute details are important. As Shelly notes: "Your children will pick up on that stress. As you juggle laundry, packing, and all the other details, remember to talk to your children about what you're looking forward to, whom you're going to meet, and

6. PRE-TRIP PLANNING

153

what you're planning to do." In other words, keep them focused on the enjoyable side while you handle the details.

Paperwork • MD

Aggregating and organizing all of your documents may not sound as exciting. Yet it's a critical step to a successful trip. Do so long before your journey begins to eliminate a lot of last-minute stress.

Passports • MD — U.S. and Canadian citizens (including infants) entering or leaving North America by air must have a valid passport. As this book goes to press, U.S. citizens can simply show passport cards when traveling by sea or land to or from Canada, Mexico, the Caribbean, and Bermuda. This identification is part of the Department of Homeland Security's Western Hemisphere Travel Initiative (www.dhs.gov). Canadian citizens may use a form of government-issued ID (such as a driver's license) to enter the U.S. by land, but require a passport for all other countries.

Make sure that everyone's passports are valid, as the first step in planning a trip outside of North America. In fact, they should be valid for more than six months beyond your departure date. Make sure you have two to four blank pages available for visa stamps. Failing one or both of these requirements could prevent you from boarding a flight. By car, not having passports, passport cards, or government-issued identification could lead to unwanted hassles and a delay getting back into your country.

Adult passports for U.S. citizens are valid for ten years. Those for children under fifteen years of age only last five years. For Canadians, passports remain legitimate five years for anyone over the age of three, while tots' are good for just three years.

On the morning before Shannan H. was due to visit her husband's family in England, she noticed that her five-year-old daughter's U.S. passport had expired. It was a Saturday, just three days before Christmas, and all passport offices were closed. After many phone calls, she was lucky to find someone who could help. "A sympathetic soul at the British Embassy managed to procure permission for my daughter to leave the U.S. and enter the U.K."

It's easy to forget the importance of a valid passport when so many other details demand attention. With the shorter expiration date on children's passports, be particularly vigilant, as these years can pass so quickly.

U.S. citizens (or the parents of a U.S. citizen) can pick up passport application forms at one of 9,000 locations. See the U.S. Department of State's website for a listing of these locations (www.iafdb.travel.state.gov). These forms can also be downloaded and sent by mail. The processing time is about six weeks. Once you submit, you can use either the status-check tool on the Department of State website (www.travel.state.gov/passport) or call the National Passport Information Center to get information on your application.

Canadians may apply in person at a local office listed on the Passport Canada website (www.ppt.gc.ca) or by mail. Don't leave your applications or renewals to the last minute. If you might be traveling within the next twelve months, send in the paperwork.

For rush jobs—expedited passports—there is an additional fee and extra shipping charges if you apply by mail. In the U.S., you can visit one of thirteen regional agencies where your passport is processed on-site. You must have an appointment to apply in person, and these are issued only if you can

6. PRE-TRIP PLANNING

155

prove (by showing an airline ticket or similar documentation) that you will be traveling within fourteen days. These applications are fulfilled within forty-eight hours. Canadians may also have their passports expedited, either by mail or at a Passport Canada office, for an additional fee.

U.S. and Canadian citizens applying for a child's passport will need:

1. Proof of citizenship (usually a birth certificate or similar document)

2. Evidence of relationship to parents (including legal documents pertaining to custody, when necessary)

3. Parental identification

4. Both parents' permission to apply for a passport

5. Two passport-sized photographs of each applicant

Both parents must be present when the passport application is submitted. If one cannot be present, the appearing parent must provide either proof of sole authority to apply or notarized permission from the other. The State Department requires legal documentation of sole authority such as a court order granting custody or a death certificate. If this documentation is not available, a Statement of Consent or Special Circumstances form (DS-3053) must be submitted stating why permission from the non-applying parent cannot be obtained.

For U.S. citizens, passports for children under sixteen years of age cannot be renewed. Once it expires, you must re-apply. Those over sixteen can renew via mail by sending Form DS-82 along with your most recent passport, two passport photos, and funds to cover the fee to the National Passport Processing Center. Canadian passports are not renewable, although you can apply for a new one using an online application, or you can mail in Form PPTC 054, which is downloadable from the Passport Canada site.

Your passport is the most valuable item you'll carry with you when you travel internationally. Keep copies of the front page of your and your children's at home (with a trusted friend or relative) and in your luggage. Some countries, such as Vietnam, require that hotels register guests with the police and will ask to hold your passport as identification. While this is a routine procedure, the U.S. government recommends you retrieve your passport the very next morning. If possible, leave a copy rather than the original.

If you lose a passport while traveling abroad, immediately contact the local authorities and the nearest embassy or consulate for your country. A copy will make the replacement process go much more smoothly. Should one go missing at home, alert the local authorities and your passport agency. You'll then have to apply for a new one.

Special Permissions • MD — When traveling with children who are not your own, you'll be responsible for ensuring that their paperwork is in order and satisfies necessary legal requirements. This includes documentation that you have permission from their parent(s) to travel with them, whether it's across state lines or from one country to another. A child leaving the country without a parent must have a signed, notarized letter from both parents giving permission. Such letters are only valid for that trip and should specify the dates and the names of the accompanying adults. Check with the child's parents well in advance of the trip, giving plenty of time to

6. PRE-TRIP PLANNING

157

obtain a passport if necessary. Do an online search for "child travel consent form," and you will find plenty of templates to help create the paperwork.

When Diane K. traveled to Belize with her son, the permission-to-travel letter from his father was not notarized. This led to problems when she was trying to enter that country. "The customs officer in Belize was not satisfied that I had permission to travel with my child. After much discussion, however, we were finally let through the border." After this experience, Diane says, "I will never again leave without having a notarized letter."

Visas • MD — A visa is a stamp in your passport or a piece of documentation that gives you permission to enter a country for a set number of days. Many countries require that you apply before arrival, while others will stamp your passport with a visa at the border. Check the embassy or consulate website for the country you'll be visiting. The International Travel section of the Department of State website also provides information on entry requirements to many nations, with contact information for the relevant embassy.

Visas are issued per passport. There are no special rules or conditions for obtaining visas for children, and their passports must be submitted to the relevant embassy with a visa application form just like yours. Note, too, that travel between certain countries can be restricted or forbidden due to strained relationships (U.S. and Cuba, for example).

Visas may be single-entry or multiple-entry. With a single-entry visa, you may only enter the nation one time using that paperwork. A multiple-entry visa is issued for a period of time during which you can visit many times.

Visas granted in advance of travel may be of longer duration than those obtained at the port of entry. For example, a thirty-day tourist visa for China, granted in Shanghai, can only be renewed twice for thirty days each, allowing you a total of ninety days in the country. Visas obtained beforehand include single-entry (valid for three or six months), double-entry (valid for six months), or multiple-entry (valid for six or twelve months) categories.

The turnaround time for visa applications will vary by country. Follow the guidelines to allow enough time for visa processing.

Vehicle Documentation • MD — A valid driver's license, registration, and proof of insurance are usually all that's required to drive across international borders. If it's a rental car, you should also carry the contract. Depending on the crossing, you may also need *either* of the following:

1. A *Carnet de Passage en Douane* (CDP) or temporary import permit. This provides a guarantee that the vehicle will leave the country within the time limit specified or all required import taxes and duties will be due. Both U.S. and Canadian drivers can apply for a CDP from the Canadian Automobile Association (CAA, www.caa.ca).

2. A return guarantee bond. As an example, this is required to take a vehicle into Mexico anywhere south of the border zone (an area up to fifteen miles south of the U.S.-Mexican border). This can be purchased online from Banjercito (www.banjercity.com.mx). The application process is available in English and Spanish.

Check the State Department website to find out which of these documents will be required for your travels.

6. PRE-TRIP PLANNING

When abroad, you'll want to bring an international driver's permit (IDP) that can easily be purchased at your local American Automobile Association (AAA) office, on their website (www.aaa.com), or through CAA. Show your current driver's license and provide a passport-size photo. The IDP is written in ten languages and should be used in addition to your driver's license.

Bills and Mail • MD — For shorter (two weeks or less) vacations, it's usually not necessary to make special arrangements for handling payment of your regular bills. For longer journeys, however, you may consider other arrangements.

Paying your bills online will help smooth out the process while you're traveling. The first step is to sign up for electronic bills (e-bills) for your utilities, mortgage, phone, credit card, etc. With this option, you'll receive your bills via e-mail rather than snail mail. Depending on the company, you may be able to set up an automated service that deducts from your checking account, or you can transfer money yourself on the telephone or online, from anywhere in the world. These transactions are most secure on your laptop connected by a cable. Wifi and net cafes can leave your data vulnerable.

If you prefer paper bills, ask a trusted friend or family member to help. You could leave blank checks (to be filled in as your debts come due) or some other payment instructions with this person, so that you don't have to worry about these chores during your travels.

To handle a credit-card bill by telephone abroad call collect (toll-free numbers do not work outside the U.S. and Canada). There is often an additional charge to pay by phone, but it'll do in a pinch, if you can't access your account online and have forgotten to make a payment.

Remember to put a hold on your postal mail or to have a neighbor or friend regularly pick it up if you're traveling for more than a few days. This will prevent your home from looking vacant.

Contact Lists • MD — Keep a list of people you want to stay in touch with on the road. If you're carrying an electronic address book in your phone, make sure you have up-to-date addresses, phone numbers, and e-mails for everyone. Back up key data on a good, old-fashioned sheet of paper.

My biggest failing when I travel with my kids is forgetting to pack a contact list for their friends. I'm used to having the little book of names and addresses of classmates on my desk at home, but it rarely makes my packing list. On one trip, my younger son wanted to send postcards to all his friends, and I had to explain that we didn't have their addresses. He was very disappointed. I tried to convince him that it would be OK and suggested that we could buy postcards, write them, and then we'd mail them when we got home. He looked at me as if I'd sprouted another head. Then I had a flash of inspiration. I had an online list in my Gmail account with the e-mail addresses for the mothers of his friends. We found an Internet café, I shot off quick notes asking for mailing addresses for everyone, and within days the postcards were winging their way to the U.S. Crisis averted—just this once.

Hot Tip! If your child is using a travel journal, this is a handy place to keep friends' addresses. Travel journals for kids often include pages meant for just this purpose.

Write down phone numbers for your child's pediatrician, dentist, and other medical providers, or add them to the electronic device you're using on the road. Although I have yet to meet a mom who doesn't know all these numbers by heart, traveling is a change of pace from your daily routine, and it's easy to forget this important information. And, in the case of an emergency, you'll be glad you have a list to refer to.

In addition to details for health-care providers, your list should include insurance information and contact information for family members. Verify that the data is current, make a copy to leave with a friend or family member, and add the list to your travel documents.

Reservations and Itineraries • MD — Keep confirmation numbers or letters for everything you've booked. This includes hotels, shuttles, rental cars, and tours. Reservations can easily get lost within a company's system. Having a printout will aid you, if there's a discrepancy with the cost or a question about the existence of the reservation.

Make copies of all important documents such as passports, airplane tickets, travelers checks, visas, and credit cards, and leave them where a friend or family member at home can access them if need be. It's easy enough to set up a free e-mail account through Gmail, Yahoo, or Hotmail that you can access from most anywhere in the world. Sending scans of these documents to yourself will ensure that you can retrieve this information quickly.

Prescriptions • MD — Even if you have enough medication to last your entire trip, keep a copy of each prescription in case anything gets lost. These can often be easily refilled at a local pharmacy when you are traveling in North America. My pediatrician's practice uses digital prescriptions, meaning he no longer writes out a paper slip. Instead he completes a form on a computer and e-mails it to the pharmacy of my choice. Even though these digital copies exist, it is unlikely that they are accessible to a pharmacist in another city or country. If your pediatrician uses this method as well, note that you may have to call, explain your trip plans, and get their input on how best to handle regular or emergency refills while you're out of town.

When we visited Italy, my older son lost his glasses. Sigh. We walked around and around the pool where he'd been playing, up and down the road, and turned over everything in our rented apartment. No glasses. I had forgotten to bring his prescription. We contemplated calling the ophthalmologist in Seattle and asking him to fax or e-mail a copy to us. But after taking one look at the cost of eyeglass frames in the nearest town (much more expensive than the forty dollars we had paid for his SpongeBob SquarePants frames at Costco), we decided to make do. His prescription is very similar to mine, and I have a small head. He wore my glasses, and I wore contact lenses. Since then, I always pack an extra pair of glasses and a copy of the prescription.

Nanny Services • MD

I can clearly remember the first time I used the nanny service at a hotel. My son was about three, and we were in Fiji with another couple and their young children. It was coming to the end of the vacation, and the adults decided we'd treat ourselves to dinner out sans children.

The hotel offered childcare services. I was a little nervous engaging a complete stranger to spend any time with my kid. The concierge assured me, however, that the agency only employed qualified personnel, and all references were thoroughly

6. PRE-TRIP PLANNING

checked. The woman who arrived at our room was a friendly, motherly lady a little older than me. She had a big smile and basically shooed us out the door, assuring us that our son would be just fine in her care. And he was. When we returned, he was sleeping soundly in his bed.

Opting to use childcare while you're traveling is a highly individual choice. For Cathy P., a full-time mom with three boys ranging in age from six years to four months, childcare at their hotel or while on a cruise is necessary for an ideal vacation. "My older boys love going to play at the Kids' Club, and my husband and I enjoy having a few hours to ourselves with the baby. On cruises, the boys can eat early at a buffet dinner, and then go watch a children's movie at the Kids' Club while we eat—that's a real treat."

Research available options, and consider the dates and times for which you may need care, as well as the likely costs. Most major hotels worldwide offer babysitting services as one of the guest amenities.

The sitters, however, are usually drawn from a local nanny or childcare agency. Before embarking, ask for this company's contact information. Then, call it directly and enquire about the cost, availability, qualifications, and experience of its employees.

If you are staying at a house or condo, booked through a rental company, the agency may detail childcare services in a guest handbook at the property.

Hot Tip! If you are renting accommodation directly from the property owner and he doesn't provide information for childcare services, call the concierge at a local hotel and ask for recommendation.

Sittercity (www.sittercity.com) is an online resource for find-ing childcare professionals, with listings for over thirty metro-politan areas in the U.S. You'll need to sign up as a member to use this service.

Consider how your children will react to meeting a new sitter. As with so many other things, a child's personality will influ-ence whether or not she is comfortable meeting and spend-ing time with a stranger. While my older son, Cillian, was always perfectly at ease, Brendan hated the idea of having a stranger around. It was helpful to supply movies, games, and books, which we brought from home, for them to play with, so Brendan was distracted.

It does help to show nervous kids the information about the fa-cilities in advance and talk it up so that they are excited before you arrive. Have a back-up plan, in case your child is resistant to the sitter at the last minute and clings to you for dear life.

While resorts, hotels, and cruise ships may very well offer childcare services, don't make any assumptions about what may be available at a "Kids' Club" or other childcare center. If you have any questions or concerns, contact the premises directly. Ask about licensing and adult-child ratios, as well as facilities for diapering, toileting, and food service. Read the terms of the service carefully to determine if the venue is right for your kid. You may find that the service requires your child to be potty trained, and they may group children by age (an important fact if you have more than one child, and they want to stay together). Advanced reservations are usually required.

Those fortunate enough to have a nanny at home should con-sider bringing him along. Be sure to discuss and document expectations and responsibilities for the trip beforehand.

6. PRE-TRIP PLANNING

165

Communicate clearly the expenses that you will be paying for and whether or not you will offer a per diem for additional expenses. Finally, decide whether to accommodate her in her own room or with your children, and create a schedule allowing her work time and free time during the trip.

7.
LEARNING BEFORE YOU GO

O NCE *you've decided where to go on your trip, the fun can really begin! Now it's time to learn, alongside your children, about the languages, geography, history, and cultures of your destination. Cultural festivals, theme dinners, family video nights, and phrase practice can all build the excitement. We offer suggestions for ways your whole family can begin learning about the places you'll be exploring.*

Ethnic Foods • MD

My children are extremely picky with food and prefer plain pasta, chicken, and some carrots or broccoli. But, I am a persistent mom who loves to travel, and I want them to be more cosmopolitan in their choices. I also strongly believe that food and culture are intertwined, and if my children won't attempt local foods in new countries, their experiences will be limited. To get them accustomed to new flavors before we travel overseas, we eat at ethnic restaurants in Seattle, and we cook with recipes from around the world at least once a week.

Food is a natural way to introduce a new horizon to your children. Some cuisines are easier than others: Italian, Mexican, Chinese, French, and Indian restaurants are plentiful all over North America. One place to start is the food court at a nearby shopping mall, where ethnic chain restaurants are popular. IKEA (the Swedish furniture store) is another option. Here, you can shop, enjoy supervised childcare, and finish up your visit with some Swedish treats at its café. Introducing your child to different foods teaches her about color and culture from around the world.

Debbie D. introduced her preschooler to a traditional Spanish dish before her family visited that nation. "About a week before we left on the trip, I made paella. That worked out really well, and my picky son was excited whenever we ordered paella in Spain."

Shopping at an ethnic grocery store or even in the ethnic-food aisles of a large supermarket is always intriguing for children. If your kids are not as interested in the healthier foods, candies and cookies are reliable attention-grabbers and can be a start. Websites such as Cooking.com (www.cooking.com) are useful resources for a wide variety of recipes. Even if your child won't help in the kitchen, she will certainly enjoy opening packages and investigating what's inside.

Cultural festivals are colorful, exciting, and often include global food vendors. In Seattle, we are lucky to host the year-round Festál (www.seattlecenter.com/events/festivals/festal). This is a celebration of traditional arts, performances, history, and foods from other countries. My children have had their first tastes of many flavors from the stalls at these events. Though we have yet to visit many of the countries, including Brazil and Japan, my boys have now been introduced to those lands. Similar celebrations focusing on a specific holiday can be found in many North American cities, including Saint Patrick's Day in New York (go Irish!) and the spectacular Chinese New Year parade in San Francisco.

Hot Tip! Invite foreign friends over for a potluck meal. Most likely, they will be glad to share food traditions from their cultures with your children.

Food is also a good way to remember a trip long after you've come home. The Greek restaurant in your city may not have tables outside with a view of the Mediterranean, but the souvlaki could taste just as good. And it'll give you and your children an opportunity to reminisce about your vacation.

Language Learning • LF

One of the best ways to really get inside a culture is to learn its language. It can be a wonderfully empowering moment when children are able to ask a vendor how much something costs or say, "My name is…". Knowing even just a bit of the local

Reasons for trying new foods before you leave home: • LF

1. It allows you to introduce new foods to a fussy eater in a safe environment. If there's nothing she can find to eat, at least you're not too far from the peanut butter and jelly in the pantry.

2. Should your child not enjoy certain flavors, you have time to plan how to manage this while you're traveling.

3. It provides an opportunity to learn to pronounce the names of the dishes that your children do like. That way, even if you can't read a menu, your children will be able to order those dishes (and probably will have fun doing so!).

4. You can learn the words for basic foods like bread, rice, and chicken. These are staples that even the fussiest child will usually eat (especially if served plain).

language will help your child be more easily welcomed and can make a lasting impression.

Fortunately, children acquire foreign languages much more readily than adults do. Their absorption skills are strongest before the age of ten. However, don't let this fact keep you from starting your older child on the path. As kids, their minds are still sponges.

It's courteous—and helpful—to be able to speak at least a few words. Pictorial dictionaries make it easy for children to associate objects with words. The field is crowded with these wonderful books. Many of the series use the word "first" in the title and the language. While you could check one out from the library, I'm a big believer in children owning great resource books. This kind of book is a natural keepsake to help them continue to learn.

Another effective—and fun—resource is the British Broadcasting Corporation's (BBC) children's language course by the improbable name of MUZZY (www.early-advantage.com). The program includes DVDs with cartoon action sequences, which kids love to watch, as well as audio CDs and a workbook. Instead of their watching one more round of the latest kidvid, pop MUZZY into your DVD player. Your kids will be rolling with laughter while learning another language.

Software is another path. My top pick is Rosetta Stone (www.rosettastone.com), which offers thirty-one languages for everyone from kindergarteners to adults. Rosetta Stone caters to different learning styles with its multifaceted approach, using images, text, and sound. The interactive nature of this software—you get feedback on your pronunciation—makes it a lot of fun. For a more affordable option, you can download language lessons from iTunes (www.apple.com/education/itunesu_mobilelearning) or Audible (www.audible.com), or borrow language tapes or CDs from the library.

Hot Tip! When looking for language tapes, CDs, or DVDs, be sure to purchase the right language or dialect. Spanish as spoken in Spain (Castilian) is markedly different from that in Latin America. The same would go for preparing for a trip to China, where the language may be Cantonese or Mandarin, depending upon the region.

Before a South American trip with her two boys, Sarah C. ordered a Spanish-language poster of foods and another depicting rooms in a house, from a teacher's supply resource, Teacher's Discovery (www.teachersdiscovery.com). "I also got a Spanish bingo game that was a lot of fun to play with the kids," she says. "I quizzed Sam and Timmy before the trip. By the time we headed out, they knew and could order foods, and they knew colors, the words for *boy* and *girl,* and some simple phrases."

While planning a trip to Turkey, Laura F. found a wonderful resource, *Point It: Traveller's Language Kit* by Dieter Graf. "It's a tiny book that has pictures of everything you could possibly need—tires, thermometer, ambulance, tampons, etc." Laura says. "You can show the picture to someone who can direct you to where you need to go."

The book helped immensely. "Eden had a high fever. I was able to tell the man at the front desk of our hotel that I needed a pharmacy. He offered to help and then drove me around town in his car until we found one that was open. At the pharmacy I was able to describe what was going on with Eden, and we got antibiotics."

For an additional learning opportunity, most guidebooks contain a glossary of phrases, such as *hello, goodbye, please* and *thank you,* in the local language. If you employ these words in daily interactions with your children, they can start learning before you go. It's also really useful to pick up a pocket-sized phrasebook that you can take along.

Hot Tip! If you'll be visiting more than one country and have more than one child, have each pick a language to be the "expert" at.

In the car, listen to a language-learning CD or tune in to a foreign radio station to have fun picking out the words you all know.

Even kids disinterested at home will pick up some of the language while they're there. Dizy B. did some language study with her son before Central America; yet, he didn't show a lot of excitement. Once there, however, it was a different story. "I took a conversational approach with him," she says. "Initially I had him ordering food and asking directions. Then, in Nicaragua, we met a guy who was a lot more fluent in English than we were in Spanish. We could ask him, 'What's this?' and the fellow would point to a table and say '"*mesa*—table."' Christopher has retained a lot of the information he learned."

Numerous total-immersion programs exist, so that teens may live with a host family in another country while they learn the language. Such an international exchange can be a life-shaping experience. I spent a summer living with a family in Mexico City when I was sixteen. I discovered how much alike we all are, and I felt close to my host family. For years after, I referred to them as "my Mexican mom and dad." Going into the exchange as a shy kid, I emerged afterward feeling more in control of my own destiny—I had acquired a solid sense of my own strengths and capabilities.

Whichever path you choose for your child to learn another language, it will offer lifetime benefits. Also it will lead them to a healthy appreciation of and interest in other cultures.

Pen Pals • LF

Helping your child find a correspondent is a great way to introduce her to a different culture.

Having a pen pal can be an exciting experience. Receiving e-mails, letters, or photos from afar builds anticipation about the place your family will visit. It can also help her see that no matter where you live, everyone shares similar issues and dreams. For children who are shy, writing is typically a lot easier than talking; a pen pal can help build confidence.

While numerous websites exist to link classrooms, it can be challenging to find one for individuals who want pen pals. Check out Student Letter Exchange (www.pen-pal.com) for starters. You might also ask at your child's school whether they already have a connection.

Help your kid find legitimate, safe pen pal websites. Some that appear to be for children have inappropriate elements, such as ads for prison inmate or "romance" pen pals. It's important that parents involve themselves actively in the search for pen pals and monitor the relationship.

Sponsoring an Exchange Student • LF

In our family, we love learning about other cultures and are raising our child to see herself as a global citizen. What better way to instill wanderlust than to invite a young exchange student to live with your family? In addition to the wonderful daily learning opportunities, your family may have a great opportunity later to visit her homeland.

The rewards are great. Just sitting around the dinner table, you can explore the differences in customs and traditions. Through a shared life, it's easy to see that all of us are so much alike. And exchange students can remind us to explore in our backyards too. We hosted Henna, a national basketball star in Finland. I hadn't been to a game since I was in high school, yet we went to all of hers in our hometown and proudly cheered her as she shot the winning hoops.

Hosting allows you to learn another language in the best way possible, through daily conversations. Some families find it helpful to assign certain languages to certain parts of the house. This prevents confusion, especially with tots, and makes sure English doesn't dominate all conversations.

An exchange student can be especially meaningful for single-child households. Most visitors are high-school age; if personalities mesh, you may even find your exchange student takes on a big-sibling role.

Exchanges don't charge fees; you're merely expected to provide the guest with room and board and to treat them like a member of your own family. The students pay for their flights, insurance, any educational costs—they typically attend the local high school—and spending money. You can also deduct fifty dollars per month as a charitable contribution, even without hosting an entire year. Some exchange programs place students for just a semester.

Check out the Council on Standards for International Educational Travel (www.csiet.org). CSIET is a private, non-profit organization that identifies reputable international youth exchange programs and promotes their value. It creates an annual list of CSIET-certified programs, available for a small fee.

Economic Differences • MD

In Puerto Vallarta, Mexico, my son asked for the first time about the differences between our level of comfort and what he had observed while we were traveling. He was eight years old and was intrigued by the people who were selling trinkets on the beach outside our hotel.

One evening, as we walked along the far end of the beach, he noticed these vendors inhabited shacks. He wanted to know why their living conditions were so poor. Although this is a complicated topic, we felt that he deserved an answer. My husband and I explained the differences around the world. We talked about our lifestyle in the U.S. and revealed that not every child has a house or school like him.

When you travel with your children, especially internationally, there will come a day when they will ask a *why* question difficult to answer. How you respond will help shape her view of the world.

Toddlers are too young to notice or understand the concept of poverty. By elementary school, most children start learning about larger issues, including the wide financial gap. Some schools even promote charity fundraising that helps disadvantaged children at home or abroad. Kids this age can understand the value of collecting diapers or peanut butter for peers in their own city. If you're headed to a developing country, start talking about societal disadvantages and preparing your child for what she might see. This will help her become an empathetic and concerned citizen.

David J. Smith's book, *If the World Were a Village: A Book About the World's People* (illustrated by Shelagh Armstrong), is a very powerful tool for helping children understand the economic complexities. He explains how the different communities around the globe can be represented in one 100-person village. The message is poignant and very easy to understand.

Jeanne D. describes how she prepared her six-year-old daughter for a visit to some remote and impoverished areas. "Before we went to Morocco, we talked a lot about how the people live and how little they have. I think that really helped my daughter adjust quickly to the living conditions there. We have always done service projects with her, such as going to nursing homes at Christmastime to serve meals and cheer people up. So we prepared her in the same way by telling her in advance about what she might see. We talked about different customs, religions, ways of living, and poverty."

When discussing these differences, remember the following:

- Don't ignore the topic, but do make it easy to understand. She will need an answer—one that makes sense to a child's view of the world.

- Present the information in a way that doesn't sermonize, so that she will stay interested.

- Be flexible in your travels, in case you need to change your plans. If your child sees others her age destitute or begging, it may be too much to process. Consider rerouting to more developed regions or, if the experience is still too traumatic, leaving the country altogether.

As Jeanne said about an African trip, "In a way, kids are kids. My daughter is used to adapting to different ways of living and often not having a language in common. She focuses more on what they do have in common, like running around, singing, and being happy. I don't think she really had a sense about the families in the desert not having running water or how that impacts their daily life. She was not bothered at all by the mud huts or dirt floors, although the bugs bothered both of us. She thought it was very cool that they keep camels and goats in their backyards, as our friends did, and she loved the food."

Hot Tip! As your children get older, consider volunteer vacations with organizations such as Global Volunteers (www.globalvolunteers.org) and Global Buddies (www.globalbuddies.net). These organizations arrange activities for adults and children and often assist people in disadvantaged regions, whether in North America or abroad. These programs are generally open to children as young as eight who are accompanied by an adult.

8.

FLIGHT PLANS

FLYING *with children requires special consideration and more attention to details than adult-only travel. Factors that may seem only somewhat important to a grown-up become greatly magnified when kids are involved. You may feel like Goldilocks, struggling to schedule a connecting flight that is neither too long nor too short, and attempting to keep your kids entertained beyond their electronic games. But the experience can be "just right" with some effort.*

Planning Your Flight • MD

All travelers have the same goal: to find the most direct route for the best price in the shortest time. When flying with children, pay extra attention when planning that route. It can make the difference between a pleasant experience and a harrowing few hours.

Some years ago, a relative asked for advice about this. I cheerily responded that all flights come to an end. With small children, especially toddlers, air transport can be difficult. These bundles of energy want to move, but are too young to understand why they must stay seated. When my boys were toddlers, they wriggled incessantly to get out of the seat belts at takeoff and landing. They jumped up and down on their seats; they spilled food and juice on themselves, me, and each other (usually not intentionally). They needed to go to the bathroom with unbelievable frequency, and they kicked the seats in front of them.

While I certainly disciplined them, this didn't alleviate the fact that they annoyed our fellow passengers. I would take a deep breath before each flight and cheer for every minute during which they behaved.

There is no magic age when flying gets easier, since children mature at different rates. For me, things took a turn for the better when my younger son, Brendan, was about four and could sit still for long periods. When he turned seven, he was old enough to carry his own bag and to keep himself entertained by reading books or listening to music. He also understood that disruptions—such as delays—are something we have to deal with calmly.

There are a number of practical things you can do to ensure that traveling with children goes as smoothly as possible.

Book Direct Flights • MD — When you book direct flights (those without a layover), you simply board the plane, try to ensure that your child has as good an experience as possible, and exit at your destination. Whether your child behaves like an angel onboard or not, the difficult part is over on arrival, and you can continue on to enjoy the rest of your trip. There is no worrying about the wait before a connecting flight.

Plan Flights Around Your Child's Schedule • MD — Book your flights based on when your child normally eats, sleeps, and plays. Though it may be easier said than done, have your child skip his afternoon nap to help him doze on overnight routes.

For international flights more than eight hours long, my children respond best when we leave late in the evening. This usually means that we arrive between eight a.m. and midday. This also gives a slight advantage over jet lag. If you can keep your child awake for all or most of the first day, his natural sleep cycle will kick in at sunset and will make him more likely to sleep at "bedtime."

Hot Tip! Infants don't have circadian rhythms. Therefore, changing time zones won't affect your baby's sleep cycle. At six months, when he is sleeping for longer lengths of time, he may become more prone to jet lag.

Plan Layovers Strategically • MD — Layovers and young children are like oil and water. You may have to wake them from naps in order to deplane, or you may have to carry a sleeping child while juggling gear (car seat, stroller, and carry-on bag) between connectons. Long layovers require that you keep small children entertained. If time is short, you'll need to be prepared. As Pippa C. says, "I've had connections where I got the kids off the plane, grabbed the stroller from the gate attendant, and just ran."

To manage layovers, keep the following in mind: • MD

1. Give yourself more time than you think you'll need between departures. This allows for flight delays and long distances between gates. Two hours is a good rule of thumb. Stay on the same carrier—or one of its partners—to simplify rebooking should you miss a connection. Leave even larger margins when dealing with budget airlines, which do not have co-operative agreements. One delayed flight could invalidate all your later tickets!

2. Research the terminals you are flying into. If you have to change terminals, factor in an extra forty-five minutes when you're traveling with a child.

3. Before booking, consider your routing options, and fly through airports that are less busy. Airports Council International (ACI, www.airports.org) publishes data on passenger traffic. Search for Annual Traffic Data under the Data Centre link on this website. The busier the airport, the more difficult it will be to navigate with young children.

4. International passengers should know where they go through customs and passport control. If you fly from North America with a domestic layover, you will not have to go through customs outbound. However, when you return, you're required to clear customs at your first North American port. This will require a longer layover to ensure you catch your connecting flight.

Sometimes, your children may surprise you. When my boys were six and ten, we flew from Seattle to Puerto Vallarta via Phoenix. Because of delays, our scheduled two-hour layover became six. We boarded the plane three times, while the pilot and ground crew tried to resolve a problem with the aircraft. These disruptions were more tiresome for my husband and me than for our children. Satisfied with plenty of snacks and their handheld video games, playtime increased with every extension of our layover, and they were perfectly content.

Booking • MD

I remember when the only way to reserve a flight was to contact a travel agent. Since the birth of Internet booking engines—such as Expedia, Orbitz, and Travelocity (www.travelocity.com)—I have purchased almost exclusively online. I enjoy the independence of being able to handle the details—even though it does take time and effort. If you have a travel agent whom you trust and whom provides good service at a reasonable price, there's no reason to abandon that relationship. After all, they provide personalized service and can assist you if something goes wrong post-reservation.

There are several options: use a booking engine; purchase directly from the airline, either online or by phone; buy from a consolidator or metasearch website (which aggregates fares from most airlines and booking engines), such as Hotwire or Priceline (www.priceline.com); or book through a third party, such as a travel agent or American Express (which also may be supported by a travel agency).

Booking Engines • MD — Travel sites allow you to enter your departure and arrival locations, using either a city name or airport code. Also input your desired dates, times, and the number of passengers. The result will be a list of possible flights, sorted by cost, duration, number of stopovers, or other factors. Some booking engines allow you to search on flexible dates one to three days before or after your target, to help find the lowest fares.

Examine the report carefully to determine whether all the taxes and fees are listed in the final cost. Pay attention to the total duration of the trip—including layovers—and make sure you can wrangle your family from one gate to another. Booking engines will include routes solely on one carrier, as well as those routes on more. While the latter may be cheaper, sometimes you can get the best price for a flight by booking directly with an airline.

Airline Websites • MD — Most, but not all, companies have websites that provide booking functions. When I bought flights in 2006 from Olympic Airlines, I was able to reserve seats online, but I had to call a customer service agent in Greece to pay (Olympic has since added online booking).

Hot Tip! Some airlines based outside of North America will not accept foreign credit cards through their websites (for security reasons). Therefore you must book through a travel agent or have a friend with a local credit card do the honors.

Metasearch Engines • MD — While metasearch engines (those that pull information from other sites), return results for the best prices, they require payment before you know all the details (such as departure time and airline). Frustratingly, fares are often non-refundable. Still, these are great options if you know your plans will not change or if you are looking for a great last-minute deal.

Other metasearch engines—such as Farecast and Kayak (www. kayak.com)—aggregate pricing information and (in the case of Farecast) predict whether rates are rising or falling. They are not booking engines, however. If you find a suitable flight, you are redirected to the airline or booking engine where the fare was offered to complete your purchase. These sometimes expire before the transaction is completed, so move quickly!

Pricing • MD — While there are no standard rules for the pricing of children's airfares, it is common to see discounts between the ages of two and twelve. You may also find special offers where "kids fly free" when accompanied by an adult who is paying full fare.

Discount or low-cost airlines such as Southwest Airlines and JetBlue have grown in popularity both in North America and abroad. In Europe, carriers like Ryanair and Easyjet (www.easyjet.com) are rarely out of the headlines, thanks to their truly jaw-dropping deals (sometimes as low as one dollar) between EU member states. The prices are right, but remember the following tips:

1. The super-low fares advertised are usually one-way and do not include taxes.

2. There will be additional fees for bags; checking in at the terminal (rather than online); and requesting an assigned seat, food, or drink.

3. If you're checking a bag, you may not be able to check in online.

4. These airlines tend to use small, out-of-the-way airports, rather than flying into major hubs. Factor in ground transport time and cost to your budget.

8. FLIGHT PLANS

5. Baggage restrictions for both carry-on and checked luggage are strictly enforced. Penalties for over-weight items can be fierce.

6. Seats are often close together and may not recline.

7. You may need to book well in advance (more than three weeks before the flight). The cheapest deals can also sell out, so move rapidly.

8. Fares may increase up to three times the bait prices during school vacations.

Frequent-Flier Programs • MD — You may have frequent-flier miles with one or more carrier, which can influence your choice. With the airline industry seemingly in free fall, consider using your miles soon, because they might be devalued at any time.

When booking with frequent-flier miles, first, determine how many miles you need for each seat. This information can be found on your airline's website. Common quantities include 20,000 per seat for destinations within the continental U.S.; 30,000 from North America to Hawaii, Mexico, and the Caribbean; 40,000 from North America to Europe; and 75,000 from North America to Asia. Because of these large amounts, you may decide to accumulate miles to book flights for your whole family every three to five years. Or you may choose to use them more frequently, by booking one seat, then paying full price for the rest of the family's transportation. Either way, you may need to consult customer service about "blackout"—no travel dates, which can complicate reservations.

You may also use frequent-flier miles to upgrade tickets from coach to business class. Having flown in all sections with a small child, I can assure you that upgrades are miles well used.

And, if you're flying internationally, your airline should allow you access to their lounge.

Hot Tip! Consider a credit card that offers frequent-flier miles with your favorite airline. Using this for purchases you'd make anyway (gas, groceries, daycare fees, etc.) will help you reap the benefits in free flights.

In Your Seat • MD

It's unrealistic (but a wonderful idea) to think that other passengers will defer to your every need. To take some of the challenge out of the experience, make sure that you and your family are comfortable.

If you book your flights far enough in advance, you are often able to choose your seats. Airlines usually hold seats for priority customers (frequent fliers) and release them to others at a later time. Some airlines now reserve aisle seats and emergency exit rows (not suitable for children) for these same V.I.P.s or for those willing to pay extra. If you're unable to request specific seats when you book, contact the airline closer to your departure date.

When traveling with children, factor in the distance to the restrooms and whether or not you want to sit in bulkhead seats—both are bits of information that you can find on SeatGuru (www.seatguru.com).

Bulkheads are the partitions (either a wall or curtain) that separate sections of the aircraft, such as first class and coach. Some people prefer bulkhead rows because they have extra legroom. Also, with no row of seats in front, no one can recline his seat into your space. All carry-on bags must be placed in the overhead bin during takeoff and landing, and despite the extra legroom, children aren't permitted to sit, lie down, or play anywhere except in their seats.

Hot Tip! When flying with a lap child, you can check in online, but you must call to request a bassinet or ask when you arrive at the airport.

Reserving a bulkhead seat is notoriously difficult. These are limited (on a British Airlines flight to the U.K., they numbered only fourteen of the 227 coach-class seats) and are usually assigned not only to families, but also to people with disabilities and priority customers.

With an infant under one year and a flight longer than four hours, it may be worth calling the airline to plead your case. For these endurance hauls, you can request a bassinet that attaches to the bulkhead wall, allowing your baby to more easily nap. If you cannot secure a bulkhead in advance, check in at the airport early (at least two hours) and request your seating preference then. For kids over five months, you have a choice: request the "car seat" rather than the "crib" type of bassinet. The latter is often far too small for babies over five months old.

When flying with kids, the actual seating arrangement is important. Siblings or friends may fight over who gets the window (or aisle) seat. And, if there are two adults traveling, you'll have to decide how to arrange two adults and children across the rows. You want to ensure that your gang doesn't annoy strangers and that you (not fellow passengers) have the pleasure of your child's drinks spilling on your lap.

While older kids are usually more autonomous and younger ones still need parental assistance, you can't rely on these generalities. My fiercely independent seven-year-old prefers to re-main beside Mom—although he would never admit it—and my older son flat out refuses to sit next to strangers. I have to consider these factors, whether I'm traveling alone or with my husband. Above all else, I avoid a seating arrangement that leaves me playing the parent-in-charge from across the aisle or from the row behind.

Hot Tip! Have older children review the aircraft seating chart with you. Talk about who's going to sit where and what to do in case of an emergency if you're not all sitting together.

One Person, One Seat • MD — Most airlines allow a kid un-der two to fly as a "lap child." This means that you will not pay for another seat, although you may be required to cover taxes and fees such as fuel surcharges, since the child is still a passen-ger. While this is a very attractive option, consider purchasing a seat anyway for kids more than six months old. Due to ris-ing fuel costs, airlines try to fill flights as much as possible. This means you will likely be seated next to or between other passen-gers. The amount of space in which to care for your baby and store your bulging diaper bag will be limited. However, if you're traveling with another adult and just one infant, and your flight is short, the lap-child option may be an attractive one.

Mariah V. was pregnant when she flew to Finland with her eighteen-month-old son, Walter, who did not have his own seat. The outbound flight was not full, and there was an extra space available. However, the return flight was full. "I had to have Walter on my lap the whole time."

Check SeatGuru to find detailed information on the cabin and seat layout for the aircraft you're flying. This site includes

8. FLIGHT PLANS

details on how much space there is between seats, and you can then decide whether or not to purchase a seat for your child. Airlines often publish on their websites the type of aircraft on specific routes.

Most airlines reveal their policies relating to traveling with infants and children. Check the Frequently Asked Questions (FAQs), or search for specific information.

Packing for a Flight • MD

One of the benefits of traveling with a child who has his own seat is that everyone gets an equal luggage allowance. Four pairs of toddler jeans weigh far less and take up a fraction of the space required for the average adult's. Therefore, you can pack some of your clothes in your child's luggage—for a while, at least.

In addition, each passenger is allowed one carry-on bag. You can also use this to your advantage by hauling extra items in your infant's allotment.

Once, while delayed on the tarmac for four hours at Heathrow Airport, we devoured all our snacks, read all of the children's books multiple times, and almost ran out of diapers. I learned to always pack extra items for these unexpected delays and to cram all spaces in carry-on bags.

You might consider carrying a special seat belt for your child. In 2006, the FAA approved such a device for kids who weigh between twenty-two and forty-four pounds, to be used in addition to the plane's seat belt. Parents will appreciate that this device is far smaller and lighter than a car seat, and is much easier to lug around. The AmSafe Child Aviation Restraint System (CARES) employs a belt and shoulder harness that goes around the seat back and attaches to the passenger seat belt, providing restraint for the upper part of your child's body. In addition to being certified for U.S.-based airlines, it is also approved for those in the U.K., Australia, New Zealand, Singapore, and Canada. The CARES device can be ordered on KidsFlySafe (www.kidsflysafe.com).

A child with the right character-logo knapsack will enthusiastically pack his own bag and proudly try to carry it. The wrinkle in this perfect plan is that he will likely want to put every single one of his special toys in that backpack. Thus it may end up weighing too much for him to haul for more than a short distance. And then you will end up carrying a kid-size backpack, in addition to your other bags.

Strike a deal with your child. Offer to pack his special travel things, so that you can pull out the items that he is least likely to miss. This approach has the benefit of lightening the load, if he's just carrying his favorite teddy or blanket.

Hot Tip! Keep your carry-ons filled with toys, books, or games in a bag that is small enough to fit under the seat in front of you. A young child's short attention span means that he'll want access to this hoard frequently.

Only car seats approved by the FAA may be used on board a flight. Check the bottom for the safety label that verifies your car seat is approved. Every airline has different rules regarding rear-facing infant seats. Check with your carrier's policy in advance to avoid having to banish gear to the hold.

Most airlines require that you gate-check large strollers. Though this is a convenient service, such items can be easily damaged. I purchased a small, lightweight, umbrella stroller for traveling and found it to be a worthwhile investment.

Carry-on luggage tips: • MD

- Carry enough diapers for the entire flight and layover, plus twenty-five percent extra for any delays or lost bags.
- Bring formula for the entire flight and layover. Then add twenty to forty percent more, in case of hassles.
- Pack enough toys, games, and books to keep your child entertained.
- Check with the airline to determine whether meals are served and whether you have enough food to keep your child happy throughout the flight.
- Decide whether you should check an umbrella stroller or take it as a carry-on.
- Make the same call for a car seat. If you do take it on board (avoiding potential damage in the cargo hold), your child will need his own seat.

Child carriers, such as the Ergo baby model, are fabulous for traveling with infants and toddlers. They're light and easy to pack into an overhead bin. (See Chapter 11, "Pack it Up," for more information.)

There are now very strict rules for both checked and carry-on luggage, and these differ among airlines. For example, most U.S. ones require that checked bags weigh less than fifty pounds. Ryanair (in Europe) mandates a maximum of thirty-three pounds (and a carry-on-baggage limit of twenty-two pounds) per passenger. That's a whopping thirty-three percent less than the allotment on most U.S. airlines. This fact is important to note for any connecting flights. Also, many airlines in North America have now added fees for checking a second bag (and in some cases, for checking the first). Fees may also be levied for oversize and overweight baggage—by the bag or by the pound—depending on the airline.

Debbie D. has learned to get around these fees, as she roams with her husband and young son. "It is possible to travel with little kids and not check any baggage, but you have to be willing to do laundry on the road and not bring a lot of gear."

If you have a stroller and check it at the gate, you may have to pick it up at baggage claim. Be prepared to carry your (perhaps sleepy) child from the plane all the way to baggage claim, and factor this into deciding the number of carry-ons you will bring.

In-flight Food and Drink • MD — Once a free perk on flights, food and drinks have become a source of additional revenue. While a few still offer complimentary snacks, it's usually only juice, soft drinks, coffee, water, and a nibble (peanuts). Depending on the airline and the length of the flight, your airline may offer food and drink for purchase.

Hot Tip! Choose water over soft drinks and juice when flying with your children. If and when a spill occurs, you won't have to deal with a messy cleanup.

While your e-ticket may indicate whether a food or beverage service is offered, it's always best to confirm this with the airline, particularly when traveling with children. If meals are not provided, consider snacks from home or pre-packaged foods purchased after security. When I travel, I usually squirrel away some of the following in my carry-on bag: nuts, granola bars, Goldfish crackers, Cheerios (when my boys were younger), and dried or fresh fruit.

8. FLIGHT PLANS

The Transportation Security Administration (TSA, www.tsa.gov) rules prohibit you from carrying liquids through security, although you can purchase drinks once you're through the screening process, and then take them on board. Rules change often, so check the TSA website before flying.

It may be possible to bring small amounts of baby formula, breast milk, and juice for your infant, as long as you declare it at security. Inspectors may ask you to drink a small amount.

Hot Tip! Most airline websites now include information on in-flight food and beverage choices—including prices. Remember the supply of these items may be limited.

In-flight Entertainment • MD — "Mom, is this a movie flight?" This is a critical question for my younger son Brendan, before we board any airline. In his worldview, there are flights with films and those without, and nothing else matters.

At home, I have strict rules for my children about TV and video games, sometimes to their consternation. Cillian, my older son, once lamented, "of all the moms in the world, why did I have to get you?" When we fly, I relax rules and game-time limits, and happily allow my children to watch kid-friendly entertainment. While we always pack books and playing cards, on longer flights, movies really make the time pass more quickly.

Unfortunately, in-flight movies help little in keeping young children entertained. (See Chapter 11, "Pack it Up," for suggestions for these youngsters.)

In-flight entertainment is available on almost all aircraft. Many airlines are experimenting with some form of video-on-demand system, where seats have individual LCD monitors, and passengers can choose among audio and video options. Alaska Airlines (www.alaskaair.com) now offers a digEplayer hand-held DVD player for rent on some routes, and Virgin America (www.virginamerica.com) shows live TV.

Many carriers list their movie selections on their websites. On older aircraft, where the flick is broadcast on shared screens, you cannot depend on the choice being either suitable for your child or entertaining to him.

If you don't want to rely on the in-flight movie, consider renting a portable DVD player from a retailer such as InMotion (www.inmotionpictures.com), which has booths at more than thirty major airports in the U.S. You could also bring your own laptop or iPod, though you'll need to check that it has the software to play a DVD. Also, consider carrying an additional battery.

Hot Tip! Many airlines now charge for headphones, particularly on domestic flights. Pick up some cheap ones at your local drug store and keep them in a drawer next to your passports.

Flying definitely gets easier as children get older. The more often they fly, the more familiar they become with seat belt-and-safety routines and what's expected of them on board. When they need the bathroom, they're old enough to go alone. My boys now understand the difference between first and coach class, and complain that we always fly coach. I've promised that the next time we travel, they can help me plan so they can see the difference in price. I'll let them pick between a coach-class seat and paying the difference with their allowances. I think I know which option they'll choose!

9.

HOME AWAY FROM HOME

THERE'S *a world of possibilities for where to lay your heads at night. On a trip with children, finding the right spots to stay requires a bit of extra planning. However, the rewards are great when you score with that perfect place that's comfortable, close to fun activities, and maybe even educational. In this chapter, you'll find ideas for some of the top kid-pleasing accommodations and budget options, as well as guidance on how to book rooms just right for your family.*

Practical Tips • LF

When traveling with kids, it's fun to base at least a part of your stay in a unique accommodation. How about an historic hacienda in Mexico, a working olive farm in Italy, or a cave in Turkey? Betsy H. and her husband, along with their three- and five-year-old sons, travel frequently to Japan to visit family. "We usually stay a couple of nights in a Japanese inn. We especially enjoy inns near natural hot springs. You wash outside in beautiful stone baths, before soaking in the springs. My sons love to play in the water and wash, scooping and dumping the water over themselves. My older one is finally becoming more comfortable with getting into hot, hot water for soaking. It's a luxury to be in places like these," Betsy says.

Kim C. and her daughter stayed at a particularly quirky, fun retreat center with tent cabins. "The cabin we stayed in had a beach theme. The floor of the cabin was covered with sand, the bed was a hanging waterbed, and there was a beach umbrella and a beach ball inside the cabin! For nighttime there were cool lanterns and even tiki torches."

The first lodging criterion is location. Look for properties near green spaces, so your young children have room to run. Places on the outskirts of cities tend to be less expensive than in-city spots. But consider whether it makes sense to save that money or to make your life easier with ready access to the sights.

It's best to start by keying your parameters into a booking engine such as Expedia, Travelocity, TripAdvisor, or Hotels.com. For more options, try searching for the location and "tourism." The official website for that region will list accommodation options. If you're traveling to Europe, also take a look at ViaMichelin (www.viamichelin.com). For more remote locations, use a guidebook to learn about options; the Rough Guides series is a good choice.

Hot Tip! Consider whether you are eligible for a lodging discount through programs such as AAA or the American Association of Retired Persons (AARP). If you're an airline loyalty program member (frequent flier) or have a credit card affiliated with hotels, check out the properties that are a part of the program, for the maximum discount.

Once you've decided where you'd like to stay, the trio of space, amenities, and budget enters the picture. Tots are easy to fit into most standard hotel rooms, since you can get a standard room and (in many countries) request a crib. With one or two older kids, you can easily find chambers with two queen- or king-sized beds or a family hostel room with two bunk beds. But with three children, there's always an odd person out. This is where you'll need to get creative. Adjoining rooms are one answer. A suite—with one or two bedrooms and a central living space with a sleeper sofa—is another option. Rental condos or houses are tailor-made for families, as they typically have two or more bedrooms and a sleeper sofa.

To save money and to avoid eating out all the time, look for accommodations with a kitchen. Buying fruit, bread, cereal, milk, and peanut butter will provide all the makings for breakfasts and lunches. Be sure to check whether the accommodation covers breakfast in the price of the room. Sometimes you can opt out of this expense; it's worth asking.

Hot Tip! Swimming pools are at the top of kids' criteria for lodging, and they allow for your gang to let off steam after a day of new experiences. If your budget doesn't stretch, look for free places for swimming—whether a nearby lake or river, in the ocean, or even at a city pool.

9. HOME AWAY FROM HOME

You'll want the comfort and security of lodging reservations for at least the first day or two of your trip, particularly if abroad. No matter how you book a room, secure a confirmation, read it carefully to avoid any misunderstandings, and communicate with the proprietor if anything doesn't look right. Taking along only confirmation numbers may get you into trouble. Having printouts of all of the important details—website information, directions, confirmation numbers, and all correspondence—makes you fully prepared for any snafus you might encounter.

Ask to see your room before you make the commitment to stay somewhere. If it's unacceptable for any reason or you feel unsafe there, don't hesitate to cancel your reservation and look for another place to stay, even if you lose your deposit.

Winging it on the road, start your lodging search the day before you need the accommodation, or at least as early as possible. You really won't want to panic into a much pricier hotel or drive into the night searching, especially with kids in tow. You can stop at a tourist office or an Internet cafe to research. Or, if you have a wireless-enabled phone, check the web and call ahead.

Hot Tip! If you book at a business hotel (in-city with a focus on conference facilities), you can virtually guarantee that the pool will be your own private oasis during the daytime. Rates at these properties can be cheaper on weekends than midweek.

Hotels • LF

Hotels are ideal for the first night or two of a trip abroad, as they're a known quantity, and offer comfort and convenience if you're dealing with jet lag. Most are well set up for family needs, with the possibilities of adjoining rooms and amenities such as cribs and additional beds for young children. Hotels run the gamut, from places with walls so thin you may think the crying baby next door is yours, to luxury properties that offer so many features and amenities you'll have to bribe your children to leave.

If you are a member of a hotel loyalty program or you have had good experiences with a particular chain, check them out first. Many brands that are familiar to North Americans can be found around the world, though each continent has its own chains too. Accor Hotels (www.accorhotels.com), with more than 4,000 properties in nearly one hundred countries, is a good resource.

Boutique hotels are unique establishments that mirror the landscape and culture. They tend to cost more, but the experience can be really rewarding, even if only for a night.

Once you have put together a short list, use TripAdvisor to check out each property. This online travel community offers advice, photographs, and user reviews. Comments vary widely; ignore the extreme viewpoints and look for the middle ground. Once you have the best price offered by the booking engines, check the hotel's website for another quote, which may be even cheaper.

Hot Tip! A phone call (or an e-mail) to a hotel gives you the opportunity to bargain for a better price. For a big family, ask the reservation agent whether she can offer a deal on a second room. For deep discounts, always ask, "Is this the best you can offer?"

Dawn L. finds that when traveling with young children, it's important to book a room with "getaway" space. "I discovered that when my kids were napping, my husband and I had two choices: reading in the bathroom or hanging out in a dark room. If I book a place with two rooms, I can do my own thing while the kids nap in the other room," she says. "If I can get a room with a balcony, I don't need two rooms—I can have my own space on the balcony while the kids nap or play." To take this route, however, do check that the balcony is safe for little ones.

Motels • LF

Motels (motor hotels) are typically a lot cheaper than hotels. And there are more of them—you can typically find them lining major arterials. This reliability doesn't alwasy translate overseas, though. Known brands can be more- or less-fancy abroad. Do your homework. Motels are all about price and familiarity.

In small towns or remote areas, motels may be the only lodging available. In cities, independent motels are frequently found in the seedier areas. Their quality varies tremendously. It's particularly important to consider the neighborhood's safety and to examine a room before committing.

Even if a property seems safe, however, you may encounter more "colorful" behavior, as their lower rates can attract noisy partiers. Use your personal radar to figure out whether a particular motel is safe and comfortable enough for your children.

Rental Properties • MD

It started with a hotel room in Disneyland, a very fussy toddler, and a sleepy five year old. With us sharing one room, bedtime became a disaster because my boys weren't sleeping on the same schedule. This made the entire stay more stressful than it should have been. To avoid this, it helps to have everyone go to bed at the same time—though this is tough on older children and limits adults from quality time together. The alternative is to book accommodations with more than one room.

Suite-hotels, condos, apartments, and houses offer alternatives, especially useful for families. Typically, such accommodation offers lots of space in each room, kitchen facilities, and separate sleeping spaces.

When Barbara R.'s family wanders, they stay in condos. "When you travel with a toddler, you don't really know what their schedule for eating and sleeping is going to be in advance. Their nap schedules may differ while on vacation than at home. They're hungry when they're hungry. Getting a condo with a kitchen made traveling much easier for us. It was also cheaper than staying at a hotel."

The longer the time away, the more important your accommodation choices. Don't assume that you can go from a three-bedroom house to sharing just one room without any issues. For me, the additional space is necessary for my sanity. My children (and husband) are neither neat, tidy, nor orderly. They have a habit of collecting junk—beach glass, interesting stones, souvenir tickets, candy wrappers, small toys—all of which they leave strewn around our living spaces. Even a one-bedroom condo allows me to retreat away from the clutter. I am a happier, calmer, nicer vacationing parent because of this.

Cillian is a night owl and will naturally go to sleep late and wake up late, while Brendan is exactly the opposite. His day starts at seven a.m., with so little variation that I often joke that we could set our clocks by him. One loves a quiet room in which to fall asleep while reading; one likes a dark chamber with some music. We can relax and enjoy our time best when we have separate spaces. This doesn't mean that we vacation in very large, very expensive accommodations. But in that one-bedroom condo, Brendan can nod off early in the bedroom, while Cillian has his quiet book time in the living room with the grown-ups.

These types of rental properties often contain kitchens or kitchenettes. Having a fridge and an oven, or even just a hot plate, makes it easier to laze through breakfast, avoid expensive restaurants, and ensure that your fussy child is getting enough nutrition. If you want a break from cooking, take a simple approach to breakfast (cereals or bagels), and plan to dine out in the evenings only. Or if your kids are crankier at the end of the day, eating in may be the easiest way to keep everyone relaxed. Be careful, though, that you don't spend your vacation doing exactly what you do at home: shopping, cooking, and cleaning.

Hot Tip! Larger rental properties are an affordable way to spend vacation time with family or friends, provided costs are shared.

While some suite-hotels and condo properties are rated similarly to hotels, many properties are not scored at all. Therefore, determining quality may be difficult. Price can sometimes serve as an indicator, but be sure to fully research any lodging.

In a popular resort area, you also could find properties using online engines. Many places are professionally run and have websites with booking options. ResortQuest (www.resortquest.com) is a good example of a management company, with lodging in the U.S., Canada, and Europe. For smaller resorts or off-the-beaten-path locations, start your search with the tourist information website for the region.

My preferred way to rent a house, apartment, or condo is directly from the owner through online resources such as Vacation Rentals By Owner (VRBO), HomeAway (www.homeaway.com), and AlluraDirect (www.alluradirect.com). VRBO and HomeAway list properties worldwide, while AlluraDirect specializes in Canadian ski resorts.

I begin researching well in advance, as this task can be time consuming. The information provided by the owner may not be very detailed—especially in terms of the size, location, and availability. Owners will sometimes link to their own website, with full details. Property-management companies often list options both on their sites and on booking engines such as Expedia. The more information you can find, the better. Google Maps (www.maps.google.com) is a fantastic tool to pinpoint the exact location.

Within some resort areas, particularly ski and beach ones, condo accommodations are timeshare or wholly or partially owned personal vacation properties. Even though these can be rented through a third party—such as a-management agency, a consolidator, a travel agent, or an online booking engine— these are the easiest to find and rent directly from owners. The resort's literature or website is likely to list all available properties, and might even provide amenity and quality information. Once you find a spot you like, you can then go to one of the owner-direct websites mentioned above and book it directly. The prices there are probably less than elsewhere.

Hot Tip! Ask for a price reduction for longer-term rentals or for a rental outside peak tourism periods for that destination.

9. HOME AWAY FROM HOME

During her travels in Europe, Jeanne D. had a pleasant surprise. "I already knew that property owners at beach resorts in the U.S. rented out properties for longer periods, at lower rates, during the winter. I guessed it would be the same in Europe, and I was right."

Bed-and-breakfasts • LF

Bed-and-breakfasts (B&B's) exist in countries around the world. They range from family homes, where the owners rent out one or more bedrooms, to small inns. Breakfast is always included, and it's usually a more substantial meal than, say, a continental buffet at a hotel chain. As a family, we enjoy B&B's because each is unique, cozy, and personable. We also love the delicious homemade meals that are the hallmarks of B&B's. I still salivate recalling the colorful fruit parfaits and cardamom-prune scones we had in Oregon.

Bed-and-breakfasts offer opportunities for relaxing rather than going, going, going. These accommodations may include community game rooms, a yard for kids to play in, and a dining room with access to tea and coffee (and sometimes cookies and cocktails). B&B's in the countryside might even have farm animals on-site. We've experienced charming spaces for kids, ranging from a loft to a bed in a cozy alcove.

It's fairly common for B&B's to not accept children under seven. (These properties reserve their spaces for those seeking quiet.) You'll need to honestly assess whether your kids are capable of using indoor voices and behaving courteously. Fortunately, some B&B's are perfect for families with even the busiest, most talkative kids. Look for those with lodging available in a separate cottage or cabin.

B&B's offer great socializing opportunities, which can be a welcomed respite to parents eager to talk to other adults. At a

206

B&B, you'll have the chance to visit with the owners and other guests. Your hosts can usually offer a wealth of information about their location. If a family dinner in a restaurant is in the cards, they can reveal their favorite places to eat.

Once B&'Bs were the budget alternatives to hotels, but this is no longer true. Inns are such a diverse lot that you can find them at nearly any price, from an inexpensive room in a home to a five-star luxury accommodation in a small lodge. Two of the best websites are BnBFinder.com (www.bnbfinder.com) and BedandBreakfast.com (www.bedandbreakfast.com), which has the most extensive international listings.

Pensions • LF

Pensions are small, family-owned guesthouses; Europe has many of these. They have fewer amenities than hotels, and they often have shared bathrooms. As at B&B's, pension proprietors fix breakfast, the accommodations are often unique and charming, and the atmosphere is family-friendly.

Laura F.'s family typically visits less-developed countries. They've stayed at numerous pensions and B&B's. "We always have a hotel reservation when we first get into a country, and other than that, we don't have an itinerary, so we just travel around and see what we see," she says. "When we get to a village or town, there are invariably pensions or B&B's listed at the tourism office. The proprietors love Eden, and if they have kids or pets, it's fantastic for her."

Lodges • LF

One of the most engaging ways to travel with kids is to take them to places of great beauty and spend plenty of time outdoors. Staying in or near natural areas allows plenty of time to hike, canoe, or bike through them. You can find wilderness

9. HOME AWAY FROM HOME

lodges in unparalleled settings around the world, from the river valleys of Iceland to the mountains of Patagonia. Lodges typically feature grand interior spaces crafted of local wood and stone. They can range from rustic facilities with shared bathrooms and tiny rooms to luxury properties. All, however, offer easy access to the wilds.

Popular during the summer for hiking, some remain open in the winter for skiing. A shoulder season trip will increase your odds of getting a room, and an uncrowded experience. For a very popular lodge, start planning up to a year in advance. If the main lodge is booked, check to see whether there are cabins or other types of lodging available. In the wintertime, check potential dates carefully: some close when snow removal proves challenging.

Adventure lodges offer not only access to wilderness, but also trained naturalists who lead interpretive activities. Their leisurely pace, and knowledge base about plants and animals is a good match for kids' interests, attention spans, and stamina. Adventure lodges keep guests busy with activities ranging from hiking, fishing, and canoeing to evening talks. Many are well known for their cuisine, which might be based on locally caught, foraged, or grown foods. At some, guests who catch a fish can have the lodge's chef prepare it for their dinner—a big thrill for a youngster who has just landed her first trout. At one adventure lodge in British Columbia, huckleberries we picked were turned into breads and sauces to accompany meals. Kirsten still talks about the thrill of seeing "her" berries served to the guests.

Hot Tip! To interest your children in a stay at a natural area, do an online search for videos on your shortlist of parks. Then plan a family video night to whip up excitement. For U.S. destinations, there's a terrific PBS-produced video series and book titled *Great Lodges of the National Parks.*

Eco-Lodges • LF

A growing phenomenon, eco-lodges occupy some of the most fascinating places on the planet, from Costa Rica to Namibia, and Easter Island to Mongolia. Such a vacation shows children that we value the world's unique places and believe in caring for the environment.

As with any new concept, there is no widely accepted definition for an *eco-lodge*. In general, though, all one's systems are green-designed. And education is always a big part of the mission.

"We try to find places with local flavor," Lisa M. says. "We prefer to stay at small lodges and hotels that are locally owned, if possible, and that are committed to helping tourism be sustainable for the country."

Eco-lodges often bring in experts on a variety of topics, from the culture of nearby indigenous people to bird-watching. Many offer an active role in conservation, perhaps helping to raise endangered or threatened species like baby turtles, or re-planting damaged areas. It's common for guests to participate in these activities, which are hugely popular with children.

An eco-lodge mitigates its impact and waste. Typically, the buildings fit into the natural environment with minimal disruption. The lodge may use "gray" water (captured from sinks and tubs) for landscaping, may offer less-frequent laundry service for towels and sheets, or may even run its own waste-water treatment system. One where we stayed drew its water from a stream and filtered it, then ran the wastewater through a treatment plant beneath the building, releasing pure H_2O again. Composting, recycling, and reusing are also among the ways eco-lodges lessen their footprints.

Eco-lodges often avoid environmentally harmful pesticides and insecticides. In tropical areas, they may furnish mosquito

9. HOME AWAY FROM HOME

nets rather than toxic sprays. Or they may have misters that emit chrysanthemum extract, a natural repellant.

Many eco-lodges are off the electrical grid, generating their own power through solar panels or some other means. At an eco-lodge in a Mexican jungle, nighttime brought hundreds of glowing votives that lined paths, and a flickering chandelier lit the communal dinner table. Organic gardens supplement meals at some eco-lodges, and proprietors generally do their best to purchase food from local growers, fishermen, and foragers.

Eco-lodges are more expensive than hotels, yet they can offer an incredible experience that helps form your children's views of the world.

Resorts • LF

While more expensive than a standard hotel, resorts offer high value for the dollar. Most give parents a chance to take a break as they offer kids' day camps, and many feature amazing pool complexes. Accommodations tend to be spacious and family friendly. In addition, most resorts offer a variety of eateries, from casual lunch spots to fine-dining restaurants.

Beach resorts—such as those at popular tourism centers in Asia, the Caribbean, Mexico, and Hawaii—are legion, yet resorts can also be found in scenic places in the mountains, at lakes, and beside rivers. The book *100 Best Family Resorts in North America: 100 Quality Resorts with Leisure Activities for Children*—by Janet Tice, Jane Wilford, and Becky Danley—is an excellent resource for this continent.

Hot Tip! To save money, stay at less-expensive accommodations throughout your trip, then spend the last few days at a resort to unwind before you return home.

Before enrolling in a daylong children's program, determine whether your kids make friends easily and enjoy group activities. They might not yet be ready to spend time away from familiar adults. You'll also want to check if the activities are appropriate for the ages of your children. Ask about the staff-to-child ratio, and determine if babysitting services are available for an occasional adults-only evening.

All-Inclusive Resorts • LF

All-inclusive resorts have the same amenities as a standard resort, but guests pay a single fee for all expenses. By spending up front, guests can enjoy the downtime, rather than worrying about mounting costs. The fee usually includes transportation to and from the resort, lodging, meals, drinks, snacks, tips, children's activities, evening entertainment, and an array of additional amenities.

For kids, all-inclusives offer fabulous swimming pools, water sports, and everything from treasure hunts to tea parties as part of supervised activities. Adult-wise, they entice with spas, golf, scuba diving, fine dining, concerts, or dancing—and the chance to remember what it was like to be together before kids.

Hot Tip! Each all-inclusive resort has a low season; to get a better rate, be flexible about timing. Try different months in the resort's booking engine to find the most alluring deal.

One of the leading all-inclusives, Club Med (www.clubmed.us), is now family friendly, with children's programs at twenty-two resorts worldwide.

9. HOME AWAY FROM HOME

Hostels • LF

Staying in hostels (which typically have two or more sets of bunk beds in a room) can be an inexpensive and friendly way to travel. You'll meet interesting locals exploring their own country and adventurers backpacking around the world.

Common rooms allow you to mingle with other guests. When Kirsten was young and I was a single mom, I needed an inexpensive weekend getaway. I booked a family room in an historic hostel at Washington State's Fort Worden State Park. This scenic spot is complete with a lighthouse, a crescent of sandy beach, and immense sweeps of grass to run around on. In the evening we lay on the parade ground and gazed at the stars. Morning brought a complementary pancake breakfast and visits with hostelers, while one of the guests played the piano.

Sarah C. says: "When we travel, we like to stay in hostels and with families. Partly, we wouldn't be able to travel for as long if we stayed in more expensive places. The nicer the accommodations, the less you experience the culture, since they don't tend to cater to locals—and our family has more fun when we're not as insulated."

Some hostels are in imaginative dwellings, ranging from castles to factories, former prisons to ships. There are even temporary hostels, set up during the summertime at college or university dorms.

Hostels have fully equipped communal kitchens for guest use, and most offer breakfast. At some, a light morning meal is included in the price, and at others you'll have to pay extra. Many hostels ask guests to clean their rooms before they leave in the morning, keeping costs down. While some have in-room bathrooms, others share these facilities. Normally, each bed has a blanket or quilt and a pillow. Guests provide their own sheets, pillowcases, towels, and soap.

You can purchase sheet sacks from a number of companies online or from hosteling organizations for about fifteen dollars. Or you can make your own by sewing along the bottom and three-quarters of the way up the side of a doubled-over, double-size sheet. You can also rent linens at hostels.

The more expensive the country, the more expensive the hostel. For instance, a hostel in Asia might cost only three dollars a night per person—an unbeatable bargain. In Paris, you might shell out thirty-two euros per night per person— still cheap for lodging in the heart of the city. However, since costs are per person, hostels work best for small groups. For example, a family of four would pay 128 euros for a night in Paris. They could probably find an inexpensive hotel or a pension cheaper. At some (mostly in-city) hostels, you have to pay for additional services, such as refrigerator space and parking.

Whenever possible, reserve a family room (i.e. private), so you won't have to worry about sharing your space with others or splitting into gender-specific dorms.

While there are numerous privately owned hostels, each with its own style and qualities, it's helpful to work with an organization with properties around the world. There are currently more than 4,000 Hostelling International (HI, www.hihostels.com) branches in more than eighty countries. HI sets standards, and offers guidebooks and online booking for most options. You can make an HI reservation online or by phone up to six months before your trip.

Hot Tip! Before you reserve a room in a hostel, check its opening hours. Some close down after breakfast until late afternoon, allowing staff to clean and prepare for the next batch of guests. This wouldn't work well for napping toddlers or those who like to rest after a busy morning of sightseeing.

Farm Vacations • LF

Rural lodging can be a great opportunity for families, particularly those who live in urban areas. The number of farms opening their gates to guests is growing. It's a win-win situation: farmers receive income that helps preserve traditional agriculture, and for kids, these vacations reveal where food comes from.

Farm stays can range from full-service inns to B&B's, guest cottages to campsites. Some are working farms, where guests can get involved with harvesting a crop, herding cows, or collecting eggs. Others offer bucolic settings without participatory activities. Yet all provide the opportunity to spend plenty of time outdoors and to get a sense of country life.

World Wide Opportunities on Organic Farms (WWOOF, www.wwoof.org) is a well-known program. In return for free room and board, volunteers help with chores. Both hosts and visitors pay a small fee to the network.

Home Exchanges • LF

Traveling with children, unless you're camping or visiting relatives, can be expensive, particularly for larger families. Home swaps are easy on the budget. Usually, families arrange to stay at each other's digs during the same time period. This not only saves on accommodation costs, but also keeps your house occupied. You pay only the price of an annual membership in an exchange program, which typically runs anywhere from $50 to $200—although some are free.

Many properties on home-exchange websites are surprisingly upscale and in gorgeous locales. With their seductive visual appeal, amenities, and promise of relaxation in a private home—for free—it's hard to imagine a better option. However, where you live makes a difference in the success rate of these services. More folks want to visit San Francisco or New York, for instance, than perhaps a small town or a remote area.

Once you are a member of a home-exchange network, search for "children friendly" options. Then ask the exchange service to contact the owners of the most appealing homes. It's up to you to negotiate the details, but the company will provide advice on how to make the trade. The service will also offer tips on avoiding the most common problems and will typically provide online tools such as contracts.

For the greatest success, start searching at least four to six months before your trip. Be realistic about what you can offer. Go ahead and contact multiple homeowners at once, rather than approaching one at a time. The more contacts you make, the better your odds of finding the right exchange partner.

Hot Tip! Seconde homes make great "swappers." These get-a-ways often are in appealing vacation spots, increasing your bargaining power. Plus, you won't have to dovetail travel times with the other family as precisely.

The greatest concern most have about a trade is leaving their home in the care of strangers. While there are no guarantees, the program administrators and users note that participants are generally conscientious. After all, you're caring for their home

9. HOME AWAY FROM HOME

215

while they're enjoying yours. Complaints appear to be quite rare. You'll be communicating frequently with your home-exchange partner before the swap, which should help ease your anxiety. If you can arrange to meet at the beginning of your trip, it can be helpful. And, to be on the safe side, it's a good idea to remove or lock up your valuables. Some people throw car keys into the deal: check with your insurance company before considering this.

Know Your Trade (www.knowyourtrade.com) offers assistance in selecting among the numerous home-exchange programs.

Home Stays • LF

A home stay allows to you live with locals, getting to know a place more intimately. This is an affordable way to spend more than a few days in one location. And many home-stay hosts have children themselves, which can add to the richness of the experience.

The quality of the sleeping arrangements is as variable as the individuals offering home stays. Some hosts may have guest bedrooms, while others may offer air mattresses on the floor. The best might even show your family around or prepare a meal that's typical of their region or culture.

Lisa M. and her children stayed with a family in a village in Ecuador for a night, an experience she learned about through Crooked Trails (www.crookedtrails.com), a wonderful non-profit that organizes family trips featuring this type of cultural exchange. "My daughter had fun playing with the kids, even though she didn't speak the language. We ate with the family and slept with them, and then my kids went to school with their kids. It was a real experience for my kids to see the way most of the world lives," she says.

Karen M.'s Story

We travel all over the world. I work for an airline, so I travel free. Then, to save on hotels, I couch-surf so my daughter and I can afford the luxury of being able to travel. My daughter was nine when we had our first couch-surfing experience.

When we were couch-surfing in L.A., the homeowner, an interesting woman who had built her own house, had other guests that night, so we got to meet people from Poland. We sat around a fire pit in the backyard and visited. My daughter lay in a hammock looking at the stars, talking to the lady's daughter. It was a chance to have some one-on-one time without feeling rushed. We must have talked for a couple of hours.

Everybody thinks I'm crazy to couch-surf, but you've really got to try it. It's important to read the profiles. There are certain people I stay away from: I'm not interested in staying with the twenty-year-olds, for instance. You have to e-mail the hosts. And you have to read comments from people who have stayed with them. I would never take my daughter into an environment where we didn't feel safe.

Be especially careful about the host families, perhaps steering clear of single men, for instance. Check out a home stay's references prior to your visit. If you arrive and feel uncomfortable about anything, don't hesitate to move along.

Some countries have official home-stay programs that you can find online. Servas International (www.servas.org) is the oldest organization, with roots in the peace movement. All Servas hosts are personally screened and approved by an experienced representative of their country.

CouchSurfing (www.couchsurfing.com) also connects travelers with free crash pads around the world. Despite the website's

9. HOME AWAY FROM HOME

name, *couch-surfing* doesn't mean you literally stay on a sofa. Accommodations can range from floor space to a spare bedroom. The website allows hosts and guests to meet and greet online prior to the stay.

During a home stay, be sure that you and your children help out in any way you can with household tasks. It's also a thoughtful gesture to offer your hosts a small gift. This could be something that's representative of where you live, or it could be as simple as a gift of fresh fruit from the local market.

10.

GETTING AROUND

S OME *of the most exciting things about traveling with children can be the actual journeying to and from your destination, and then making your way around once you arrive. What child isn't thrilled by the clang of a trolley bell, the whistle of a train, or the horn of a ferryboat? Beyond flying, there are many wonderful opportunities to get the most out of your trip and to ensure that your children have a safe and fun adventure.*

Cars • MD

Within North America, sometimes you can't beat the feeling of piling everyone into a fully packed car and just hitting the road. This can accommodate your family's need for independence, flexibility, and—maybe—a little bickering in the backseat. Abroad, renting a car removes the constraint of having to rely on public transportation, which can be challenging in a foreign language.

Practical Matters • MD — Allow common sense to prevail: Give your car a once-over, making sure everything is tuned up and in good working order. If you don't have a manual for your car, pick one up from the dealer or order it online—you'll be glad you have it should anything go wrong. Check that your spare-tire kit is complete, including flares and tools. For itineraries with extreme weather conditions (snow or desert), pack appropriate gear, including blankets or sleeping bags, a collapsible snow shovel, and extra water and food. A membership to AAA or CAA is a worthwhile investment, as these services offer roadside assistance to their members.

Be sure that the kiddie equipment is in good condition, including car and booster seats, and harnesses. Make sure LATCH (lower anchor and tethers for children) anchors are securely in place. Car-Safety.org (www.car-safety.org) has a handy diagram explaining how to install both these devices. Remember that different states and countries have varying requirements that may effect your decision to use a child or booster seat. For travel within the U.S., there's a nifty reference table of booster-seat laws by state at Saferoads.org (www.saferoads.org). Each state listing then provides further links to the actual.

Keeping children entertained on long car trips can be challenging. I've used books, music, movies, and games to pass the time. Marie W., who has taken many cross-country drives with her six children, has perfected her skills. "I pack a little backpack for each child, with pencils and paper, and something unique that child will enjoy." She also recommends audiobooks and bringing a portable DVD player. Interestingly, she, rather than the youngsters, chooses the audiobooks and music during car trips. "No one is ever happy with my choices initially, but everyone has to listen. I recently played *The Curious Incident of the Dog in the Night-time,* by Mark Haddon. The kids became so engrossed, they frequently did not want to get out of the car at rest stops."

My boys love handheld video games and portable music players with headphones. But we also have never taken a road trip without a bag or two of books spilling about on the rear seat. And when all else fails, if your kids can stay awake long enough, there are always games, jokes, and songs.

Car Rental • MD — When I rent a car in the U.S., I shop early for the best price available. I use metasearch engines such as Priceline and Hotwire, where discounts of up to fifty percent are possible. With these sites, you must pay the full cost in advance, and the rental agency's name is withheld until you have finalized the purchase. Note that you cannot make changes to your rental with these sites, but can do so if you book directly or through one of the booking engines. There may be additional charges for any changes.

Hot Tip! Eco-friendly cars are now available at some rental-car agencies. Check Hybrid Rental Car. (www.hybrid-rental-car.com) for a list of companies that offer alternatives to gas-only vehicles.

If You Rent a Car Seat

Debbie Dubrow, author of Delicious Baby (www.deliciousbaby.com), suggests:

1. Inspect the seat. Look for any evidence of cracking, twisting, worn harness webbing, broken buckles, or other distress. Close the seatbelt buckles and pull hard to make sure that they do not detach.

2. Look for latch belts. All car seats should have a these built-in; a latch is the preferred way to install any car seat.

3. Examine the expiration date of the car seat on the manufacturer's label on its side or back. If there is only a manufacture date, don't use a model that is older than five years.

4. Check the size. Most have height and weight information printed on the side. Make sure that the car seat suits your child.

5. Get the manual. The car seat booklet will help you install and use the seat properly. Most agencies attach the manual to the seat in a waterproof pouch, but some store them separately. If a manual is not available, you can ask the agency to print one from the manufacturer's website.

6. Don't be shy. If the first seat you are given does not have a manual or is not in good condition, ask for another one. In some cases, you will be able to go in the storage room and choose your own. Look for seats that are newer (sometimes they are at the bottom of a pile or in the back of the room).

7. Check for recalls before you travel. Contact the Vehicle Safety Hotline at 888-327-4236 or the National Highway Traffic Safety Administration (www.nhtsa.dot.gov).

8. Get help from the right person. Ask whether there is a certified car-seat technician on site to help you install the seat safely. Don't assume that other employees will have the proper training (or authority) to affix it correctly.

Although most rental-car agencies offer car seats for an additional fee, bring your own whenever possible, whether traveling domestically or internationally (and especially to developing countries). This avoids potential issues with availability, quality, and installation. Always remember to tote the base of the infant car seat with you. Though it's not required, it does help safe installation. It's also easy to check at the airport with the rest of your luggage.

For rentals, make your request well in advance, and specify whether you need an infant, regular, or booster seat. You will usually need to install the rented car seat yourself, since in some places, employees are legally barred from helping you.

Hot Tip! Car seat safety standards are very stringent in the U.K. and Europe. If you can confirm availability in advance, using one provided may be better than taking your own. Not only will it lighten your load, but your own car seat may not meet local laws.

Expect to pay a daily rate of five to twenty-five dollars per seat per day, and familiarize yourself with the local laws for child safety seats. In most of the U.S., some form of car seat is required for children up to six years of age and sixty pounds, or eight years and eighty pounds. In Europe, the law is eleven years or seventy pounds. There are no international laws or standards governing child seats. Many developing countries are just starting to adopt such safety measures, such as the one that became law in India in 2006. Before heading abroad, contact the rental-car agency to find out what the rules are and whether or not car seats are available. Larger companies may include general information on their websites, though that data may not be location-specific.

Hot Tip! Have one adult handle the rental-car pickup at the airport, while the other deals with the baggage carousel. The lots are often offsite with a shuttle. Splitting the duties means you don't have to cart your kids and your luggage onto the shuttle bus. Many agencies, however, require all drivers to sign paperwork and present their licenses in person. Leave enough time to double back, if need be.

Some credit card and frequent-flier loyalty programs have partnerships with rental-car companies. These usually allow you to earn miles with your chosen airline. The American Express Rewards program is noticeably different in that a cardholder accumulates "reward points" and can then convert these points into vouchers for rentals.

For a month or longer in Europe, you may be able to use one of the buyback programs offered by Renault (www.renaultusa.com) and Peugeot (www.peugeot-openeurope.com). With these, you lease the car and sell it back to the manufacturer (or agent) later. Full insurance is generally included in the agreement, and rarely are there limitations on where you can drive the car (unlike rentals that have a mileage limit or regulations about border crossings). For example, twenty-one days in a Renault Clio may be $799 with this program, compared to a rental price of $1,500 for the same model.

Before road-tripping, however, consider the safety of the streets and other drivers. Be particularly vigilant in developing countries where traffic rules are often far more relaxed than in North America and Europe.

Trains • MD

My kids love trains. Taking them is not part of our normal life, so perhaps the novelty value is still quite high. Or maybe it's due to their enthusiasm for the ubiquitous *Thomas the Tank Engine* books, movies like *The Polar Express*, or the Harry

Potter series featuring the Hogwarts Express. They enjoy being able to move around and investigate the length of the train and see what treats are for sale in the dining car. In carriages with compartments and tables, you can almost see their minds buzzing as they imagine themselves as a character they've seen or read about.

When we travel as a family, we like to ride public transportation as much as possible. Not only is it relaxing, but it reduces our costs, because we don't have to rely on expensive rental cars. Within North America, we often use transit systems such as the BART (Bay Area Rapid Transit) in the San Francisco area or the "L" in Chicago. But our train travel is not limited to this continent.

When headed abroad, I automatically begin researching what public options are available and never assume that we will need a rental car. In Europe, India, and Japan, traveling by train is a viable option, even with very young children, as their services are extensive and (relatively) comfortable.

Start online. JohoMaps (www.johomaps.com) has links to both urban and intercity rail maps for many countries worldwide. You can find maps and books on international metro systems on UrbanRail.net (www.urbanrail.net). The bibles for rail timetables are the Thomas Cook guides (www. thomascookpublishing.com). In addition to their popular *European Rail Timetable* edition, they also publish guides for America, Africa, Asia, and Australasia. The Trains at a Glance information provided by Indian Railways (www.indianrailways. gov.in) is an excellent resource for that country. These websites generally list current fares and schedules.

Train travel can also mean saving money on taxis. Major stations usually stand in the heart of a city, making hotel access cheaper and easier than getting there from an airport.

I prefer to book tickets in advance, either online well before we leave home or from the station a day or more before our train is due to leave. For more fluid plans, you still may be able to get tickets a couple of hours before departure (though this can be more stressful, if there's a chance that tickets will sell out).

Rail passes, such as Eurail's, are popular as they provide a variety of cost-saving options. For example, you can purchase a SaverPass for a group of two to five people traveling together in Europe. If your kid is eleven or younger, this option may not be the best, as you can purchase a child's fare ticket for him: typically fifty percent off the adult rate. Fly/drive packages—rail passes cum car rental, for a limited number of days—are also available.

While the Eurail pass may be the most well known, similar deals are available in Japan, India, Australia, and New Zealand. Often you can purchase combination passes that include rail and bus or rail and ferry services. In Africa or Asia, expect to purchase individual tickets. Always ask about the cost of a round trip fare: sometimes these can run cheaper than a one-way!

Hot Tip! Consider taking an overnight sleeper train. Your family can doze off in one country and wake up in another. This will also save on accommodation costs. Consider packing sleeping bags, though, as night services only provide sheets generally.

Ferries • LF

Boats are relaxing and convenient—you and your children can sit back and enjoy the scenery, have lunch in an onboard café, become mesmerized by the ship's frothy wake, and laugh at the "silly walking" of leaning into the wind on deck. Kids absolutely love the adventure of traveling on water and this mode also gives parents a break. I like to think of ferry transportation as a "mini cruise" without the huge expense. And it's a great way to meet the locals.

It's cheapest to walk onboard as foot passengers. Otherwise, ferries charge by the size of the vehicle, and it's common for the fee not to include the driver or other passengers. Tolls are often higher in peak season (summer in North America). This can add up, particularly on longer routes. As just one example, for a family of four traveling with their car from Port Hardy to Prince Rupert, British Columbia, aboard a BC Ferry in the summertime—a fifteen-hour daytime voyage—the cost is nearly $800.

Kids on lengthy voyages get bored. Fortunately, longer ferry trips typically offer cabins with sleeping berths. These are worth the expense when traveling with children; it beats trying to sleep on lounge chairs next to strangers, and it affords you peace of mind. You won't have to constantly supervise your children as they wander about in public spaces. And you can get some rest yourself without worrying whether your children are safe. A cabin also gives your gang a fun getaway spot and a comfortable place for naps.

Cabins on board ferries can range from a cramped cubbyhole near the engine room to a spacious stateroom with an expansive window and a balcony. If you can at all afford it, a cabin with a view is highly preferable to staring at four blank walls. That is especially true for daytime routes. However, *any* cabin is better than none.

Berths are mandatory on some ferry lines that offer overnight voyages. Despite the cost, it's usually less expensive than staying at a hotel in a major city.

Book as early as possible, as tickets for longer routes—especially international ones—may sell out. Shorter crossings often run more frequently; in these cases, you typically can buy a ticket at the terminal. Arrive at least a half hour before sailing, and preferably earlier, particularly for popular routes in the summertime. Check the ferry's website to see the suggested wait times.

Hot Tip! If your ferry route will cross an international border, be sure to keep your passport handy for customs and immigration. In some cases, officials may hold your I.D. until just before arrival.

Part of having a successful shorter ferry ride is advance preparation. On some vessels, you are not allowed to return to your car once you've gone upstairs to the observation deck. Bring all the items you'll need for the duration of the trip. Assemble these in daypacks or totes before the ticketing booth, and be sure not to leave any valuables in your vehicle.

If your children are prone to motion sickness, be sure to bring whatever preventative works best for them (such as ginger, Dramamine or a wrist-pressure band), in case of swells. Also pack snacks, drinks, or whatever else you'll need for the duration of the ferry ride, like diapers, warm layers, cameras, and even binoculars.

Since water reflects sunlight, you can get a burn much faster on a boat than on land—it's similar to the reflection from snow—so you'll need to include sun protection in your carry-aboard bag. (See Chapter 12, "Health and Safety," for tips.) Also pack windbreakers so everyone can comfortably spend time outside: gusts are particularly strong at the front of the ship. The stern will be more sheltered from the wind, so it's a great place to enjoy the scenery.

Hot Tip! When traveling by boat, it's far better to pack your own picnic lunch, even if that means swinging into a grocery store en route. Ferry food, at its best, is cafeteria food, and most of the time it's just fast food—and high-priced fast food, at that.

Ferry rides bring together locals and tourists, and it's likely your children will find playmates on board. For your peace of mind, dress your children in bright, easily identifiable colors. Then they're easier to spot while playing with other kids, or if your older child takes your younger one around the deck or to the restroom.

Do your homework beforehand. Some less-developed regions of the world have services with inadequate safety systems. This can lead to overcrowding, vessel maintenance problems, and even the carrying of toxic materials on passenger ferries. Conduct an online search to see if the system you're considering has a record of safety issues. When boarding, if you discern that the boat is overcrowded, disembark immediately. It's far better to lose a fare than to worry once you've left port.

If ferries are a novelty for your family, you'll want to review some safety issues with your kids prior to boarding. For starters, no one exits the vehicle until all the cars around yours have stopped. One more cardinal rule: Tell your children not to play near railings, as they could easily fall through the sometimes large gaps. With the wide-open spaces inside a ferry and the allure of amenities—such as a games arcade, cafeteria, and gift shop—there's a lot to tempt kids. Ask younger ones to stay in sight at all times. If they're old enough to be on their own, tell your kids to always stick together in pairs. For teens, it works well to set a return time (or times) before they set out to explore.

Hot Tip! Window seats typically go fast. To secure one, have your daypacks filled with everything each family member will want on-board. As soon as it's safe to get out of the car, hustle everyone upstairs. If that's not possible, send one adult upstairs to stake out a good spot. Foot passengers should aim for the front of the line in order to board early.

Shorter ferry routes, such as those between Spain and Morocco or between France and England, are often served by hydrofoils. These ultra-high-speed vessels are exciting to ride, and they're great fun for kids. You may pay more than for a conventional ferry, but it will shave off a considerable amount of travel time, affording you more travel time.

Some ferry systems are extensive, with a multitude of routes to different destinations. In the Pacific Northwest, Washington State Ferries (www.wsdot.wa.gov/ferries) thread their way to scenic wooded islands in Puget Sound. Ferries in British Columbia (www.bcferries.com) carry passengers to 285-mile-long Vancouver Island, the charming Gulf Islands, and remote mainland destinations. In Alaska, ferries (www.dot.state.ak.us) ply waters where waterfalls tumble and whales breach. The three-night sailing up the Inside Passage allows passengers to pitch tents on deck—or sleep in lounge chairs under heat lamps (cabins are twice as expensive). Nicknamed "the poor person's cruise," this epic journey blends scenery with soft adventure.

In Europe, three regions boast extensive ferry systems: the Baltic Sea, the North Sea, and the Mediterranean. To book passage on any one of about 1,500 ferries in Europe, see Ferrylines.com (www.ferrylines.com). A Ferry UK (www.aferry.co.uk) claims to be the largest online ferry network, serving more than 800 European routes. Island-hopping in the Greek islands—with their picturesque whitewashed villages, aquamarine bays, and

Joanne D.'s Story

In Vietnam, we were on our way by boat to a remote village. It was the only way you could get there. It was pouring down rain, and all kinds of foreigners were in the boat with me and my eight-year-old son, Bryce. We were all crunched inside the cabin, with plastic flaps pulled down over the windows to prevent water from spraying on us.

Finally the rain let up a little bit, and the boat operator opened the flaps. We had been so confined, and when they lifted up the tarps, it was just glorious outside—really green and lush and mountainous. The locals had built beautiful gardens alongside the river on super-steep slopes. They used intricate fencing to separate the crops; it's amazing to think they could grow gardens on such steep slopes.

Bryce poked his head out and was fascinated by the boat's wake. He wanted us to take a video of the waves. He had such wide eyes as he looked at the scenery—it was so beautiful there. He really loved the experience.

archaeological sites—is a top draw. Check out Greek Ferries (www.greekferries.gr).

Hot Tip! Ferries on many longer crossings have children's play areas and video arcades to keep young ones busy. Just in case your ferry doesn't feature a play space, you'll need to be prepared with books and portable travel entertainment.

There are also ferry systems throughout Asia. As just one example, Japan has thousands of islands and a massive network connecting them. For ferries in Japan, see Japan-guide (www.japan-guide.com) and click on "Travel."

Local Transportation • MD

Taking local transportation can be one of the most exciting and interesting ways to get around at your destination. Your child will love feeling the wind on his face as you zip through Bangkok on a *tuk-tuk* or peer down on pedestrians from atop a double-decker bus in London.

In developing countries, these services are part of the tourism industry's backbone, and often support locals and their families. It's a wonderful opportunity to teach your children about saving money, since such modes are usually far cheaper than a taxi. Plus, your family may get to know the residents that you're supporting (as there's often the opportunity for one-on-one chatter with your driver). You can sometimes get a completely different perspective on a city or town.

When we visited Puerto Vallarta, Mexico, we stayed quite far from the town proper. Although there were usually taxis waiting outside the hotel, we took the public bus, enjoying the sights and sounds of the markets and children playing in the schoolyards that we passed. The bus stop in town was at the edge of a thriving neighborhood of small streets and ethnic stores that Cillian and Brendan found fascinating. We had been in Puerto Vallarta almost a week before we even discovered the tourist-centric promenade where cruise ships docked. What a surprise!

No matter where you are, these alternative modes of transportation generally make a smaller carbon footprint than taxis and rental cars (another lesson for your child), and can make for some of the best memories of your trip.

11.

PACK IT UP

PACKING *doesn't have to be stressful if you plan ahead. We offer plenty of proven tips to smooth any wrinkles in the process, and our master checklist can save you time while helping you establish a simple, pre-trip routine. Happy packing!*

Practical Packing Tips • LF

If you have an infant or toddler, it is likely that you are surrounded by a mountain of kid gear that makes your daily life more manageable. While these conveniences may seem indispensable, parents have been successfully rearing children without portable swings, bouncy seats, and high chairs for a long time. Probably you can make do with less. Unless you'll be hiring sherpas to transport your luggage, you'll need to pare down to the essentials. See our Packing List later in this chapter for helpful hints.

Until my daughter was a middle-schooler, I would just pack my suitcase two-thirds full of my own clothes and reserve the rest for her, these kids outfits were small and easy to fit into my case. But if you have more than one child, or older children, they'll need their own suitcases.

It's best to start packing a week or more before your trip, particularly for early starts. Young children love to get involved with packing. We all know that "helping" often means that they assemble completely impractical items—perhaps the contents of their toy bin, but no clothes. It's a fun experience, though, to watch your little one purposefully going about selecting items—and it can reveal what they consider important. Of course, the final packing is up to you. You'll just need to be sure your youngster is preoccupied or off to a play date.

Even if your child is approaching a responsible age—say, when she's a tween—you would be wise to check over what she is planning to take. The essentials may elude kids until they're well into their teen years. Don't let her make it out the door without the necessary items, or you'll be adding to trip hassles and eating up valuable vacation time tracking them down.

When I am preparing for a trip with my husband and daughter, I allot each of us a large plastic bin a week before, along with a packing list and a blank, lined notepad. This allows each of us to organize our own clothing and gear. When an item goes into the bin, it gets checked off the list. And if any of us think of extra things we'd like to take, we write them down on a notepad. After the trip, I add these to the master family list. By placing potential travel items in a bin, we can just toss in things as we think of them. The larger capacity allows you to easily remove items and add others as you decide on the best combinations. Of course, a day or two before departure, it's time for the suitcase-fit test.

If the duration of your trip is a week or less, determine the right clothing by checking the daily forecast on Weather.com (www.weather.com). For longer trips, plan for the average conditions at your destination. Remember that it rains in even the sunniest places sometimes.

In the tropics, the temperatures may be hot, yet rainstorms are common. We'll leave our raincoats at home, but take small umbrellas. Ponchos are another great way to entirely cover up little ones who can't manage umbrellas, and these garments take up minimal space.

Pack carefully to avoid unnecessary wrinkles and to fit more in. One method is to roll your clothes into tidy logs. You can also use packing cubes, soft-sided containers that hold clothes and accessories; these allow easy access without pulling everything out of your luggage. Make your own with one- or two-gallon zip-top bags. Compression bags are similar, but you can squeeze the air out, to maximize space. You can find these at outdoor or container stores.

My daughter and I have soft-sided suitcases that are expandable. When we leave, the bags are in their most compact state.

As we travel, we simply unzip the folded fabric, instantly creating more room for souvenirs. If you don't have this option, be sure not to pack to the brim—leave extra space for the return leg of the journey.

Hot Tip! If you go on a trip that will tempt you with fragile art, pack a nylon fold-up shopping bag into your suitcase. With a carry-on-size wheeled suitcase and a daypack for the outbound leg, you won't have to check bags. On the return, simply check your suitcase, and you can hand-carry the shopping bag with its precious cargo.

Clothing • LF

On most trips, we end up bringing more clothing than we need—there always seems to be one or more orphan outfits that aren't used at all. It's better to pack light, so your bags are easier to handle. Besides, buying locally made clothing helps support the economy there, and these items make great souvenirs.

Our children grow out of their clothes at an alarming rate when they're young. It's virtually guaranteed that when you are packing, you'll find that there are garment and footwear gaps. When my daughter was young, she sometimes needed new shoes every four to six months. Nearly always, I would be alerted to this by, "Mom, my toes are hurting. I can't wear these shoes." Of course, this was always just as were setting out on a trip.

Sandals are another issue—you will typically need to buy a new pair for your growing children every year. Look for ones that are comfortable enough for walking and for the beach. For all footwear, check out the sizes at least a month before departure, so they'll have time to break in new ones, if needed.

The same goes for clothing. Have your kids try on garments at least several weeks before a trip, so you'll have time for Plan B. It can be hard to find kids' clothes for a different climate. Most stores sell summer clothes in the spring, so in the fall or winter months, you may find stores are filled with odd leftovers—with the emphasis on "odd."

My daughter and I still convulse with laughter when we recall one summer trip. We just couldn't find the time to get a swimsuit for her before leaving. I figured we could buy one at our destination. Unfortunately, the only place that stocked any in the summer was a Wal-Mart, where the sad dregs in her (teen) size ranged from a shapeless black sack that we dubbed "the burqa" to a Vegas showgirl bikini, complete with fake jewels on the top. Nowadays I start thinking about clothing needs at least a month before a trip.

Hot Tip! Place online orders early in case anything is out of stock, or the sizing is off and you need to return an item. Also, allow plenty of time for shipping.

Sometimes our kids' favorite clothes are beloved for a reason other than comfort. In these cases, you might have to gently talk your daughter out of taking that sequined top that rubs on her collarbone, or discourage your son from bringing his scratchy, polyester, cartoon-character shirt. New clothes, in particular, with their irritating tags and stiff material, won't typically be as comfortable as well-worn ones. If you do buy new garments, run them through the wash before packing them. This removes the chemicals that make them stiffer (for display purposes), which could cause a rash. Even better, shop at a consignment or thrift shop to fill in wardrobe gaps. You can find brand names at these places, the pre-worn clothing is more comfortable, and it can impart to your kids the value of buying secondhand.

No matter how long your trip, pack just one week's worth of clothing and then launder on the road. (See Chapter 13, "While You're There," for tips.) Darker clothes won't show dirt or stains as readily, but may be impractical in warmer climates.

You'll get more mileage out of layers, such as shirts, vests, T-shirts, fleeces, and sweatshirts, rather than a heavy parka. If you have a young daughter, consider pairing a sundress with leggings and a sweater to extend its use.

Also, choose garments that don't wrinkle as readily. As a test, grab a handful of the fabric and squeeze it, then smooth it out. If wrinkles stay in, you'll know that it's not the best choice. Patagonia (www.patagonia.com) carries synthetic children's clothing that works well for travel. You can also find a good selection at outdoor gear stores such as REI. Also, check out TravelSmith (www.travelsmith.com) or ExOfficio (www.exofficio.com).

Now for a word about underwear. On the road, silk or microfiber beat cotton; the lightweight fabric is comfortable, and it dries much more quickly. You can hand wash it in the evening, and it will be dry by the next morning. You can find these undergarments at an outdoor clothing store or online. Unfortunately, they're available only in adult sizes. However, since most of these fabrics are stretchy, it's likely the smallest size will fit your tween or teen.

Laura F. has another take on the underwear issue. "The one luxury I afford myself in packing is bringing as many pairs of underwear as my daughter will need for the trip. For me, vacation and hand-washing someone else's dirty underwear are mutually exclusive," she says.

Whenever I'm traveling outside the country, I try to blend in—and I must do it pretty well, since locals often try to chat with me in their language. To accomplish this camouflage, I avoid styles that would tip off others that I'm from North America: no white tennis shoes, logo T-shirts or baseball caps, and no flip-flops (unless at the beach).

Most cultures allow more leeway for children's wear—for instance, kids can wear sneakers for most occasions, rather than hauling several pairs of shoes on a trip. But to play it safe, use the same parameters for your kids. Globalism means that seasonal styles tend to be pretty much the same, whether in Paris or Peoria.

Dawn L.'s young daughter dressed up all the time. "She insisted on wearing only dresses for two or three years, the sparklier the better," Dawn says. "She was obsessed with princesses." But all that changed on a family trip to Kensington Palace in London, where Princess Diana's clothing was the centerpiece of an exhibit. "We came to a riding outfit, and Adrienne asked 'Why is that here? Princesses wear pants to ride horses?' The day we got home, Adrienne went into her closet and put on a pair of pants. It was worth the whole trip that she would finally wear pants!"

It's important to be respectful of the culture you're visiting. If your journey includes a local church, temple, mosque, or other religious building—even in a Western nation—it's thoughtful to avoid jeans or shorts, tank tops, or flip-flops. In more conservative areas, you'll need to pack clothing that offers more coverage. Read up on the local etiquette in advance, both for a better understanding of what to pack and just to be more in-the-know. (See Chapter 14, "Responsible Travel," for more information.)

Hot Tip! Carry a scarf for you and your daughter. In some countries, women must cover their hair and shoulders or legs when entering a church or temple. This light item can easily be tucked into a daypack, and doubles as sun-protections too!

Be sure to pack one nice outfit for each family member. You never know when you might want to have an evening out. The clothing doesn't have to be fancy. For a girl, packing a skirt would be adequate, and for a boy, consider taking along a pair of neat khakis and a polo shirt.

Winter Clothing • LF — For cold climates, dress kids in multiple lightweight layers that allow them to shed or add items as they need to, depending on their level of activity. Wool and cotton should be banned for such a trip, as they retain moisture, leaving the wearer cold and damp. Today there are numerous synthetic-fabric garments for children that do a much better job of keeping them warm.

Hot Tip! Inexpensive nylon-coated jackets and rain pants may be easier on your budget. If you spend the extra money for a synthetic, breathable, waterproof gear, the odds are that your child will outgrow it before the next season. But it will still be in good shape, allowing you to sell it to a consignment store and recoup up to half of the cost.

Clothing layers should include a moisture-wicking inner layer, such as polypropylene long underwear; a middle insulating layer, such as breathable fleece; and an outer shell. If you can afford the extra cost, it's best to go with breathable fabrics, such as a synthetic, moisture-wicking, waterproof coat.

Don't forget waterproof pants if your children will be spending any length of time in the snow, whether it's for skiing, tubing, or snowball fights.

Hot Tip! Even for a brief hike, it's essential to be prepared for weather changes. At high altitudes, in particular, the conditions can shift quickly. Pack a windbreaker (or a rain poncho), a fleece jacket, a hat, and gloves or mittens into everyone's daypack. REI and other outdoor stores carry garments with zip-off pant legs and sleeves for versatility. And, of course, be sure to bring snacks and plenty of water.

Look for garments that are lightweight and compressible, so they are easy to stow in your child's daypack. All fleece isn't equal: The best fleece hats are those made with wind-stopping fabric. Gloves or mittens should have a breathable, waterproof outer fabric—such as Gore-Tex—and be fleece lined. Proper socks are often overlooked; many synthetic, moisture-wicking fabrics can keep children's feet warm. You might also try heating gel packs inserted into their boots.

For a tween or a teen, clothing choices can become even more of a struggle, as the style code stresses "cool" over comfort. This could mean walking around without a coat or even in shorts when it's cold or rainy. If your young person dresses this way at home, the consequences are few—maybe she'll become chilled, weakening her immune system, and she'll catch a bug. This is unfortunate on your usual turf, but if you have a busy travel schedule, it can be dire, causing you to change plans or even shorten a trip. Therefore, it makes sense to strike a bargain with her before you head out.

Toiletries • LF

Purchase your favorite shampoo, conditioner, lotions, and such in travel sizes, or transfer the contents of family bottles into empty, tinier ones. If your child is young, you can just put her toothbrush and toothpaste into your toiletry kit. But once she gets old enough to yearn for independence or to crave more lotions and potions, she'll be happier with her own bag. It's a good idea to pack toiletries in your carry-on, if flying, so that you have them handy. Though rules from the TSA change frequently, liquids, gels, and aerosols currently need to be in three-ounce containers and placed into quart-size zip-top bags for going through the security line. (See Chapter 8, "Flight Plans," for more details.)

Most mid- to higher-priced hotels provide shampoo. Fewer places offer conditioner, however, so take along some for travelers with long hair that tangles easily. Many properties in Europe no longer give guests little bottles; instead, you'll find a dispenser on the wall. On a trip with my husband and daughter, it took a while for us to discover this, hiding behind the shower curtain. Also it wasn't obvious that the liquid was both shampoo and soap.

For dental equipment, glasses, or contacts, be sure to pack the requisite accessories. For instance, if your child wears braces and a retainer, be sure she takes a pick, wax, floss, a retainer-tightening key, and elastic bands. Such items might not easily be found at a pharmacy at your destination. Spectacle-wearers should tote along the glasses case—and prescription or spare glasses.

Girls new to menstruation may not be tuned in yet to tracking their periods. Monitor this for the first few months until your daughter gets the hang of it. That way, you'll know whether she needs to take feminine supplies on a trip. If there's any doubt about the timing or if her cycle is still irregular, you'll need to carry supplies just in case. And if your daughter's period hasn't started yet, but she is eleven years old or older, it's a good idea to take along some supplies just in case it starts. On a trip, you may not have ready access to a pharmacy or grocery store. First-period kits, such as one put out by Dot Girls (www.dotgirlproducts.com), are compact enough to make sense for traveling.

Accessories • LF

Do take scarves and a few pieces of costume jewelry to vary the look of your outfits and extend their usage, but leave the precious items at home. Even inexpensive jewelry that simulates "real" bling (cubic zirconia, for example) should be avoided, so as not to tempt thieves.

If your child is accustomed to wearing a favorite gemstone ring or gold necklace, explain why it's important not to wear it. You might even strike a bargain and promise to buy a piece of locally made jewelry while you're there.

Creature Comforts • LF

Kids of all ages should take a comfort item on the trip, whether it's your young teen's diary or your toddler's beloved blankie. Moms of larger families say they limit their kids to one treasure apiece, so they can keep track of the objects of affection. But if an only child wants to take her three favorite stuffed animals, and there's space in her daypack, well, why not? By having more than one favorite along, she has more play possibilities.

Everyone should have a little piece of home that helps them feel more secure when traveling. For parents, it may be a down travel pillow, fleece throw, or perhaps a favorite tea or coffee.

Food • LF

When my daughter was a toddler, we never traveled on a family car vacation without an avocado for her. Strange? Maybe. But no stranger than the food fixations of many a pint-sized person. At least she would consistently eat this nutrient-laden

11. PACK IT UP

243

food. This was essential as we couldn't ever guarantee that she would eat available items in the store or restaurant at our next stop.

As parents, we've all seen kids melt down because they were hungry and we weren't prepared. Nibbles ensure a better experience; snacking gives kids the extra energy boost they need to keep on balance emotionally. The key is to always keep an emergency stash, just in case you don't have access to stores at any point on your trip. For example, in some countries or regions, grocery stores close in the late afternoon or on Sundays.

Nutritionally, look for low-sugar, low-salt snacks without preservatives. I always leave room in my carry-on on a trip's first day for a small, insulated lunch sack filled with perishable goodies such as fresh fruit, carrots, string cheese, hard-boiled eggs, cheese and crackers, muffins, or individual yogurts. I pack these alongside frozen juice packs (except when flying, since these are prohibited through security), which keep the food cold.

Thereafter, you'll need less-perishable snacks. Foods that travel best include nuts, dried fruit, pretzels, Goldfish crackers, jerky, trail mix, granola, and energy bars.

Take note that power bars may be good for you, but unless they're tasty, your child won't eat them. For the best nutrition, it pays to read the labels and select products made with whole foods. Don't rely on kid-friendly labels; even products made specifically for children often are full of sugar and chocolate. One standout is Lärabar, a nutrient-dense energy bar of unsweetened fruits, nuts, and spices, in a wide array of flavors, such as "cherry pie" and "lemon." Another "good for you" brand is Kind Fruit + Nut Bars. Chefs can also make their own energy bars; there are numerous recipes available online.

Electronics • LF

Unless you're planning to work, it's best to leave the laptop at home. Most mid-priced hotels, B&B's, and even hostels have an online computer station, and you can find Internet cafés around the world. If you must haul the laptop, don't forget to pack the charge cord, and if possible, a spare (charged) battery and travel adaptor plug. Most models have an in-built power converter, but check this too.

Cameras • LF — Cameras—digital, video, and otherwise—are essentials for recording the special moments of your trip. For the youngest children, inexpensive disposables are best. As your child and her photo-taking capabilities grow, you'll undoubtedly upgrade cameras a few times to point-and-shoot and then perhaps even a digital SLR. (See Chapter 13, "While You're There," for more information about photography.) When packing, include all of the components, such as the docking station or charge cord and an extra memory card. Rotate two or more cards through the camera. That way, if one corrupts, you still retain some shots.

MP3 Players • LF — Whether or not you take MP3 players is an individual matter. Some families ban these devices figuring that if a child is plugged in, she is tuned out and will miss important details of the trip. Plus, it can become a struggle to monitor and negotiate usage. However, electronics are a big part of life for most teens—and their parents. MP3 players can be invaluable for whiling away wait times, such as on flights or long car drives, when you might get tired of reading or playing games and need a bit of personal space. The beauty of MP3's is that you and your children can listen to your own favorite music, podcasts, or audiobooks without inflicting your choices on the others.

Cell Phones • MD — When traveling, cell phones are an important tool for keeping in touch with friends and family at home (and perhaps with other members of your group). However, your normal models may not work abroad or even in a different state. Additionally, the cost outside your calling area can be exorbitant. Before you leave home, check the area covered by your cell phone service provider and determine any associated roaming charges. If you are traveling overseas, verify that your cell phone has the technology to work in another country. Purchasing a cheap pay-as-you-go phone there may be easiest. These often work on SIM chips, which can be purchased for different countries: instant local calling! (To learn more about cell phones, see Chapter 13, "While You're There.")

Noise-canceling Headphones • LF — Since buying a set of noise-canceling headphones for my husband, I've somehow ended up wearing them much of the time. These devices are, in my book, an essential for long-distance air travel. You know that sensation you get from long-term exposure to jet engines? It's like getting your sea legs after being aboard a boat—your ears are humming, and you feel wobbly and fatigued? Noise-canceling headphones eliminate the constant low-pitched droning sound that becomes tiring hour after hour, and you arrive feeling refreshed and ready to go.

These units are expensive, so unless your children travel frequently, it won't make much sense to buy a set for them. But I'd highly recommend one for yourself, to give your ears a break. You can use these units in combination with an MP3 player to listen to music or podcasts. Bose (www.bose.com) and Audio-Technica (www.audiotechnica.com) are the leaders in noise-canceling headphones. For maximum comfort, be sure to buy an over-the-ear style.

Keeping Track of It All · LF/MD — Electronics are a mixed blessing when traveling with children. The self-entertainment value that comes with a Nintendo DS or an iPod is priceless. However, once you've packed everyone's digital cameras, MP3 players, cell phones, chargers, headphones, games, and maybe even laptops, you'll have a bundle of cords to deal with and numerous gadgets small enough to lose or break easily.

Ideally put each cord in a separate, labeled, zip-top plastic bag, and then cram all those into a larger plastic sack—or better yet, into a packing cube, which is tougher. Where possible, share cables among appliances (no need to haul three iPod chargers, for example).

Use dedicated traveling cases for handheld video games. There are many options available on Amazon (www.amazon.com) or at any electronics store. Ideally, the case should hold the device, its power supply, and some games—everything packed together, so it's immediately obvious if something's been forgotten. Bulkier headphones take up a little more space than the earbud style, but are less likely to get lost or broken and are easier for children to use.

Most countries have different electrical systems, with distinct prong configurations. For international travel, purchase a universal converter set, available at a travel store or online.

Take extra disposable batteries with you, rather than relying on finding new ones on the road. Even better, take along a battery charger—it's more environmentally friendly.

Hot Tip! Purchase a Power Monkey from Magellan's (www.magellans. com) so that you have an additional power source while traveling. This battery pack comes with a selection of socket adaptors and device connections, allowing you to recharge almost any device in any country.

11. PACK IT UP

Set ground rules about electronic entertainment devices before your trip. You could determine a daily time for each member of the family to decompress in her own way, including playing video games, checking e-mail, and making phone calls. There should be a consensus among everyone with regard to when electronics are appropriate.

Entertainment • MD

The trickiest part of traveling with a preschooler is packing enough toys, books, and games to keep her amused en route. Some moms encourage new, wrapped toys to distract and amuse. I have found that plenty of age-appropriate books and games from home is sufficient. Coloring and puzzle books, as well as simple card games, are always a hit. Reusable sticker books have an added bonus in that you can use them on the way out and on the way home. As kids get older, Mad Libs (www.madlibs.com) make for laugh-out-loud moments, and they can have hours of amusement with any of the Klutz (www.klutz.com) products.

I consistently overpack my carry-on bag of tricks. Certainly, I pay the price with aching shoulders on the first day or two of our vacation. But keeping my kids amused and entertained is worth the effort. I pack enough books so that I don't go mad from reading the same story over and over and over. Also, I introduced my children to audiobooks at an early age. And, when they were young, picture books with a "turn-the-page" recording were very popular, as the kids felt they were reading solo.

I like to encourage that independence. Even though most of the entertainment equipment is usually in my backpack, each kid has his own knapsack for his key items. I never allow those to get too full, lest I have to shoulder it.

When it comes to traveling, the fact that most children enjoy the same book multiple times is a bonus. That way, you can take just a few of their favorites. These are probably the same volumes you're already reading at bedtime, so it'll be easy to continue that comforting routine in a strange place

Once a child is an independent reader, it's a double-edged sword. They love to read, but they want to take all the Flat Stanley, Magic Tree House, or Harry Potter books with them. To avoid back strain, find out if there is a secondhand bookstore on your route and whether it stocks children's books. You may want to introduce your children to the idea of trading-in at home before you try this elsewhere.

That said, buying new tomes on the road can add to children's excitement—and up the educational souvenir quota! Most countries have discounted "media rates," should you decide to ship home printed materials.

In addition to books, we carry board games. While there are travel editions of many popular ones, these can be expensive. For games like Othello and chess, you can simply put the pieces in a zip-top bag and tuck the board into the side of a suitcase, leaving the box at home. Scrabble is the one game that I do recommend in the travel edition, as it comes in a zippered case with snap-in tile racks. These allow you to keep track of all the bits and to pack the game away without having to restart it.

For younger children, the ThinkFun puzzle games can provide hours of independent play. These include Rush Hour, Hoppers, or River Crossing. The games have little bags for easy carrying or a snap-in compartment within the game board for cards and pieces. Just perfect.

We rarely play cards at home, but I always throw a pack in my bag when we're traveling. A rousing game of Snap! can while away time in an airport—and will attract other children, too. Children six and older can grasp the basics of solitaire, and even though poker has a somewhat unsavory reputation, it's a fun family game—especially when you're anteing in loose change from another currency. Some other card games that my kids really enjoy are Set and Quiddler, both from Set Enterprises (ages six to adult), Rat-a-Tat-Cat and others from Gamewright (ages four and up), and Haunted Castle by Ravensburger (ages four and up).

Camping Gear • LF

Sleeping in the great outdoors requires you squeeze additional gear (tent, sleeping bags, pads, and more) into backpacks. This can be especially challenging with children if they're unable to carry much weight.

Airlines may have shrink wrap or thick, tough plastic bags to protect backpacks and other delicate gear. These ensure that any loose elements don't fall off and get lost, and they cut down on wear and tear. Call ahead to determine whether thee services are available. If not, you can buy backpack travel covers online. Some have straps to convert them to oversized duffle bags.

Leave fuel canisters at home; most brands are easy to buy, even overseas. If you are taking a camp stove on a plane, make sure it is very clean and doesn't have fumes. Also remember not to take Swiss Army knives or camping hatchets in your carry-ons. The TSA website details what is allowed aboard an airplane.

Silvana C. uses sturdy duffle bags to carry outdoor gear. She suggests taking the lightest tent possible, since the airlines have weight restrictions. Or just leave it home. Silvana says:

"Many KOA campgrounds have cabins, so you don't need to bring a tarp and tent."

Laura S., her husband, and children frequently fly to destinations, then camp. They stow sleeping bags, tents, pads, and other gear in sturdy cardboard boxes, making sure the dimensions fit the checked-baggage requirements. They seal the parcels with packing tape and affix a printed label with their destination and home address. When they arrive, they simply collapse the boxes until the trip home or use them to organize gear in their rental vehicle. They take along extra tape and home-address labels for the return trip.

It's easy to take too much on a camping trip. "I thought if we could fit it all into our packs, we'd be able to carry it," says Dizy B., who, along with her thirteen-year-old son, Christopher, went on a three-month trip through South America. Adding to the complexity, they took along their surfboards. "Even though we walked around the house and the yard several times, the first time we actually had to walk somewhere with our packs and surfboards, we realized it couldn't easily be done. On our trip, we just put our heads down and went. It was sheer determination and exhaustion." Dizy and her son ended up purging belongings throughout their trip. "It was hiking boots here, a sleeping bag there—people were very appreciative, but it's a choice I wouldn't make again," she says.

Specialized Gear • MD

On a car trip, you should be able to fit some extras, such as skis, skateboards, customized bicycles, or musical instruments. When your trip entails a flight, you'll need to pre-plan and be creative with hobby gear. For larger unwieldy items, it's a lot easier to rent at your destination. If you're determined, check

11. PACK IT UP

with your airline about its luggage restrictions and additional fees for extra bags, before heading to the airport. A second (or third) checked bag per person may cost far more than renting the items.

In some cases, you may need to carry gear for both you and your children. For example, you may need specially-sized clothes, boots, or accessories. Bring smaller, fragile items, such as snorkel gear, in your carry-on. Check larger or bulkier items in specialized cases, or in well-padded duffel bags.

Unless it's unavoidable, never check a musical instrument. Stringed ones are particularly vulnerable to breakage and are difficult to appropriately cushion. Alert an airline representative at your gate about bringing the instrument onboard. Be prepared to count it as one of the two carry-ons passengers are allowed.

Gear for Young Children • MD

In Peru with my husband and older son, Cillian—just two at the time—we carried very little specialized gear. We used a Kelty Kids carrier and didn't take a stroller or a car seat. We didn't bring a travel bed with us, nor did we do anything special in terms of food. I left my diaper bag and used my daypack instead. I did, however, bring a bundle of books, including puzzle and coloring ones, some pencils, and small toys.

Because I didn't overstuff our bags with extra diapers, we needed to buy them along the way. I learned that putting your nose to a small child's bottom, then making a face, is a universal way of communicating a diaper issue. I still don't know the Quechua words for *pharmacy* or *diaper,* but I was able to sort out my little guy's needs almost as easily as if we'd been at home.

My light packing habits may be a little extreme, but it's not difficult to find a balance between what you rely on normally and what you really need while traveling (without packing the kitchen sink). So many products are available for babies and toddlers. Some are necessary, like car seats, while some are truly discretionary, like $400 strollers. What to do with all this gear when you're preparing for a trip? The simple answer is to pack light, like we did in Peru. This may mean purchasing something just for traveling—such as a cheap, light, umbrella stroller. In most cases, however, it means simply limiting what you bring.

To begin, see our packing suggestions at the end of this chapter. Determine what products are necessary and which ones are discretionary. You won't want to carry it all, but critically check the list and ensure that you're only taking what you really need. A lot of daily infant and toddler products, such as a diaper-pail, are labor-saving devices—and are truly intended for use only at home.

Consider borrowing or renting larger equipment, like a crib, at your destination. Within the U.S., a wide variety of baby gear is available from Baby's Away (www.babysaway.com) outlets in twenty-nine states, and orders can be placed online. Alternatively, use Internet services such as Jet Set Babies (www.jetsetbabies.com) or Tinytotsaway (www.tinytotsaway.com), to order equipment and supplies for delivery to your destination.

As you go through your checklist, consider every caretakers' priorities, anywhere: warmth, sleep, feeding, potty, and comfort.

Once children get a little older, life on the road gets easier. By age four, your little gal has left the terrible twos behind and is more even tempered. You need very little specialized gear, and your little one can be more involved in the process of getting ready to travel.

You can (and should) involve your child in preparing and packing for the trip. It's totally impractical but very fun to say, "Mommy's packing; you need to pick what you want to bring with you," just to see what she chooses. I do remember having trouble holding a straight face when my then three-year-old returned with his entire collection of soft toys and his bedding.

I usually allow two piles per child: one for check-in and one for carry-on. This works for flying, as well as car, boat, and train trips (where you might want quick access to toiletries and a change of underwear). I make everyone responsible for his own overnight or carry-on bag, and traveling has improved tremendously as a result. No longer do I have an upset child because, "Mom forgot my ..."

I used a bright, kid-sized, pull-along duffle with both of my boys in their preschool years. They enjoyed having their own bags to pack and trundle along "just like Mom."

The upside of kid-size luggage is that its small capacity helps your budding Christine Columbus sort out what she wants to pack from what will actually fit in. Samsonite's Sammies is my favorite among the many kid brands available today. The colorful bags are styled as animals—including tigers, ladybugs, and turtles. There are backpacks and duffels to match the eighteen-inch, pull-along suitcases. You'll want to outfit your child with a piece of luggage that's also easy for you to carry. Because there's no easy way for an adult to manage the short tow bar on a kids' bag, choose one with a strap that can be attached to your luggage or, alternately, a shoulder strap for adult use.

Luggage for kids by Trunki (www.trunki.net), a U.K.-based company, is available in many North American retail and on-line stores. These sturdy travel bags double as a ride-along for your preschooler and are approved as carry-ons. There's also a strap suitable for kids pulling or adults carrying.

Warmth • MD — Always pack a sweater or warm coat for your child. Regardless of the weather forecast, your baby or toddler is more susceptible to changes in temperature than you are. If there's an unexpected drop, you don't want to be caught un-prepared. Even if you're traveling someplace warm, it's good to have something for late-night or early-morning outings. Both Brendan and I are early risers and many times we have had breakfast outdoors or taken a walk together in cool, crisp air while the rest of the family has slept.

Hot Tip! Wear layers of clothing, including sweaters and jackets, on your flight. This conserves space in your luggage.

Sleep • MD — Portable cribs are usually available in all types of accommodations in the developed world. Unless you are staying in the same place for the duration, bringing your own crib may be more trouble than it's worth. I'm a fan of co-sleep-ing (sharing a family bed), which is the easiest option for par-ents with small children. If you do carry your own crib, look for gently used products online or at a secondhand store to save some money on this travel gear.

Toddler beds are not as readily available as cribs in hotels or other lodgings. I opted against a portable toddler bed with both my children, since we often took long international flights with at least one layover. Instead, we pushed beds against walls and, for added safety, piled pillows and blankets to create a barrier between the sleeping preschooler and the exposed side of the bed.

Feeding • MD — If your child is still taking breast milk, feeding couldn't be easier while you're traveling. The two leaders in pumps, Medela (www.medelabreastfeedingus.com) and Avent (www.avent.com), each offer products suitable for the road. Don't forget to bring breast-milk bags with you. They're lightweight, take up very little room, and you won't have to hunt for them in a strange supermarket or pharmacy.

Once infants are weaning, food becomes more of a concern than perhaps at any other age—and even more so when you're traveling. You may have legitimate concerns about what to bring and whether you can depend on purchasing familiar foodstuffs. Fortunately, baby products, including food, are available everywhere. The brands may be different, but you should have little difficulty in finding products in supermarkets abroad that are equivalent to the ones at home.

Hot Tip! Bring only a few days' supply of all your feeding and diapering essentials with you. This will save you the effort of dragging too much stuff through security and onto an airplane. You will have time to settle in, orient yourself, and find a supermarket before you need to stock up again.

For solid foods, consider packing a hand-cranked food mill, such as one from KidCo (www.kidco.com), and making your own baby food. Sassy Baby's (www.sassybaby.com) partitioned containers are good for dry foods such as cereal. The company also offers a container that allows you to pre-measure up to six servings of dry formula, so that you can pack away an unopened tin of formula to use when you arrive.

If your child has food allergies or other dietary restrictions, be prepared to bring any specialty foods with you. Unless you know a reliable outlet, it's safer to take what you need. A little research can go a long way. I used soy formula with both my children to protect against milk allergies. I would search for a natural-foods store at our destination and call ahead to make sure that a similar formula was available. If not, I knew in advance to pack my own.

The road from milk-fed to proper table manners is long and messy, and I can't think about toddler eating habits without chuckling. They're definitely no tidier on the road. You'll want to bring bibs, utensils, and plastic serving dishes to keep clothing clean—particularly relevant when you're living out of a suitcase. Items great for travel include Take & Toss sippy cups from The First Years (www.learningcurve.com/thefirstyears), funky toddler cutlery such as the Beetle Spoon and Spork available at Hog Wild Toys (www.hogwildtoys.com), and Snack Traps (www.snacktrap. com), toddler-friendly containers for dry cereals and crackers.

Potty • MD — The big developmental milestone in the preschool years is potty training. Accidents will happen when traveling—even for those kids who rarely have them at home. Pack some disposable undies or nighttime training pants just in case. I used the Dri Nights Waterproof Mattress Protector (available through One Step Ahead) both at home and on the road with my children. It is triple layered: soft on top, absorbent in the middle, and waterproof on the bottom. It also has extra-long side "wings" for securing the protector in place, and since it's not bulky, it's easy to pack at the top of a suitcase.

Though I didn't bother in Peru, a good diaper bag can be vital. Today, there are excellent products available, such as the Baby Sherpa Diaper Bag Backpack (www.babysherpa.com). Don't forget a portable changing pad that will provide a clean surface for diapering, no matter where you are. Skip Hop has a stylish version in five colors that you can find online, or check out an eco-friendly model from One Step Ahead.

Comfort • MD — Many parents swear by their baby slings. And since a sling is really just a long piece of cloth, it's a versatile tool to have on the road. Mariah V. took one to Nepal with her then five-month-old son. She says, "It folds up really small, so it's easy to have in your backpack. You can use it as a blanket as well as a sling, and if you need to lay your child on the ground anywhere, you can use the wrap for that, too."

Kid carriers really help to encourage daytime naps-on-the-go. They are also more convenient than a stroller, which can be a hindrance on cobblestone streets, sandy beaches, and rutted country roads. Even at home, I used my BabyBjörn (www. babybjorn.com) front carrier constantly when my boys were really young. For older infants and toddlers, soft carriers— such as Ergo's (www.ergobabycarrier.com) and Beco's (www. becobabycarrier.com)—are very popular choices.

Moving up from a BabyBjörn to a backpack-style model (such as a Kelty Kids carrier, www.kelty.com) is a natural step. With your toddler on your back, you have both hands free to pick up or pull luggage, hold an older child's hand, or have access to your passport. If your kid falls asleep, she is safe, secure, and supported. Using a carrier is not always smooth sailing, though. My younger son did throw up on me once—a nasty experience. That we were boarding a nine-hour flight at the time was particularly annoying. It was the first and only time

I have flown business class international, and it was the most uncomfortable flight I have ever experienced.

After I bought an umbrella stroller, (a simple one from Kolcraft), it lived in the trunk of my car for a long time. It was small enough to fit into the overhead bin; light enough to carry with one hand when not in use; and cheap enough so that if it were damaged or lost, the cost to replace it (twenty dollars) was very low. For a more permanent stroller at home and away, consider one from Maclaren (www.maclarenbaby. com). These have a compact umbrella-style fold, which makes them a good choice for double duty.

Gifts from Home and Memory-makers • LF

Presents are a wonderful way to teach graciousness while traveling. By taking small items for other children, your kids can practice thoughtfulness and maybe even make new friends. You'll also want to bring gifts for the parents of families you may meet.

In places where poverty is common, appropriate presents include colored pencils (beware of crayons if you're traveling somewhere hot—they can easily melt all over the contents of your suitcase), sketchpads, coloring books, sticker books, Beanie Babies, and small craft kits. One of your best resources will be your local drugstore, with its enticing display of inexpensive children's toys.

Dawn L. regifts party favors. "My kids go to tons of birthday parties, and they come back with lots of trinkets. I have a box that I toss all of those in, along with the leftovers from making goodie bags for their parties. When we travel, I pack it all up."

Think regionally when selecting gifts for the families you'll be visiting. Sports team or local-themed T-shirts, key chains, and

Kimm S.'s Story

We always carry little city or state lapel pins that are made for the tourists to our city. We take a bag of twenty of them on each trip.

On a trip to the Netherlands, I told Emma: "These are for giving to special people on the trip. You get to decide who to give a pin to, because we don't have enough to give one to everyone." We were biking and had stopped in a park with a little bridge over a canal. There were swans in the canal, along with a couple of cygnets. A girl and her mother were watching the swans. We had some bread to feed the birds, and naturally the girl wanted to feed them, too. As they were feeding the swans, Emma gave the girl a pin.

On another trip, we were lost in Tokyo as we were looking for a noodle shop. A man we asked for help walked us clear across town and found us the best noodle shop. Emma gave him a pin. That's her job. It's a good way to start a conversation!

playing cards are popular ideas. A small photography book on your region or country allows travelers to share home with new friends. Many people in other countries are fascinated with Native Americans. Consider taking along a small handicraft that is representative of these cultures. When selecting gifts, think about your own culture, as well; if you live in the Pacific Northwest, for instance, vacuum-packed smoked salmon would be a thoughtful offering.

If you'll be traveling by air, wrapped gifts may be opened at security.

Whenever I've traveled to another country, I have always taken along a small photo album with pictures of my family, our house, and our neighborhood. This is a great conversation starter, and it helps new friends feel more comfortable asking questions about our life. You can ask your children to select photos they would like to include. You can even give them a digital camera and turn them loose on a shooting expedition. As an alternative, you can simply take postcards of your city and local wildlife.

While gifts and photo albums allow you to become better acquainted with those you meet, writing can help your children remember their trip experiences. Plan to take a new journal for each child. Bound blank books are a good choice for longer journeys and older children, yet you don't have to spend that much money. A small spiral-bound, lined notepad works fine and could be more convenient size-wise. Be sure to equip yourself with a journal as well, and take time daily to record your thoughts and impressions. Seeing you do this will encourage your children follow suit. You may be amazed by just how much your child absorbs. My daughter has been keeping journals of trips since she was very young, and we both enjoy looking back over these. I like to think of them as the most important treasures gleaned from a trip.

Packing List • LF

It's a great idea to devise a packing plan on your computer that you can refer to for future trips, adding and deleting as your children get older. Refining the idea a bit further, consider one for summer and one for winter. E-lists are easy to update as your child grows and has different needs and interests. The following examples are good starting points. The intent is not to haul everything suggested; these are much more comprehensive than you would ever need or want on a single trip. However, they can help you remember important things that might work well for your family.

Clothes • LF

- belt
- cardigan or pullover sweater
- casual dress or sundress
- casual pants or capris
- casual tops
- dress shoes
- dressy blouse or shirt
- extra bra
- five full changes of clothes, socks, shoes, a jacket or sweater (for your toddler)
- gym clothes (top, shorts, sneakers, socks)
- jeans
- light outdoor jacket
- pajamas
- scarves
- slacks
- shorts
- skirts
- socks
- suit jacket
- sun-protective clothing (pants, shirt, and hat)
- swimsuit (in a plastic bag)
- tank tops
- tights and/or leggings
- underwear
- walking/hiking sandals
- walking shoes
- waterproof windbreaker or rain poncho

Personal-care Items • LF

- alcohol wipes
- at least three bottles and/or sippy cups (one clean, one dirty, one in use)
- baby monitor
- birth control/condoms
- braces and/or retainer supplies
- clothesline, sink stopper, laundry soap (in double plastic bags)
- conditioner
- contact lenses and solutions
- dental floss
- deodorant
- earplugs
- empty plastic bags for dirty/soiled/wet clothes and dirty diapers
- face lotion
- feminine products
- first-aid kit (See Chapter 12 for a specific list.)
- hairbrush
- hair accessories
- hand lotion
- hand-wipes (two to three packs if you have a toddler)
- insect bite reliever
- insect repellant
- lip balm

- lipstick
- makeup
- nail clippers /file /tweezers
- over-the-counter remedies
- plastic outlet covers
- prescription medications
- razor
- shampoo
- soap
- spare glasses
- sunglasses
- sunscreen
- toothbrush
- toothpaste
- tissues
- two to three days' worth of diapers
- two to three days' worth of formula and /or baby food
- vitamins
- waterproof mattress pad

Documents and Accessories • LF

- address list (for postcards)
- binder with flight and lodging confirmations and directions
- binoculars
- books /magazines
- business cards
- camera
- cell phone (and charger)
- electricity converter /plug adaptor
- eye mask
- flashlight or microlight (keychain-sized flashlight) and batteries
- fold-up nylon bag (for taking gifts home)
- frequent-flier card
- gifts for new friends
- guidebooks
- inflatable pillow (for long trips)
- journal and pens
- maps
- MP3 player
- noise-canceling headphones
- passport
- phrasebook
- sleep sack and pillowcase (if staying at hostels)
- small photo album or picture book of your city
- small spiral notebook (for expenses)
- snacks
- travel umbrella
- travel alarm clock
- wallet /purse with driver's license and credit cards, and foreign currency in small denominations if going overseas
- watch

11. PACK IT UP

Entertainment Packing List • MD

For Toddlers and Preschoolers:

- coloring and puzzle books
- favorite soft toy or blanket
- playing cards

- reusable sticker books
- small toys for on-the-go
- washable markers

For Elementary-school Ages:

- activity books from Madlibs
- books, books, and more books!
- games from Klutz
- handheld video game players with charger, batteries (if required), and games.

- MP3 player with audio books and music
- Thinkfun games
- travel versions of favorite board games

12.

HEALTH AND SAFETY

S TAYING *healthy on the road requires preparation before you leave, taking into consideration your destination and activities. This process is relatively simple if you're traveling within North America or to other developed areas, and if you and your children are healthy with all vaccinations up to date. Less-developed regions require you to consider additional vaccinations and insurance. No matter the destination, be ready for the most unlikely events by having your family's health and medical information at your fingertips. This ensures the safest journey for your precious cargo.*

Medical Records • MD

Prior to your trip, you'll want to first organize your family's medical records into four categories: emergency contacts, vaccinations, insurance, and prescriptions and medications.

Emergency Contacts • MD — Begin by creating a contact list that includes your own doctor(s), your children's pediatrician, and any dentists and ophthalmologists your family visits. Add any specialists seen in the past twelve to twenty-four months. Include your insurance provider and a brief medical history for each person, listing all known conditions and allergies, any current prescription medications, and any major illnesses or operations.

Vaccinations • MD — Each year, most schools require an updated vaccination record for all students. Add a copy of this to your child's medical bio. Any additional shots received should be recorded on an International Certificate of Vaccination (commonly called "the yellow card"), which is issued by your doctor or travel clinic.

If you're headed to a developing country, check the Centers for Disease Control and Prevention website for information on what diseases may be prevalent, as well as for recommended vaccinations.

In addition to educating yourself on the CDC's website, consult with your doctor and pediatrician on how to best prepare everyone, since your physicians will know your family's medical history. Mariah V. visited her five-month-old son's pediatrician before going to Nepal. "I was able to ask my son's doctor what types of shots we needed. She then researched which vaccinations were safe and came up with a plan for administering them."

If your youngster has not yet completed his cycle of childhood immunizations, your doctor may recommend accelerating the schedule. Information on the American Academy of Pediatrics' vaccination requirements can be found at the Childhood Immunization Support Program website (www.cispimmunize.org).

While some vaccinations are available in oral form (far more appealing to children), most are given as injections. Depending on where you are traveling, shots for hepatitis A and B, cholera, typhoid, yellow fever, and Japanese encephalitis may be suggested (or required, in the case of yellow fever). These inoculations may require one or more shots administered over a number of weeks or months. Give yourself plenty of time so that you can stagger any vaccinations your child might require.

For areas where malaria is prevalent, consult with your doctor about you and your child's options. Anti-malarial drugs such as chloroquine must be specially prepared for kids, while others are not available to children due to the high possibility of adverse side effects. Those under eight shouldn't take doxycycline, for example. Nor should older travelers who have a heightened possibility of sunburn. See "Insect Repellents" later in this chapter for non-drug mosquito-fighting options.

No matter what vaccinations you ultimately decide upon, it's unlikely that your health insurance will cover those specifically recommended for travel.

Prescriptions and Medications • MD — If anyone in your family is on medication, carry enough with you for the duration of the trip. This may require a phone call to your insurance provider, explaining your travel plans and getting authorization for additional refills. Ask your doctor to provide

12. HEALTH AND SAFETY

267

you with a paper copy of the prescription, as well, in case you do need to restock it along the way.

Hot Tip! Medication should always be packed in carry-on bags, in case your checked baggage is delayed or lost.

In North America, you may simply be able to visit a branch of the pharmacy where the prescription was originally filled— these chains share a database and thus have your information already. Elsewhere, you must provide the pharmacist with your doctor's contact information so he can then authorize the refill.

Abroad, refills may be a little more complicated if your medication isn't available over-the-counter (which is the case for most prescriptions in many developing countries). This will require you to see a doctor for a new prescription. (See "Finding Medical Help Abroad," later in this chapter, for more information on locating a doctor.)

Should your medicine be considered a controlled substance (this includes narcotics and psychotropics found in ADD and ADHD medications), check the guidelines issued by the International Narcotics Control Board (www.incb.org). At a minimum, you must carry a copy of the prescription to prove medical use.

Insurance • MD

Sort out insurance coverage, particularly if you are traveling to underdeveloped or remote regions.

Medical • MD — When Cillian was eighteen months old, he fell down some steps at a friend's house in Oxford, U.K. Concerned that he might have broken his arm, and mindful that we had a nine-hour flight home the next day, my husband called the emergency room at a local hospital for advice. We were encouraged to bring him in. After studying his X-rays, the staff determined that he had a minor fracture and put a cast on his arm. We paid for the visit, got copies of the X-rays for our pediatrician in Seattle, and were able to claim the out-of-pocket expenses from our insurance after we had returned home. The most difficult part of the entire experience was the flight. Poor Cillian couldn't get comfortable, because his favorite thumb was in a cast and unavailable for sucking.

In the case of an accident, many insurance policies cover travel outside of your home state, as well as overseas, and may reimburse you for emergency and urgent-care expenses. Check with your provider whether your family is covered at your destination. And keep in mind that your coverage might not include certain activities, such as adventure sports, scuba diving, or rock climbing.

Travel • MD — Consider travel insurance, if there is any possibility that you may have to cancel your trip at the last minute, after you've spent a heap of money on a tour package, or non-refundable hotel or air tickets. For a relatively small fee, you'll be reimbursed for costs of a thwarted adventure. Depending on the policy, other benefits may include baggage reimbursement, and medical, dental, and evacuation coverage.

Evacuation and Transportation • MD — Though no one wants to consider the unthinkable, it's imperative that you have an emergency plan, especially if you are the only adult traveling with your child.

Evacuation insurance covers an injured or ill person's transport to a medical facility. If you're traveling in a remote area of Bolivia, for example, you might consider being removed to Rio de Janeiro, Brazil, where the standard of medical care may be better. Such an evacuation could run upwards of $60,000: a cost mostly covered by insurance.

Often included in such policies are repatriation (being sent home) or an emergency reunion. This allows a support person—such as a friend or family member—to be transported to the ill or injured party. An example would be when an adult is incapacitated and the child cannot be left alone. Another provision often covered is the return of children to their home in such cases. Plans vary, so check all the options available.

A good resource is the Travel Insurance Review, which includes information about companies. Check the Family Travel Insurance Coverage Matrix (www.travelinsurancereview.net/family-travel-insurance), which offers summary information on family-friendly benefits from major travel insurers. The Travel Insurance Review does not provide rates, but you can comparison-shop on SquareMouth (www.squaremouth.com). These websites make finding and pricing different coverage options easy.

Be sure to read your policy carefully before you leave home, and note all pertinent contact info. Melanie E. traveled to Mexico with her two-year-old son. When she needed to call her insurance provider, she did not have a phone number that worked outside the U.S. "The insurance paperwork showed a toll-free number, but did not include the actual area code, so it was useless to me since toll-free numbers are not accessible outside the U.S. [or Canada]."

You'll want to make multiple copies of all your paperwork, including emergency contacts, medical records, vaccinations, and insurance. Carry at least one copy, and leave another at home with a trusted friend or family member. Alternately, if you'll have access to the Internet, consider an online medical records service such as iHealthRecord (www.ihealthrecord.org) or Medical Summary (www.medicalsummary.com). You can store all the details online and then just carry a wallet-size card containing emergency information.

Finding Medical Help • MD

It isn't as difficult as it might seem to find an English-speaking, Western-trained doctor abroad. One way is to become a member of the International Association for Medical Assistance to Travelers (IAMAT, www.iamat.org). While donations are welcomed, membership is free and allows you access to a directory of physicians and medical facilities in 125 countries. IAMAT inspects facilities continuously to ensure quality medical care. U.S. embassies and consulates also provide referrals to Western-trained and English-speaking doctors. Make sure you include contact information for the embassy or consulate with your travel documents.

When a child is sick, speed in finding a remedy can be lifesaving. That might mean you have to accept help from whatever medical facility is available—even if it does not meet Western standards. Pippa C. describes how her eighteen-month-old son Grant fell ill on a game reserve in South Africa. "He got very sick, very quickly." Though a doctor had administered antibiotics, he was not responding, and the facilities were not sophisticated enough to determine why. With the baby's fever at 107 degrees, the doctor urged Pippa to take Grant to Johannesburg, eight hours away. This was the right advice. "In the city, the doctors quickly established that Grant had strep throat and were able to treat him promptly."

12. HEALTH AND SAFETY

While Pippa didn't run into a language barrier, her problem was getting to a suitable hospital. Ultimately, doctors determined her son had an allergy that rendered the antibiotics ineffective. Without an embassy or consulate nearby to consult with, sometimes it takes motherly persistence to find the right answer to help your child.

Staying Healthy on the Road • MD

In an emerging nation, the risk of illness is higher than in the developed world. If your child is sick, you will focus on nursing him back to health over everything else; the Great Pyramids can wait. But if your family can avoid illness in the first place, your travels will be that much more enjoyable.

Before departure, bone up on your first-aid skills and learn about common travelers' ailments at your destination. Then, ask your doctor for advice on how to handle these should your child fall ill.

Once you're on the road, simple precautionary measures can help the whole family stay in top shape.

Water • MD — We're so accustomed to having fresh, clean aqua piped into our homes that it can come as a surprise that water could be a concern. Waterborne bacteria, viruses, and parasites cause numerous illnesses, from diarrhea to hepatitis. Many of these diseases can become very serious very quickly for children. It's extremely important to be vigilant about safe drinking water for your family.

In developed countries, it's usually safe to drink tap water, including that which comes from your hotel room or from drinking fountains—unless there are signs indicating otherwise. Teach your children to look for such notices; even if they can't read the words, there's usually a graphic that they can understand.

Except for some touristy cities, water in underdeveloped countries is generally not safe, not even for brushing teeth. Keep a bottle filled with treated water for just these purposes. Metal ones, such as those from SIGG (www.mysigg. com), are better for the environment than plastic ones. Many come in kid sizes with attractive designs that your children will love. Thoroughly clean your reusable bottles as bacteria can grow inside.

Buying bottled water, be sure that the cap is sealed before you make your purchase. Check for any sign of tampering or re-sealing that may indicate that the container was refilled with the tap water you're trying to avoid. In a hot climate, it can be difficult to have enough water on hand to keep your kids cool and hydrated while also trying to be kind to the environment with as few plastic bottles as possible. Do your best. Involve the children in packing their own water bottles in daypacks and looking for (safe) public drinking fountains from which to refill. Children learn about the environment at school and will likely be willing participants in protecting the planet—one less plastic water bottle at a time.

If your accommodation has a restaurant or an in-room kitchen, fill your bottles with water that's been boiled for at least one minute. This will make it safe to drink (though it may not taste any better). You might also ponder a small, portable, water-purifying system or iodine tablets. Both of these can be purchased at your local camping store or online.

Ice cubes can be tempting. When I do allow my children the occasional soft drink, I request the drinks without ice, rather than risk the consequences.

12. HEALTH AND SAFETY

273

Hot Tip! Use a SteriPEN hand-held purifier to ensure safe drinking water. This uses UV light to eradicate parasites, bacteria, and protozoa from water. It's small, lightweight, and easy to keep in a purse or daypack.

Food • MD — Like water, food safety is a concern for every traveler and, again, is most commonly an issue in the developing world. No matter where you are, it can be fun to discover new foods sold at street stalls. The kids will be intrigued by the colors and smells of grub cooked out in the open. However, if the dish is not freshly prepared, find another vendor, as flies and mosquitoes are quickly attracted to food that is left sitting. Even if your children are hungry, it's better to find a more re-liabale chef.

The simple rule for food safety is to boil it, cook it, peel it, or forget it. This means that hot, thoroughly cooked food is safest, and that you should avoid raw vegetables and fruit except for those that you can peel.

Keep alcohol-based sanitizer or wipes on hand at all times, and make sure that you and your children use them before eating. Wipes are especially welcome with an infant or toddler, who get grubby quickly and frequently. Not only are these items great for little hands, but you can wipe down utensils at restaurants if cleanliness is questionable.

For a traveler with stomach issues, the acidophilus found in many live-culture yogurts will help fight off the bacteria that makes you sick, though it has shown little effect as a deterrent.

Exercise • MD — When my boys were younger, they were such tumults of energy that I got my exercise chasing after them—even if it was just around a playground. Now that they are older, we consciously schedule plenty of physical activities into our traveling days. This is especially important when we are all adjusting to a different time zone—a full day walking and sightseeing will wear a child out, help him sleep better, and ultimately speed up his recovery from jet lag.

My kids love to play in water, and I encourage it often when we travel, whether it's at the beach, at the hotel's pool, or at a public facility. On days when we are involved in more sedentary activities (such as a guided bus tour or when we are in transit), we always make time for exercise so that the boys have a chance to stretch and work off their energy.

If your child has a pet activity, research options at your destination. Providing him with an outlet to do something he already enjoys will make him feel more relaxed and at home wherever you are.

Child Safety · MD/LF

If you could glue your child to your side for the duration of your trip, you wouldn't have to worry about his safety. While I have considered it at times, that solution is beyond practical on many levels (bathroom visits come to mind!).

All parents worry about losing their kids, and that anxiety can be magnified when traveling in unfamiliar surroundings. Much of the time, these fears are unfounded. When Sarah C. told her friends that she was taking her children to off-the-beaten-path places in Mexico without her husband, they asked, "Aren't you afraid?" What she discovered was that the locals were eager to help out, to get to know her family, and to even watch the kids while she attended to the business of travel. "Everyone we met bent over backward for us. They're so family-oriented there, and people would play with the kids while I was registering at a hotel. Safety was never an issue for us."

But, you can't always rely on the kindness of strangers. While some children will quietly sit in a stroller or hold your hand obediently, others are runners—kids who will wriggle out of your grasp in a moment and sprint. Active toddlers are particularly difficult to watch in busy locations. Though tethers allow a child to roam while also keeping him within your reach, you may be averse to these, and your little one may resist wearing one. The SafeFit Grow-With-Me Backpack with Harness (www.safefit.com) is a neat compromise. It'll feel like a big-kid backpack to your child, but you'll be able to take advantage of the additional tether.

You will likely have to move the furniture around at your accommodation to ensure a mobile toddler stays safe. Be aware of things that can fall or be pulled down (lamps) or catch little fingers (doors, drawers). Be sure to tie any blind or drape cords up securely.

If you're the only adult traveling with your toddler, be sure that doors and window locks are secure, since you might be sleeping or distracted (perhaps in the bathroom) when your child is awake. Pack baby-proofing gear from home including closet locks. Debbi T. creatively stays aware of her daughter's activity. "I tie a small bunch of bells on the hotel door, so I'm alerted if Jora tries to open the door."

For an older child who likes the independence of exploring at her own pace, identity bracelets offer the most basic level of security. When Laura F. traveled to Serbia and China, she got the kids these to wear. The bracelets had space for a list of emergency contact numbers in the U.S., including their grandmother's and neighbors'.

Hot Tip! Check out Spot Me ID (www.spotmeid.com) products for low-cost solutions such as ID bracelets, lanyards, and temporary tattoos (for your cell number).

Transmitter-receiver technologies are the next step up. On the less-expensive, simpler end of the spectrum are audio-alert devices such as Mommy I'm Here (www.mommyimhere.com), with its teddy-bear-shaped receiver that your child clips to his shoe or belt. When the parent presses a button on a hand-held unit, the child's unit chirps. For children up to age ten, ionKids (www.ion-kids.com) features a tamper-proof bracelet and a base unit. With the press of a button on the monitor, the bracelet answers with a loud beep.

Some cell phones are more than a communication device. AT&T, Sprint, and Verizon all offer GPS tracking services for models with the appropriate technology. For this option, check before a trip to see if your service provider works in that region or country. (For more information about using cell phones abroad, see Chapter 13, "While You're There.")

Never leave young children alone in your accommodation. At twelve, my older son is responsible enough to stay in a hotel room on his own, while his dad and I eat dinner at a nearby restaurant. But only if we have cell phone coverage, so that he can contact us immediately. If you choose to hire a nanny, find a trustworthy agency. (See Chapter 6, "Pre-Trip Planning," for information on sitting services.)

Travel Health Issues • MD

It's worth remembering that children who are often ill at home are more likely to experience issues on the road. Fortunately, my kids are healthy, and in twelve years of travel, we've had only one broken bone to deal with.

12. HEALTH AND SAFETY

A passport-sized book—*The Pocket Doctor* by Stephen Bezruchka, MD—is an excellent reference for summary information on diseases, immunizations, and medications for international travel. It is also a quick guide to diagnosing and treating common (and uncommon) medical issues that may occur.

Common Travel Medical Issues for Kids • MD — Changes
in cabin pressure during takeoff and landing are painful for little ears. Nurse an infant or give him a pacifier to suck on to help relieve the pressure. For older children, dispense gum or hard candy or have them make funny faces by yawning wide. Hysteria induced by tickling should be a last, loud resort (at least laughing is more pleasant for other passengers than crying).

If your child is susceptible to motion sickness, have him take some Dramamine or ginger before you head out on the water or after their symptoms have begun. I've found that Sea Bands Acupressure Bracelets (www.seaproductsonline.com) also work well. These elastic bracelets include a small button that you strategically place on your wrist to relieve nausea.

Diarrhea can go from a discomfort to a serious condition very quickly, because it's easy for a small child to become dehydrated. Give a sufferer plenty of liquids and oral rehydration solutions, such as Pedialyte, if necessary. Most bouts are resolved without medications, but if the condition persists (longer than eight hours), see a doctor as quickly as possible.

Avoid traveling to extremely high elevations without allowing kids to properly acclimatize. Infants and toddlers are not able to communicate about the headaches, nausea, or lightheadedness common with altitude sickness. According to *Best Hikes with Children in Colorado* by Maureen Keilty, spend two or three days acclimatizing and then (above 9,000 feet) don't ascend more than 1,000 feet per day.

Children love playing in the snow and frequently do not want to stop for cold, or wet clothing. However, this leaves them susceptible to frostnip and possibly frostbite—although this only manifests after prolonged exposure. I entice my children inside with hot chocolate or another warm drink. Thankfully, those are easy to find in cold places around the globe.

Sun Precautions • LF — Time outside is an important part of childhood. It helps nurture a love of nature, and develop their imaginations when they play with "toys" such as sticks and rocks. Plus it develops their bodies, as they run, jump, and climb. And exposure to the sun provides the vitamin D our kids need for strong bones.

When I was a child, summers were spent almost exclusively outdoors, and we all sported glowing tans, considered a sign of good health. Now we know that unprotected sun exposure can lead to cancer. Recent research shows that more than eighty percent of solar damage occurs during the first eighteen years of life. Just one bad sunburn in childhood can double the chance of skin cancer later.

While some sun without protection unleashes the benefits of vitamin D production, the amount needed for this is minimal—around ten to twenty minutes daily. After that, make sure they don't burn.

This is true no matter where or when you travel: Kids of every complexion need to be protected—dark-skinned children can just as easily develop sunburns as those with paler skin. Yet, kids with very fair skin and hair, moles, or a family history of skin cancer need to be extremely cautious. Since our actions are more powerful than our words, it's a good idea for parents to use sun protection consistently, as well.

The American Cancer Society has a handy mnemonic for re-membering how to limit exposure to damaging rays:

- Slip! on a shirt—wear protective clothing when in the sun.

- Slop! on sunscreen with an sun-protection factor (SPF) of fifteen or higher.

- Slap! on a hat to shade the face, neck, and ears.

The most crucial window is between ten a.m. and two p.m. The American Cancer Society suggests that parents teach the shadow rule: If it's shorter than you are, the sun is high in the sky and the UV rays are intense, so you'll need to limit expo-sure. Children younger than six months old should be kept in the shade, regardless of the time of day. You can purchase a baby sun shelter for any beach time.

Sun-blocking products range from lotions and gels to sprays and even wipes. Be sure to look for products that offer full-spectrum protection. SPF only refers to UVB (ultraviolet B or medium-wave) protection, not UVA (ultraviolet A or long-wave) protection. While UVB rays are responsible for sun-burns, we now know that UVA light also damages skin cells. Unfortunately, the market has not yet caught up to the science, and only a few countries require UVA blockers in their prod-ucts. Be a savvy consumer and look for full-spectrum safety for your kids.

Skincare products for children are gentler on more delicate skin. To sidestep the possibility of allergies, avoid sunscreens with para-aminobenzoic acid (PABA). For sensitive skin, seek out products that show the active ingredient titanium dioxide, a chemical-free block.

In addition to applying sunscreen, don't forget to use lip balm—with an SPF of fifteen or greater—to avoid dry, cracked lips. Look for children's sunglasses that provide one hundred percent UV protection, and outfit your kids with broad-brimmed hats or ones with brims and back flaps.

Hot Tip! Blue Lizard Australian Suncream is the gold standard of sunscreens for kids and the darling of dermatologists; it provides excellent protection against full-spectrum UV light. Its unique bottle, which changes color from white to pink or blue when exposed to UV light, is both educational and fun. It's not only available in Oz; you can buy it in pharmacies throughout North America.

Different cultures have different takes on exposure to the sun. In some countries or regions, tans are highly prized, while in others, tradition dictates pale complexions. If you have any concerns about finding sunscreen, it's best to pack your own.

Paula B. and her family were in a remote area of Thailand when she needed to buy some sunblock. She learned the local word and asked for it at a store. "I got whitening lotion," she says. "The locals avoid the sun, primarily because it's so hot, so we were unable to get sunblock anywhere."

As handy as sunscreen is, studies show that most products can damage delicate coral reefs and marine life when they wash off. For beach vacations, sun-protective clothing is a great alternative. It's a lot less messy and uncomfortable than sunscreen—some of which can feel greasy. And these garments are amazingly versatile working well in many situations beyond the beach. Sun-protective garments such as long-sleeve shirts and long pants can come in handy for many applications, such as hiking or even when strolling through a city.

12. HEALTH AND SAFETY

Sun-protective clothing has a UPF (Ultraviolet Protection Factor) rating of thirty or above, which takes into account both UVA and UVB rays. These garments are gossamer light, and the shirts are often constructed with vents, for added cooling.

Sun Precautions (www.sunprecautions.com) was the original innovator, and oddly enough, the FDA considers their products "medical devices." These items protect by means of a tight weave, a process now duplicated by numerous other brands. My daughter and I have used Sun Precautions active shirts for years now. After many washes, they are still silky soft and in remarkably good condition. They come in a variety of colors, but those in white are great for reflecting the sun's rays.

Coolibar (www.coolibar.com) is the Cadillac of the genre—it's the only garment maker whose products are recommended by the Skin Cancer Foundation. Coolibar's clothing (including swimwear) uses a proprietary process, maximizing protection through microfibers containing titanium dioxide. At the lower end of the range, Land's End offers affordable sun-protective swimwear for kids as young as toddlers. All of these clothing lines also cater to adults. ExOfficio also has beautifully made sitems for adults that would work well for most teens.

You might consider a hybrid approach to sun protection, as my daughter and I do. We wear sunscreen for the first hour or so, and when we want a break from the rays, we put on sun shirts and pants. We even wear these garments throughout a day of sightseeing.

Hot Tip! When snorkeling with your kids, in addition to eco-friendly sunscreen, wear sun shirts on top of bathing suits to avoid burns on the arms and upper back, the most exposed body parts.

Insect Repellents • LF — My husband swears that I could benefit science by demonstrating my abilities as a human mosquito magnet. It's true. If there's a mosquito within a mile, it will find me. The itching is bad enough, but in some places, mosquito bites can also spread diseases such as malaria, encephalitis, West Nile virus, yellow fever, and dengue fever.

Your best defense is to wear an insect repellent, as well as light-colored clothing (darker hues attract mosquitoes): long-sleeved shirts, long trousers—and knee socks for those pesky insects that fly up pant legs. Avoid wearing anything with a scent, such as perfume. (Keep this in mind if your child uses a body spray or cologne.) It also helps to avoid being outside when mosquitoes are most active, in the early morning or around dusk.

Hot Tip! Be sure to pack a soothing product like Burt's Bees Bug Bite Relief with tea tree oil, or any of several other available brands.

Picaridin is a great kid-friendly choice for mosquito repellents, and it also guards against ticks, flies, and other biting insects. Odorless and not greasy, it does not irritate skin, and has an excellent safety record. Unlike the old industry standard, DEET, picaridin has been classified by the EPA as "not likely to be a carcinogen." In Europe, it's know as "icaridin."

Studies demonstrate that picaridin is just as effective at preventing mosquito bites as DEET. While both chemicals are nearly one hundred percent repellent for a full two hours after application, the World Health Organization recommends picaridin to ward off malaria-carrying insects. Some brands carry both DEET and picaridin products, so read the label carefully.

12. HEALTH AND SAFETY

The CDC recommends picaridin, oil of lemon eucalyptus (a plant derivative), or DEET as insect repellents. Citronella and soybean oil are other natural options that are safe for children. You might also try Bite Blocker (www.homs.com), an all-natural, organic insect repellent touted by Dr. Andrew Weil; it's said to be ninety-seven percent effective. In general, natural options aren't as effective as picaridin or DEET, but they're worth a try for the less chemically inclined.

Do not use DEET if you and your children are going to be playing in water, as it's toxic for some fish and plankton. Also avoid it around infants of less than two months. Be aware that you can't use an adult DEET product on children; the American Academy of Pediatrics recommends those for children aged two to twelve years contain no more than ten percent DEET. Be sure not to apply it around the mouth or eyes, and avoid also your children's hands, if they are apt to put their fingers in their mouths.

Buzz Off clothing is impregnated with the insect repellent permethrin. Originally designed for outdoor enthusiasts, these garments are now being made for children. The EPA lists permethrin as a possible carcinogen, although it states that short-term use is "below the level of concern." It's worth noting, however, that permethrin is toxic to honeybees and aquatic life; some of the chemical rinses off in each wash cycle. And wastewater treatment plants are not set up to detect and eliminate the chemical.

First-Aid Kits • MD

With youthful ignorance, I traveled widely without a first-aid kit, before I became a mom. Such folly! Today, I couldn't imagine packing a bag without the homemade one I store in a kitchen closet. Packaged first-aid kits are widely available from local pharmacies, outdoor adventure stores like REI, and online. However, I prefer the zip-top baggie approach: You assemble a medicine chest quickly from products you probably already have on hand. The see-through plastic makes it easy for you to quickly eyeball the contents if you're rushing out the door.

My first-aid kit contains:

- acetaminophen (paracetamol)
- aloe vera gel or similar sunburn relief product
- alcohol-based hand sanitizer
- antidiarrheal medication
- antifungal and antibiotic ointments
- antihistamine
- adhesive bandages and a roll of cotton gauze
- blister kit (moleskin)
- cotton swabs

- cough drops
- decongestant
- Dramamine or similar motion-sickness medication
- insect repellent
- insect-bite relief
- ibuprofen
- nail clippers
- sunscreen
- scissors
- tweezers
- tissues

For younger children, you might also want to add:

- diaper-rash cream
- gripe water or other colic remedy

- teething gel
- infant /child rehydration formula (Pedialyte)

Before I pack the kit into my luggage, I throw out anything that is out-of-date and replenish any necessary supplies—especially adhesive bandages. It never ceases to amaze me how many of these my kids go through. But, it is astounding how having the right patterned Band-Aid can make all the difference to a "mortally wounded" toddler!

When you're buying over-the-counter medications, choose the chewable form—both for child and adult dosages—as these tablets are easier to pack. Finally, carry an antibiotic ointment such as bacitracin. These are usually sold in ten-packs (in one gram allotments) and are handy for traveling.

13.

WHILE YOU'RE THERE

WHETHER *you're traveling within your own country or abroad, experiencing this wonderful world with your children is exhilarating. You may teach them how to bargain at craft markets, carefully counting their Monopoly-like currency, or you may allow them to write on the family's blog or join a family-friendly tour to fully explore cultural sites. Whatever you do while you're there, it will surely be rewarding and educational for all.*

Currency • MD

Most children aren't taught about money until second- or third-grade math class. Until that time, children have a very loose understanding of bills, coins, and their values. By eight, most children grasp different currencies, but few have enough experience to comprehend foreign exchange rates. As a parent, ensure they don't inadvertently pay too much when using their pocket money.

Generally, I have an idea how much spending money they will have for each trip. They may save up their allowances for a few weeks, and then do some extra chores or accept a parent challenge—such as reading ten books—for some additional money. We don't give them the cash until we arrive, where we convert it into the local currency. Ideally, this money goes toward treats and gifts.

Even though a purchase in another currency can be confusing, I've never seen a merchant take advantage of a kid. Usually people are more than willing to help a child with her transaction.

Hot Tip! Have your children keep a few small-denomination notes as souvenirs. They're great mementos, easy to add to a journal, and sometimes when currencies change, they become an historical, as well as a personal, record.

When I travel, I withdraw cash from an ATM at the airport upon arrival. This is an easy way to get cash in another currency provided you have alerted the bank to your itinerary (otherwise it might freeze your account for fraud). Talk to you bank and credit cards' customer service before departure. Some companies charge only a "foreign transaction" fee (as much as five dollars). Others ding you for this, plus a percentage of the amount. Ouch! While some currencies, such as the Indian rupee, are not available outside of their country of issue, you can order most currencies from your bank. Alternately, an exchange service, such as Thomas Cook, can usually be found in the international terminal of most airports. It's helpful to have a few bills for snacks, drinks, transportation fares and bell-hop tips.

I caution you not to carry a wad of cash, because if it's lost or stolen, it's gone with no hope of recovery. Instead, carry small amounts of the local currency with travelers checks as a backup. That way you can allow your kids to be in charge of some of the family money, with little repercussion if it's lost.

Although ATM's are plentiful in cities and larger towns worldwide, don't expect to find them in remote areas of developing countries. Budget, withdraw, and use a money belt, neck pouch, or leg pouch to keep cash safe on your person.

Outside North America, your debit card may not work in all ATM's. There are two major service networks: Mastercard/Cirrus and PLUS/Visa. Check that the logo(s) displayed at the terminal match at least one on your ATM card. Usually, machines simply eject non-compatible cards, but it's not unheard of for one to take the card, which could be quite a hassle.

While on the road, I use my credit card (so that I can accumulate mileage) for more expensive purchases, such as accommodations and car rentals. While these are convenient, fees of up to three percent are common on foreign currency transactions. If you plan to shop, check your card issuer's policy on surcharges for foreign currency transactions. (At this writing, Capital One does not charge additional fees for foreign purchases. Bank of America does.) Avoid cash advances, since these also have additional fees and high interest rates. Despite the drawbacks, some frequent travelers still rely on credit cards for security reasons. A thief can run up a balance, but that's preferable to one cleaning out a bank account via a debit scam. Those worried about such schemes often open a distinct travel account, protecting their main one.

While not as widely used as they once were, travelers checks can come in handy. And, despite what some commercials might have you think, Visa is not accepted everywhere. In countries with volatile currencies—usually developing nations or ones experiencing significant political upheaval—it is sometimes useful to pay for travel expenses, such as accommodations, in U.S. dollars. This makes payment easy, with no currency conversion necessary.

American Express offers travelers checks in some foreign currencies, which you can get prior to your departure. There may be a fee for this service, and the exchange rate will be based on the day of your purchase. These are most helpful if you're only dealing with one monetary system (to one country or to the Eurozone).

Hot Tip! Leave copies of the numbers for your travelers checks, both at home and in your luggage (or e-mail them to yourself). If you get separated from both your money and your luggage, you'll still have access to this info.

Convert your travelers checks at a bank. A *bureau de change* or *casa de cambio,* which are popular terms for exchange locations, may not only charge you a fee, but you'll probably get a less-favorable rate.

In developing countries, electricity may be spotty or non-existent in some areas, making it impossible to rely on ATM's or credit card machines in shops and restaurants. Beyond these obvious infrastructure issues, power outages can happen anywhere, making travelers checks a good backup.

Handheld currency converters are available for about fifteen dollars, and often include a calculator and alarm clock. Magellan's Travel Supply carries a variety of these.

Staying in Touch • MD

Communicating with people at home is much easier today than when I was backpacking through Europe in the early '90's. Now, I travel with my cell phone handy and check e-mail at Internet cafés whenever I wish. Like most, my children are pros at using these media to stay in touch, and this skill easily carries over to traveling.

E-mail • MD — It seems like even the most remote village has at least one Internet café now. But, if you've become used to free, wireless access at your local coffee shop—as I have—don't expect this same cheap connectivity in other countries. I was surprised at how much it cost to get online on our last trip to Europe. This included using a wireless service on my laptop, as well as accessing the Internet on the café's PC's.

With e-mail, remember to stay focused on your travel experience rather than on the computer. For the first few days, I feel a strong urge to check my e-mail "just to make sure everything is OK," but by the third or fourth day this doesn't seem so important. My children are still young enough that they don't have a strong desire to check their accounts often on the road.

However, if your teen e-mails with friends at home, it's likely that she will want to continue doing so while traveling. Talk with her about this before you go. You'll need to agree on some ground rules for when and how she accesses e-mail, and who's going to pay for any expenses.

Blogs • MD — Blogs are a great way to broadcast your stories (and photos) with many people without having to send and reply to individual e-mails. A blog is like an online diary where you can document your trip in real time. These can either be open to the public (searchable) or read by invitation-only: perhaps a safer option when pictures of minors are posted. Consider setting up your blog prior to your departure, so that you won't be learning the finer points of the platform on the road. To create a free blog, try TravelBlog (www.travelblog.org), TravellersPoint (www.travellerspoint.com), or Blogger (www.blogger.com).

Blogs are extremely easy to create and maintain through one of these sites. If you have school-age or older children, everyone can be involved in a family blog or even in writing their own. On extended trips, daily or weekly entries might replace some school writing assignments for your kids.

Your children can also share their travel activities and photos with friends on social networking websites such as Facebook (www.Facebook.com) and MySpace (www.myspace.com). You'll have to caution them to keep good Internet safety practices, such as not publicizing their exact location or travel plans.

Hot Tip! WebWiseKids (www.webwisekids.org) is a good resource for information on Internet safety for parents and children.

Phones • MD — Years ago I turned off my cell phone and left it at home when abroad. I would then use a prepaid cell—if I needed one at all. Now, since GSM (Global System for Mobile communications) technology is standard on most models, using your own cell phone when you travel is easy. You will, however, need to confirm two things: what frequencies it uses and whether it's locked or unlocked.

Quad-band phones are capable of connecting worldwide. *Quad* in this case refers to the number of frequencies (four). Check with your manufacturer to see if yours will work in the relevant country.

Even if your cell phone functions outside North America, it may be prohibitively expensive. Roaming charges for international calls can cost a fortune—unless you use a SIM (subscriber identity module) card purchased at your destination. These are removable chips inside your phone that access a local phone service. This is an excellent way to cut costs on calls within the country you're in (and sometimes it's even cheap to call home!). However, your cell phone must be unlocked (not tied to a specific network), in order for you to install a different SIM card. You can have your phone unlocked by calling your service provider prior to your trip. Should the company refuse, you could buy a cheap handset abroad.

Hot Tip! Some North American cell phone providers have special packages for calling internationally from your cell phone. These include options for making calls to, as well as from, other countries. Some allow you to subscribe to the service temporarily.

There are numerous reasons you may want to carry one (or more) cell phones: Your family members can contact each other if you've split up to pursue different activities; you can be contacted by a sitter or childcare facility while they are watching your child; your child can contact you, if you get separated by accident; and you have the ability to book hotels without dragging a tired toddler in search of a room.

You might also consider purchasing a prepaid phone card and using public phones. International services such as those available on CallingCards.com (www.callingcards.com) can work from a public phone or a landline. Some, like the special cell phone packages, allow you to call to as well as from other countries. Shop around, as rates vary tremendously. Costco sells a card that charges just three-and-a-half cents per minute domestically, with excellent foreign rates. Your phone service provider may also offer a card for use abroad.

With the explosion of cell phones, the number of telephone booths is diminishing. Best bets for finding them include post offices, rest areas, gas stations, and convenience stores.

Purchasing a prepaid phone is another way to make low-cost calls in another country. Most cell companies offer these pay-as-you-go models—and many have outlets at airports, making it convenient for you to pick up a cheap handset on arrival. Otherwise, look for one at a mall or shopping area. Those with no monthly access fee are ideal: you only pay for the calls made. Purchase a phone, buy some credit—usually sold with the phone—and off you go. Just make sure you can dial internationally, if that's important, before leaving the shop.

Text Messages • MD — I use text messages frequently—at home and while traveling—because they're a quick and easy way to send short messages. I subscribe to a plan that includes messaging, because I send so many texts. Without such a service, you may be charged per text sent or received—which can add up pretty quickly, especially if you're traveling with a teen.

Older kids love texts. At my son's middle school, cell phones must be turned off and stored in lockers to deter texting during class. This passion carries over to travel as well, since they'll want to stay in touch with friends. I've journeyed with teens who seem to spend half their day furiously pecking into their phones. (See Chapter 4, "Challenges and Solutions," for ideas on how to manage your teen's cell phone while traveling.)

Writing • MD — We have a family routine of picking a fun postcard to send to ourselves. If we mail it early in the trip, it's waiting for us when we get home. My kids can spend hours choosing postcards for their friends, but they can be reluctant to actually write anything. Having your kids compose postcards to themselves is a great way to get a reluctant scribe started. Once the first card is written, the next one, two, or ten are easy.

Before you depart, put together a list of correspondents, and print their contact information on mailing labels. This allows you to keep track of those whom you've already mailed and to avoid any disagreements with your kids over sending postcards to "my new best friend," for whom you don't have an address.

Shopping • MD

The most important thing an adult can do about kids and their vacation cash is to refrain from bailing them out. If, after spending all of her allowance, she finds a must-have souvenir, book, or toy, hold your line and don't open your wallet. Otherwise, she'll learn that the "Parental Bank" is an on-demand lender—and that, I'm sure you'll agree, is not a good life lesson.

Sometimes, this approach can fall apart gloriously, such as the time we were in Italy. Since it was so hot, every time my kids begged for gelato, I complied, completely forgetting that they were supposed to buy their own treats. In the end, I was broke, and they returned to the U.S. with almost all their pocket money. Now I've learned to be more vigilant.

Laura F. traveled to Turkey with her six-year-old daughter Eden, who loves stuffed animals. "We let her buy what she wanted; however, when her pocket money ran out, we didn't give her any more."

Being careful with money doesn't mean you have to be a kill-joy parent. Your child will be getting an allowance when you resume your regular life. Sometimes an agreement to repay a purchase is all that's needed.

Markets • MD — My kids love visiting markets because there is so much to be discovered and examined. They can wander and explore, yet still be within my sight. In resort areas, the main street or boardwalk may be lined with store after store of touristy goods. Some shops sell more exclusive (and expensive) art, jewelry, or clothing—definitely not in the price-range of a ten-year-old's vacation allowance. Depending on where you are, there may be a craft or traditional market somewhere in the area. These are the ones my kids love most, for the vibrant colors and unusual items. Check your guidebook or ask at the tourist office for directions. You can finish up your shopping expedition with a snack at a café, sharing stories about all that you've seen, and then make plans to purchase your favorites. Just be aware of markets' closing hours: often early in the afternoon.

I wish I had a catalog of all the odd and useless items my children chose as souvenirs. On one trip, we returned with an oversized magnifying glass, a Venetian carnival mask, Yu-Gi-Oh cards in Italian, key chains (because, really, we needed three more), and some interesting rocks. When you go souvenir-hunting with your kids, allow them some creativity and independence, as this is an important part of the vacation experience. It will be a good lesson to let them have control over how they spend their own money. And, you never know when you might need another key chain featuring the Leaning Tower of Pisa.

Bargaining • MD — You need to be on your toes when you introduce a child to the idea of haggling at a market. She will need to be comfortable with the currency and able to do relatively quick calculations to compare costs and value—or have you there to help with this. In Mexico, we walked all around the stalls before allowing our boys to start negotiating with vendors. The point was to show them that the same products were available at many outlets, usually for different prices. This gave them some ideas on how much (or how little) to offer to start the bargaining process.

Broadly speaking, sellers ask double the amount they are willing to accept. Depending on your skill and your desire for the article, you might be able to bargain down to half price. You'll need to know—and to teach your child—that walking away is a tool in this dance.

While it can seem petty to haggle over a few cents or a few dollars, bargaining is about more than just saving money. It's a game and a way to interact with the locals. The seller is not going to give you something at a loss. Allow the back and forth to happen. If there's a language barrier, write down your bid on paper or in the dirt, and let the seller counteroffer. Stay patient, pretend to be disinterested, but continue to haggle, and eventually you should reach a mutually satisfying price.

Our then eight-year-old son became an expert bargainer in Mexico. My husband took him to a craft market and "taught" him. Then we watched at arm's length as he haggled to his heart's delight for every little purchase.

That said, in the developing world your child's purchase just might determine how much the seller's family eats that evening. This lesson is an important part of educating her about bargaining. She needs to understand that she shouldn't engage with a vendor if she doesn't really want to buy anything. What may be fun for her is someone else's livelihood. She needs to know that once she begins, if a fair price is offered, she will need to buy the item.

Tipping • MD — Tipping etiquette varies tremendously around the world. North Americans are accustomed to fifteen to twenty percent as a standard tip, while a German waiter will be happy with ten percent, and an Italian barista expects only the smallest coins set on the marble bar. In many countries, the tip is included in the bill. Your guidebook will provide information on local customs. Unless you don't mind parting with your cash, check the tab or simply ask. Also watch out for "cover charges" at restaurants: these slim down the tip expectations greatly.

Organized Tours • MD

I completely enjoyed the half-day cruise we took in Kauai with our boys when they were four years and three weeks old, respectively. I was at first skeptical about how my husband and I would manage an infant and a preschooler on a boat. Because of the tour's shorter length (four hours), it worked out really well. We got to see the Na Pali coast—which would have been impossible for me to hike three weeks postpartum—with dolphins swimming alongside and views of a beautiful sunset.

While we are usually very independent in our travels, sometimes an organized tour is simply the only way to experience a region. Many natural and archaeology sites must be visited with an organized tour (Kakadu National Park in Australia, for example). This will introduce your children to a living classroom. Doing so with a knowledgeable guide can mean the difference between thoroughly learning about an area and just looking at pretty buildings.

This is particularly true when visiting large, complicated sites, such as the Forbidden City in Beijing, where a guide can provide the highlights in an entertaining fashion (making it a more kid-friendly experience). Even the most entertaining tour leader, however, faces a tough audience in a cranky toddler. By eight years old, most kids are able to comprehend some of the finer points of once-in-a-lifetime sights.

Hot Tip! When you take a tour with a small child, stay at the back of the crowd while the guide is talking. Then other participants can hear and see, even if your tot is having a moment.

Eating Out • LF

We were dining at a lakeside café in Tivoli Gardens, Denmark, when we noticed crowds gathering. Then a small raft launched bearing an effigy of a witch. I asked local diners what was going on, and we learned that this was Denmark's traditional midsummer celebration. As dusk fell, the platform was lit afire, and we were handed a sheet of music. We joined in with a chorus of hundreds of people, singing a poignant midsummer song about nature's renewal. It's a meal we won't soon forget.

Dining out abroad can sometimes be like attending a theatrical event—only it's real life happening around you. Of course, these experiences won't occur in chain restaurants; get out into the areas where locals gather.

Part of the fun of travel, for me, is the chance to eat out. It's a great break from making and cleaning up family meals every night. Plus, it's fun to try out foods we wouldn't normally make at home. However, it can be challenging to find good places. Fortunately, a number of online sources can help with planning.

Chowhound (www.chowhound.chow.com) is an online discussion board that spans North America and numerous countries abroad. It's especially great for places with authentic regional cuisine, such as kebabs in Istanbul or *pastelillos* (pastries stuffed with meat or fish) in Puerto Rico. Within the United States, Yelp (www.yelp.com) offers reader reviews of restaurants in cities and small towns across the nation.

Vegetarians should check out Happy Cow (www.happycow.net), which has an international database. Even if you're omnivores, meat-free restaurants offer healthful foods that can be a nice break while traveling.

Guidebooks are another good resource for dining spots. Lonely Planet even identifies which restaurants are "touristy" or "non-touristy." Steering clear of the central eateries usually steers you toward more authentic local foods. Or, for finding good spots on the fly, ask resident parents about their favorite family-friendly dining spots.

Sometimes while traveling, it's a great break to stop in to a familiar fast-food restaurant. Occasionally this will be your only option. Once, in Europe, we arrived in the small town where our hostel was located, only to find everything shuttered for a national holiday. We've never been so happy to run across an open Burger King.

Burgers and fries crop up around the world, with the spread of American fast-food chains and copycats. When the options are limited, or as an occasional treat, fast food can taste really good. Even these places are paying attention to our desire for more healthful grub and are responding with new options. Look for green salads (and use less dressing than provided), grilled chicken or fish sandwiches, fresh fruit, yogurt, baked potatoes, or wraps.

Most chain restaurants have children's menus. While the choices are certainly kid pleasing and are fine for the odd meal, much of the fare is deep-fried. If you'll be traveling longer than a few days, ordering something for your kids off the regular menu is a good break from the monotony. Since portions at family restaurants are often huge, you might consider splitting an adult entrée with your child. A standard shared meal for my daughter and me is a Caesar salad, and a chicken or fish entrée. For further good nutrition, choose milk or juice for your kids.

Sampling New Foods • LF — It's fun to try out regional foods, and you'll want to share the chance to sample them. Granted, you might have difficulties persuading your finicky six-year-old to tuck into the more-exotic offerings, such as deep-fried scorpions in China or the rounded nether regions of a cow in Mexico. But every cuisine has a kids' specialty. You may not always find it on the menu, though. Hence the key question: "What do you have for children?" Your waiter will undoubtedly offer several agreeable choices. If you have a certifiably balky child, prepare her in advance by talking about how the foods will be different, yet much more interesting, than the ones from home.

Hot Tip! If your child is choosy about food, be sure to carry along "emergency rations" of dried fruit, an energy bar, or nuts, in case your young one decides not to eat what's available.

Since you'll likely encounter unfamiliar dishes and ingredients while traveling, it helps to have an "eating policy" in place. The "no-thank-you bite" works well: The child is required to taste the potentially offending substance, and she can then decide if she would like to consume more. It takes the battle out of eating and avoids the problems inherent in forcing a child to finish an objectionable food. It can take a number of trials before a child finds a new taste acceptable. Just be sure not to comment about your child's choice.

Unless your trip is lengthy, there's no need to worry if your child's diet isn't as nutritious. Laura F.'s daughter typically eats just two foods when they travel—chicken and chocolate. "I figure that two weeks of that out of the year isn't going to kill her. It works for us," Laura says.

Budget-Conscious Dining • LF — The price of eating out varies tremendously, depending on the value of your currency and which country you're visiting. Eating out (in non-tourist spots) is very affordable in many developing countries.

Visiting Vietnam with her four girls, Jenny B. had a memorable meal at a little nook with spartan furnishings—plastic chairs and tables on a dirt floor—where cooks barbecued over a small fire in the middle of the room. "Food came to us slowly, dish by dish, and it was delicious: Strips of barbecued beef were wrapped in banana leaves, and a chicken-noodle soup came with a plate of peppers, cilantro, basil, and slices of lime," she says. "We ate like royalty, all for about fifteen dollars. It made a big impression on our children and helped them realize that things aren't the same everywhere in the world."

In some countries, restaurants feature discounts on a particular "daily dish" or offer cheaper meals if you eat early—say, before six p.m. Fortunately, this timing is perfect when traveling with kids. As an example, in Australia, some restaurants serve two-for-one meals for the first wave of customers. Midday meals usually cost less than dinners, yet the menus often have the exact same dishes. By eating your main meal in the middle of the day, then planning on sandwiches or a hearty snack in the evening, you can really save.

Some North American restaurants offer free meals for children. Usually it's one free kid's meal for every adult meal purchased, and the deal is frequently available only one day of the week (usually excluding weekends). Coupon Divas (www.coupondivas.com) lists chains throughout that offer free kids' meals. For U.S. restaurants, check out Family Friendly America (www.familyfriendlyamerica.com).

Unless you're traveling where restaurant meals are very inexpensive, it's cost-effective to have accommodation with a kitchenette. While this style of lodging is more expensive than a standard hotel room, you'll quickly make up for it by preparing your own meals. "We like to splurge, eating in a restaurant," Laura S. says, "but with five people it gets expensive and tiresome—and the younger the kids are, the more you still want to accommodate lots of different tastes, so we cook in more often than not. We grocery shop locally, and get weird food and cook it on our own schedule, instead of eating in a restaurant and having to entertain the kids while we're waiting."

Hostels usually provide a shared kitchen. These are typically spacious and well equipped, so that several families can prepare a meal at the same time.

Look for lodging spots that offer breakfast. B&B's are known for their homemade fare (and the food often reflects the local cuisine). Many hotel chains supply breakfast, as well. It can take some ingenuity to sort through the stacks of white bread and sugary boxed cereals to find the more healthful options, but it's worth it. Some hotels also offer eggs or waffles.

Abroad, you'll likely have much more interesting food for breakfast than at home. A typical morning meal in Bali, for instance, is banana pancakes and a fresh fruit salad. Yum!

If your hotel doesn't offer breakfast, find a grocery store where you can purchase fruit, cereal, and milk. If you don't have a refrigerator, scope out where to buy milk in the morning. When staying somewhere for a few days, I've even been known to purchase a cheap foam cooler at a grocery store. In it I keep milk and other perishables, nestled in ice from the hotel's machine. Don't forget to pack your own dishes and cutlery, for in-room snacking.

Hot Tip! Have a bakery breakfast. To accompany the pastries, many bakeries sell milk, juice, or even hot chocolate. You can boost the healthfulness with a piece of fresh fruit purchased from a store or market.

Picnicking is one of the most fun ways to cut corners on costs. A moveable feast can be as simple as buying locally made bread and cheese, and some fresh fruit. Dining al fresco at the seashore or in a park has a way of staying in your memory, long after you've forgotten the name of a nice restaurant. Taking your kids into a foreign grocery store is a worthwhile adventure in itself; it's fascinating to see the different foods and to try to figure out what things are. Grocery stores also often have delis, where you can buy ready-made salads, sandwiches, or hot foods.

We visit farmers' markets wherever we travel, for the fascinating variety of new ingredients, the ultimate in freshness, and the cost savings. Standouts include the spiral-cut, deep-fried potatoes of Michoacán, Mexico, and the fresh-picked, cinnamon-sugar almonds of southern California. Many sellers offer free tastes. In tropical countries, we've tasted numerous fruits that are unknown to Western palates, such as *mispero*, a small gold fruit that tastes like apricots, and pink-colored *mamey*, which flavor-wise resembles a pumpkin.

Splurge Time • LF — It's always good to be able to splurge on a nice restaurant at least one night. Plan ahead for this since the stakes are higher financially. This is one time when I'm careful to do my research prior to a trip, so I can be sure of a positive experience. I always make a reservation at least the day before. As at home, only you know your children's ability to sit through a fine-dining experience, so be realistic.

In some countries, haute cuisine with kids is easier than in others. In general, destinations that are very family friendly cater to youngsters even in more elegant settings. Barbara G. says, "In London, you don't walk into a nice restaurant with a kid. In Spain, no one batted an eyelid."

Hot Tip! It's easier to eat out with your kids at a restaurant that has sidewalk dining. This way, if your kids are a bit noisy, it doesn't bother other patrons as much. Plus, the bustle of a street scene can keep your children more engaged than a quiet, indoor space can.

Even if you suspect your kids would have a hard time sitting still for a special dinner out, don't rule out the possibility. It's only through practice that kids learn new behaviors. Each time you eat out is a stepping-stone—at some point they will be mature enough and may surprise you with good behavior. "I have to balance what I want and how far will I go to impose my children on the people around me," Barbara T. says. "It's different every trip, since our children's ages and demeanors change constantly."

Photography • LF

A child with a camera is an engaged child, more apt to see small, interesting details that an adult might miss. Of course, for children, taking pictures is more about the process than the end result. When my daughter was a tween, we were viewing her underwater images after a trip to Hawaii. Her conversation went something like this: "See this? That's an eel…I think. Or maybe this is the eel over here. Well, maybe I wasn't aiming the camera right, but I think this is a small fish, here."

Most young kids simply don't have the technical and artistic abilities to create compelling shots, let alone always get the subject inside the frame. However, the point isn't to produce a neat stack of beautiful, scenic images. Rather, it's to nurture the importance of travel by recording places where they've been.

The right camera choice doesn't always have as much to do with age, as with your child's interests, motor skills, and temperament. An artistically inclined child who focuses well on a topic would probably do better at photography than one who has a hard time standing in one place. Yet, through practice, any child can create images that are special.

Decide between a disposable, a point-and-shoot film, or an inexpensive digital camera. In my experience, disposables are ideal for young kids. They're inexpensive, readily available, lightweight, and easy to use—and they produce images that are of acceptable quality. They also come in waterproof versions, for playing at the beach or snorkeling. If your child leaves behind a disposable camera, it's easy to shrug and buy her another.

While point-and-shoot film cameras might sound like an inexpensive solution, these simple cameras aren't very economical. It's common for children to snap happily away, focusing on their fuzzy slippers, the TV screen, or maybe an interesting rock, creating numerous duplicate images. At seven to ten dollars to develop a twenty-four-exposure roll, the cost can quickly become prohibitive.

Hot Tip! Consider sharing the family's digital camera for a year or more, before giving your child one of her own. This way she can learn the ins and outs with your guidance.

Digital cameras take surprisingly good pictures with a minimum of expertise needed. Prices continue to fall for these; you can get a serviceable one for less than one hundred dollars. With digital, you won't end up paying for film development, although you will have to spring for flash cards, batteries, and a camera case. (Digital cameras often come complete with USB connection cords, so you can download images to your computer.)

"Our kids have had their own digital cameras since they were six," says Lisa M., a professional photographer. For the most part, they manage their own photography needs. "They welcome my help with editing, adjusting the exposure a bit, and cropping, but they're responsible for downloading their own flash cards and putting in batteries," she says. "They sometimes take crazy pictures with close-ups of nostrils, but I feel that it's best not to curtail their creativity; I let them capture whatever they're feeling. They especially enjoy taking nature and wildlife shots and include their favorites in school projects and in greeting cards they make on the PC. They love taking video, too."

Lisa encourages her kids to keep in their computer a set of "best of" images from family trips, so they can readily share ten or twenty pictures.

Hot Tip! If you give your child her own digital camera, be sure to get a brightly colored case, so it's easy to spot and won't be left behind as easily.

If you're ready to buy a digital camera for your child, first consider the features. For the standard four-by-six-inch print, look for a camera with at least two megapixels. A four-megapixel camera can create prints of up to five-by-seven inches; for eight-by-ten-inch prints, the camera will need to have eight megapixels. Just be sure to steer clear of gear sold in toy stores; these aren't so much real cameras as they are toys.

A zoom lens is versatile: It can be used, in effect, as binoculars, to view distant objects. It's especially handy if you have a fledgling bird-watcher in your family. With more-inhibited children, a zoom lets them get close to their subjects without feeling intrusive. One with an amplification of 3x (3:1) should be just fine for most uses.

A few tips can go a long way. Basic pointers for young children should include:

- Invisible fingers—keep digits away from the lens.
- Bright faces—keep the sun behind the photographer.
- Intact bodies—no headless torsos.

- No tree-people—make sure no one in the photo has a tree, column or other human growing out of her head.

For older children and teens, you can teach them:

- Straight-on pictures are boring; angles are fun.

- I Spy: Look for small details that will ruin a shot, such as trash or a telephone pole.

- Place subjects slightly off-center. For example, position the frame so that someone walks toward the center of the image, rather than away from the center.

- Dawn and dusk offer the richest colors.

- Cultural sensitivity: Respect the local people, and don't take pictures without asking permission or receiving a nod of approval.

After a trip, make sure your children's cameras are stored in a safe spot, and immediately download the images or process the film. The more you procrastinate, the easier it is for a camera to become lost somewhere in your child's room.

To preserve trip memories, take film to a photo processor or use an online program—such as Flickr (www.flickr.com), Shutterfly (www.shutterfly.com), or Snapfish (www.snapfish.com)—to upload and print digital photographs. Each of these also allows you to share images with friends and family in an online album. This is a great way for your kids to stay connected with grandparents, and other family members and friends.

Laundry • LF

When packing for your trip, it's best to take clothes that will dry quickly, if possible. Avoid cotton underwear, which can take days to dry. There are a number of companies specializing in lightweight, quick-drying travel clothing. (See Chapter 11, "Pack It Up," for more information.)

Light packers will probably need to do laundry after about a week of traveling. I always take washing supplies, so I'm prepared to clean underwear and small items in a sink. This extends the days we can get by without doing a full load of laundry. Do keep in mind the time needed for your clothes to dry before you're on the road again. It's a good idea to build in two consecutive nights in one place every few days, so you can launder.

Laura F. says, "We always take soap and do a lot of laundry in the sink. We usually travel in the spring or summer, and we take lightweight things that we can hang-dry in a day."

Joanne D., who traveled with her son throughout Southeast Asia, says: "We did our own laundry most of the time. We brought our own scrub brush, as well as a clothesline and clothespins, and we bought local detergent. We washed our clothes in the sink and hung them to dry in our guesthouses. If it's humid, clothing takes longer to dry, so we turned on the ceiling fans to help the clothes along."

Following are some items to take along that will make sink laundering easier:

- Zip-top bags are essential for any trip, especially those times when swimsuits are still damp or the underwear washed isn't quite dry, yet you need to hit the road. You won't want to leave the items sealed for long, but it will work for a day, and at least you'll be keeping them separate from the rest of your clothes. Zip-top bags don't take up much space, so take four to six.

- A one-size-fits-all stopper from any drugstore turns your sink into a laundry basin. I can tell you from experience that these work a lot better than a doubled-up washcloth (fine in a pinch).

- A travel-size bottle of liquid detergent or a plastic bag with the powdered type—enough for several loads—saves you the time and hassle of scouting out detergent at your destination. It also guarantees that your children won't experience rashes from a new brand. Just be sure to double-bag the detergent. And try to use as little as possible, so it's easier to get the soap out when rinsing.

- A portable clothesline expands the drying area; hotel shower-curtain bars don't have enough space for more than a few wet swimsuits.

Hot Tip! Stain removers in travel sizes, such as OxiClean Spray-A-Way, work well for spot jobs, such as cleaning up drips from a chocolate ice cream cone or spilled ketchup.

When you need to run a full laundry load or two, look for a Laundromat or laundry service. Coin-operated machines are common in developed countries, but in many other parts of the world, small family businesses will take in your laundry and return it, neatly folded, the next day. At most hotels in Asia and Central America, your laundry will be taken to a local family, or it might be washed by staff on-site. (You might even see your kids' clothes, and your undies and bras hanging on a clothesline on the hotel's rooftop or out back.) Your accommodation's staff should be helpful in pointing you toward the best option.

Hot Tip! Use solar power to dry your clothes. The sun coming through a car's windows is more than adequate for drying even jeans in a day's time, if the garment is spread out on top of luggage.

When traveling in Vietnam, Jenny B. found that her hotel's laundry service was relatively expensive. "So we loaded our laundry into a *cyclo* (pedicab) and had the driver take us to someone who did laundry," she says. "After a little customary haggling, the laundress agreed to do the equivalent of four loads of laundry for about three dollars."

Laura F. always packs an empty duffel bag in her suitcase. "We throw all of our dirty clothes in the duffel bag at the end of our trip, leaving room in our suitcases for any new stuff we may have purchased. We check the duffel as a separate bag, and when we get home, the duffel bag goes straight into the laundry room."

Bathroom Breaks • MD

"What's up, honey?" I asked my younger son, Brendan, as he came out of the bathroom at a café in Nicosia, Cyprus. He was looking no more relieved than when he went in, not two minutes earlier. It was obvious he hadn't done his business, and he was looking quite distressed. "It's not a proper toilet, Mom," he said. I guessed immediately what was wrong: The bathroom at the café did not have a Western-style flush toilet, and he was confused. Instead, it was a squat toilet, which can be anything from a ceramic hole in the floor, with ridged treads to prevent slipping, to a simple hole in the ground.

The condition and style of lavatories differs around the world—something a child may find alarming and upsetting. I hadn't even thought to talk to my son about toilets before Cyprus. Indeed, had we stayed in the tourist areas, we probably wouldn't have had any need to have that conversation. But we had wandered out of the main tourist region and were having coffee at a neighborhood café with facilities that were perfectly fine for the locals.

Squat toilets are disconcerting for kids (OK, for parents, too) at first. It helps to have a little potty talk in advance of your trip. Young children face the challenge of learning how to use a squat toilet without needing a complete change of clothing every time. The simplest approach is to have them take off all their clothes below the waist (but leaving their shoes on). An older child will be able to simply roll up her pant legs—but remind her to secure the contents of her pockets. Where squat toilets are common, toilet paper is usually not available. You can either carry your own or, though it may be a hard sell, suggest that your kids clean themselves using the water from the spigot that's always located next to a squat toilet.

Hot Tip! With help from a guidebook or some online research, you can quickly find out what type of toilets you'll encounter at your destination.

In some countries, even when flush toilets are available, the plumbing system may not be as robust as those found in North America. Teach your kids to look for signs requesting that you place your used paper in a bucket or garbage can rather than flushing it.

You and your kids may be surprised that in some countries, toilets are fantastically high-tech. Kimm S. describes her daughter's reaction to the elaborate devices in their hotel in Kyoto,

Japan. "Emma was fascinated by the many buttons, the different spray functions on the bidet, and the multiple options for heating the water."

You never know, but dealing with toilets may be one adventure you hadn't counted on in your travels!

14.

RESPONSIBLE TRAVEL

OUR *children develop their sense of ethics by observing the choices we make. When we demonstrate our values through responsible travel, we teach our children to treat our planet and its people with respect. In this chapter, we provide tips for how to be culturally sensitive to people around the world. We also suggest our families can help safeguard the animals, plants, and landscapes we enjoy. In addition, we explore volunteer vacations and delve into the complex, but important, topic of carbon offsets.*

Respecting Other Cultures • LF

Responsible travel means more than caring for the environment. It means respecting the unique character of the places you visit. It's an opportunity to share with your children how other people live.

If your kids are aged four to ten or so, the book *Children Just Like Me,* by Anabel and Barnabas Kindersley, is a wonderful resource. It depicts youngsters from more than 140 countries, organized by continents. It's a personal narrative book, with photos of individual kids who discuss the foods they eat, their homes, their schools, their friends and family, and even their pets. The children's favorite games and their hopes for the future are also included in this beautifully photographed and sensitive book.

As there are so many issues woven into the fabric of daily life, it's best to pick up a book about the culture of the country you'll be visiting before you head out. The book series *Culture Smart! A Quick Guide to Customs and Etiquette* has guides for nearly seventy countries, from Australia to Vietnam. *Culture Shock! A Survival Guide to Customs and Etiquette* is another such series.

Clothing Advice • LF

Clothes represent our culture, and views of our country are formed by people abroad when they see how we dress and act. When I was in my twenties, I backpacked through Europe for several months and learned that I was accorded more respect if I wore culturally appropriate clothes. Walking through the upscale shopping district of Zurich in a T-shirt, shorts, and hiking boots, with a backpack, brought looks of distaste from merchants. Yet, by changing into my best clothing when I got to the hostel, I later returned to the same district, and received warm and welcoming expressions. We could talk about how unfair it is to be judged for our appearances, but the fact is when we're traveling, we're the ambassadors, and how we look and act reflects on our country.

Series such as *Culture Smart!* or *Culture Shock!* offer insights into what clothing to pack and wear for specific occasions. Even if you have studied up, it still pays to be aware of how others dress, as cultural norms may vary from place to place. If local women wear skirts that cover the knees (as is common in Kenya), be sure that you and your children dress accordingly.

No matter where you're traveling, if you plan to visit a church, cathedral, synagogue, or any religious site, be sure not to have bare shoulders or bellies, or to wear flip-flops. Cathedrals in Europe, while popular with tourists, are nonetheless houses of worship, and they require appropriate clothing. Each country has its own take on what is appropriate attire inside a religious building. In Italy and Spain, for example, knees and arms must be covered. You may be denied entrance if your clothing is unacceptable.

Hot Tip! There's no telling when a cultural opportunity might arise; even if you're planning a casual vacation, take at least one nicer outfit for each family member.

Reaching Out • LF

The major sights alone don't give you a good idea of the soul of a place. Nor do resort communities show the real face of a country. It's when you meet the locals that you can learn about what life is like there, in all its nuances. Granted, there's nothing wrong with choosing a destination for its plethora of family-friendly swimming pools, beaches, and entertainment

14. RESPONSIBLE TRAVEL

options. But if your schedule allows, try an excursion into the countryside, or take a meet-the-people tour. (To learn more about interacting with locals, see Chapter 5, "Friends and Family.")

Thoughtful Photography • LF

Equipped with a camera in an unfamiliar place, it's easy to focus on the unique streetscapes and architecture … and to then point the camera at the scene's people. Let your children know that, just as it's impolite to stare at others, it's also rude to treat people as objects, taking their pictures sans permission. If you or your kids come across a particularly intriguing person or situation and wish to take a picture, just ask. I've always found that the request comes across better if you smile.

The best approach is to get to know the individual, so that he is no longer just a random subject for photography. Think about it. At home, would you walk up to someone on the street and snap their picture? Most people would be put off by the rudeness and would want to know why you're shooting. But if your children take the time to approach the person thoughtfully and chat with them—after they've gotten your permission to do so—it's a different story.

Your request can sometimes be met with an outstretched hand seeking money. It's best not to pay for photographs. However, if it's a vendor at a market, do buy something as a small token of appreciation.

Different Ways • LF

Sometimes we are more of a cultural shock to the locals we're visiting than vice versa. In remote areas that Westerners don't commonly visit, talk to your children about how they may be the center of attention. Explain to them the need to respond warmly and openly, if the locals are drawn to them.

When Joanne D. traveled to a far-flung village in Vietnam with her young, fair-haired, blue-eyed boy, the villagers wanted to touch him and take pictures of him. "Friends had told us ahead of time that this might happen," Joanne says. "We were curious how Bryce would tolerate it. He was very gracious and didn't get frustrated or upset. He actually enjoyed it."

Economic Differences • LF

Before you embark, it's a good idea to chat with your children about cultural similarities and differences. This is particularly true when you'll be visiting a less-well-off country, where your children will be exposed to poverty. It can be an emotionally jarring experience to see beggars for the first time. While most North American cities have panhandlers, in many parts of the world, children are among those asking for money, which is particularly unsettling.

It's tempting to give money, yet doing so perpetuates the cycle of exploitation. Instead give to organized charities. To lessen the pain of seeing such poverty, donate to one that benefits the children of the country, prior to your trip, and talk to your gang about the donation. This way, when your kids see children with outstretched hands, they can feel good knowing that your family has helped.

Another way to assist is to plan ahead to visit a school and distribute supplies to the children there. Taking toys or supplies to an orphanage is a further opportunity to contribute; these can be found even in tourism hot spots. My mother, who regularly visits Puerto Vallarta, Mexico, always packs a duffel bag with small stuffed animals. She buys the Beanie Baby-style

14. RESPONSIBLE TRAVEL

toys at thrift shops and takes them home to wash before packing them.

Protecting the Environment • LF

As humans march into the twenty-first century, the fragile network of nature's systems is becoming increasingly evident. Furthermore, that it's stretching ever tauter, even breaking in places, due to the added stress of climate change. If we want our children to enjoy the splendors of the natural world, we must do all that we can to safeguard the environment.

Just the act of traveling with our children can help them gain a personal stake in protecting the unique landscapes and cultures, so visiting natural sights is valuable. But sometimes our actions unwittingly add to the burden on the environment. And we're not alone. Tourism, especially travel to more remote regions, is burgeoning, and the effects can lead to real problems for the host countries or locals.

Water has become an increasingly precious resource. The demand worldwide has tripled in the last fifty years, and at the same time, hydroelectric dams have diverted water, draining rivers. Scores of countries are over-pumping aquifers, trying to meet their growing water needs. And more than half the world's people live in countries where water tables are falling, including China, India, and the United States.

Before embarking, learn whether there are water-conservation restrictions or guidelines, and then follow them. Even if an area is not water-needy, by conserving water, you treat the environment with respect and teach your children to do the same.

Start in your room. No one I know uses a towel at home only once before washing it again. Just because we're staying at a hotel or B&B doesn't excuse us from considering the environmental effects of all that soap and potable water going into the wastewater stream. Many properties these days allow you to hang towels back on the rack for re-use. If your accommodation doesn't offer this option, there's an easy way to ensure that towels and sheets aren't replenished each day: Just hang the "Do Not Disturb" sign on the doorknob.

While traveling, be sure to have your children follow the same eco-conscious guidelines as normal, or learn new good habits. Here are some water-conscious tips for home and away:

- Five-minute showers should be the norm.

- There's no need to flush a toilet after every use. Your children will likely be amused by the old adage, "If it's yellow, let it mellow; if it's brown, flush it down." (Of course, if you're potty-training, it's probably best to wait until your child has set habits before offering this tip.)

- Do not allow the faucet to run while brushing your teeth.

- Be sure to turn every tap off completely. You'll need to check after young children have tried, as they likely don't have the arm length or height to screw them completely shut.

Consideration for water doesn't end when you close the hotel door. On a trip to sun-baked Phoenix, I was stunned to see a family allowing their children to play in the pool shower, leaving the tap running full-bore as they darted in and out of it, and then jumped into the pool. The message a quintet of kids was getting is that there's always more than enough, and it's OK to waste.

14. RESPONSIBLE TRAVEL

Trash • LF

Starting when they're young, we parents teach our children about the importance of properly disposing of trash. This same edict applies when traveling, even if the local culture doesn't care for its environment the way we might expect. In some less-developed countries—and, actually, in cities across the United States—you may find much more garbage strewn about than you're accustomed to seeing. People in poorer areas are often more focused on finding adequate food and dealing with the many issues of poverty than they are on how to dispose of trash.

While traveling through such places, we need to be especially sure that we don't contribute to the debris, and that we use proper receptacles.

Disposable batteries are a worldwide problem, as they leach toxic chemicals into landfills. Purchase rechargeable ones—nickel-metal hydride batteries are the best for the environment—and pack a charger. Ones with a "quick charge" feature are best for traveling, as you won't have to wait around in the morning for them to finish.

Use reusable bags for items you buy, and say no to plastic sacks. When you arrive, shop for a couple of sturdy cloth bags in which to place your purchases. If you have a spare hour, it can be a powerful feeling to help clean up a beach. These same cloth bags may prove helpful with this.

Joanne says she talked with her son, Bryce, a lot about the environment while traveling through Southeast Asia. "Pretty much everywhere we went, there was garbage alongside the road, and there were piles and piles of plastic bags. It was a good opportunity to teach Bryce how important it is to keep the planet healthy. We talk about it at home, but there was the problem right in front of us."

At home, recycling is easy—we just place our bin filled with paper, plastic, glass, and metal at the curb, or drop it off at the supermarket or dump's receptacles. On the road, however, it can be really hard to find ways to recycle. I've been amazed at how few hotels offer recycling. If there is no obvious system where you're staying, do check with management to see what you can do. Perhaps, with enough visitors seeking an answer to this question, the hotel may decide to give recycling a try.

Walking Lightly • LF

If your trip will include a visit to a natural area, it's useful to brush up on how to care for these environments. Let your children know what part they can play in preserving our natural resources.

Teach your children to follow trails so that vegetation is left to grow. Also let them know that they should not pick plants. This is particularly true in delicate habitats, where it may take as much as a century or more for grasses and other flora to regenerate.

On a beach vacation, keep your children away from all coral. These should never be touched; each has a mucus membrane on its exterior, and even the slightest contact can remove the protective coating, making it more prone to disease or death. Even stirring up a sandy bottom can coat coral, smothering it. Reefs can take decades to regenerate, and with climate change, coral is already under increasing stress.

Sunscreen contains chemicals that cause the bleaching and oftentimes the death of those animals. Up to 6,000 metric tons of sunscreen washes off swimmers each year worldwide, causing the potential for great harm. Sunblock products that contain titanium dioxide or zinc oxide do not have this effect. (To read about sunscreen alternatives, see Chapter 12, "Health and Safety.")

Protecting Animals • LF

Animals should be left alone to follow their natural behaviors. They require energy to engage in courtship, breeding, and feeding. Any interruption causes them to stress, which can lead to an energy deficit similar to a food shortage. Teach your children to stay a respectful distance from critters, and never block their escape routes.

Even if it looks like a wild animal needs your help, it most likely doesn't. Your interference could create real problems. Kirsten once found a seal pup on the beach without its mother. For all purposes, it looked abandoned. Yet I knew that young seal pups often rest while their mothers feed. If their space is encroached upon, the mother may be too alarmed to return to them. We enjoyed watching the pup from a respectful distance.

It's particularly important to never get between a parent and its offspring; all animals become fierce when protecting their young, and the situation can be dangerous. However, even if it's not, the intrusion can be disconcerting to the mother and possibly lead to abandonment of the baby.

Just what is a respectful distance? It's where animals follow their natural behavior and aren't disrupted by your intrusion. If they show any signs of disturbance, such as moving away from you, leave the area immediately but slowly, so as not to disturb them any further.

Unless you're traveling in bear country (in which case you need to make noise to alert the animals to your presence), it's best to be as quiet as possible when in a natural environment. This is both for the animals' sake and yours—you'll see more wildlife that way. You'll need to explain the importance of being respectful when in the home environments of animals. Then remind your kids of this as frequently as needed when on a nature excursion.

Hot Tip! A pair of binoculars or a zoom lens can allow your children to see wildlife "up close" without stressing those animals.

Whale-watching tours are a popular way for tourists to get up close to these magnificent marine mammals. It may seem to be a perfect activity for families, since it involves animals and an active search for them. Unfortunately, the more popular these tours become, the greater misery whales have to endure, as no regulations limit the number of vessels in a given area. It's commonplace for a pod of whales to be surrounded by a flotilla of loud boats, jockeying for the best viewing position.

The Marine Mammal Act specifies that boats stay at least 300 feet from whales (or any sea life), but many tour operators circumnavigate this rule by buzzing ahead and placing themselves in the path of the approaching animals. It's common for whales to be corralled by boats, all of which create painful sounds. (Sound is magnified underwater.) Whales use sonar to locate their food, and the underwater cacophony makes this task much more challenging. And recent studies suggest noise may be a factor in beachings.

Instead of a whale-watching tour, consider going to headlands where whales are commonly sighted. An online search can quickly yield the top land-based spots. Or, do your own

14. RESPONSIBLE TRAVEL

sightseeing aboard a ferry that has a regular route near whale-watching territory.

Other marine creatures also need the same consideration. When exploring tidepools, teach your children not to disturb the colorful life in these miniature seascapes. Be especially cautious during low tide, when many plants and animals are left high and dry for a few hours; this is when they're the most vulnerable. Children should not handle seastars or any other marine critter; picking them up causes them to halt their natural activities, which can ultimately lead to their deaths. They should be left alone where they are found. Also, caution your children not to step on exposed sealife during a low tide.

Hot Tip! Teach your kids about sealife by visiting an aquarium. These often have touch pools where your child can learn about marine life in a controlled environment.

Low-impact Transportation • LF

If you have a choice between motorized or self-propelled recreation, choose the human-powered option. Two-stroke engines (found on older personal watercraft) are polluting, and even with a newer model, most mechanized recreational vehicles are loud, encroaching on the serenity of a place and scaring away wildlife.

Bicycling, kayaking, or canoeing bring a much greater chance of encounters with wildlife. You'll also be setting a good example for your kids, by declining gas-fueled machines for recreational purposes. As a bonus, these sports will help your children develop coordination and give them a sense of mastery.

Adventure travel companies or resorts sometimes offer helicopter sightseeing or heli-skiing tours. It's best to avoid whirly bird travel, however, since these flights can seriously disrupt critical wildlife habitats. For this reason, heli-skiing is banned in France and most of Italy.

Carbon Offsets • LF

Climate change is making itself known in myriad ways around the globe. Becoming aware of our personal contributions to this trend is important, as the solution must come from everyone pitching in. By traveling, we add significantly to our carbon footprints. Check out The Nature Conservancy's carbon calculator, (www.nature.org), or go to Carbon Footprint (www.carbonfootprint.com) for more information.

Air travel, in particular, burns an immense amount of fossil fuel. The gas needed to power a jet is about the same as if each passenger drove in an individual car to the same destination. While the carbon dioxide released by jets depletes ozone, other aircraft emissions have particularly powerful climate-changing effects, because of the elevation at which they are emitted.

Add in regional transportation costs, and travel obviously has a huge impact on our planet. This doesn't mean we should stay at home, though. After all, by exposing our children to other places in the world, we are building the foundation for the next generation's understanding of and commitment to solutions for worldwide problems.

To mitigate air travel, you can purchase carbon offsets through an increasing number of airlines or through travel companies. Here's how it works: You contribute to companies or organizations that use the funds to avoid, reduce, or absorb greenhouses gases. They may do this through renewable energy generation,

14. RESPONSIBLE TRAVEL

327

such as wind farms or solar panels; by encouraging energy efficiency, such as less-wasteful appliances or light bulbs; or by planting trees or other green schemes to absorb CO_2.

More and more airlines are offering carbon-offset programs to their passengers. You can take advantage of this when purchasing fares. It doesn't have to be expensive—you may pay as little as an additional two dollars per ticket. Check with your airline to see if they offer this option. In addition, you can also purchase carbon-offset credits when booking through Expedia, Orbitz, and Travelocity.

While there's no firm evidence that an individual traveler's carbon offsets makes a dent in climate change, each of us certainly should do what we can. In a general sense, change only comes about when, one by one, we take on a small solution to the problem.

If your airline does not have a carbon-emissions program, you can purchase carbon offsets independently. Tufts Climate Initiative (TCI, www.tufts.edu) has made a complex topic accessible to non-academicians on its website. Even better, it reviewed companies that sell carbon offsets, saving consumers time and effort.

Ecology-minded Lodging • LF

Help the environment further with an environmentally conscious accommodation. Eco-lodges, found in remote spots around the world, protect and enhance their unique landscapes. They also work closely with local indigenous populations. Designed to be in harmony with their settings, eco-lodges try to live lightly on the land, from energy- and water-saving techniques to environmental education for guests.

(To learn more about eco-lodges, see Chapter 9, "Home Away from Home.")

In response to growing environmental concerns, some rental companies now have electrical, natural gas, biofuel, or hybrid cars (which typically have both an internal combustion engine and an electric motor). Agencies featuring eco-cars include small, independent ones—such as Bio-Beetle on Maui, which claims the first (starting in 1998) biodiesel fleet—and some of the largest companies, such as Budget (www.budget.com) and Avis (www.avis.com).

If you can plan ahead to mitigate some of the effects, you can enjoy your journeys while feeling assured that you're pulling your weight when it comes to the environment. Even better, you can help your children understand the importance of treating our planet with great care, a gift that will hopefully continue into future generations.

14. RESPONSIBLE TRAVEL

15.

RETURNING HOME

E ASING *back into daily life will be less stressful if you prepare for your return before you
depart. And once you do walk in your door,
there are some great ways to remain immersed in
the warm glow of vacation.*

Easy Landing • LF

Before you leave, arrange for transportation home from the airport. Ask a family member or good friend to pick you up at the airport, train, or bus terminal. If you have small children and are roaming sans car seats, ask another family with young children to pick you up, so you can use theirs. Alternatively, you can have your "support team" drive your car, if you plan ahead to hand over the keys.

Be sure to give your flight number to whoever's collecting you, so she can track the progress online.

Just in case your ride can't make it, have a backup plan and the phone number of a shuttle service handy. Carry your cell phone, whether or not you'll be using it while traveling, so you can dial immediately upon arrival to confirm your pickup.

Clean Entry • LF

Smoothly integrating back into daily life is dependent in part on how well you prepare your home. Before a trip, while we're handling last-minute packing details, I always make time to clean the house. It's a great feeling to return to a tidy house with space to easily unpack the suitcases and deal with laundry. It also helps set a more serene mood.

Hot Tip! After a trip, don't be the only one performing the tasks related to getting back into daily life. Give yourself a break and ask your children to help out, too, by unpacking their own luggage and assisting with any small tasks.

If at all possible, set aside the day after you return to unpack, organize, and deal with anything that's come up while you were gone. Consider this as a vacation day. Having this "mental health" break especially makes sense if you have a demanding job and would otherwise have to cope with the end-of-trip details, while you're juggling child, work, and household responsibilities.

Jet Lag • MD

I've come to expect jet lag, since our most frequent destination (Ireland) is eight time zones from Seattle. When traveling in both directions, I know that everyone's sleep patterns will be disrupted for at least a couple of days.

Jet lag happens when our circadian rhythms—our natural inclination to be awake when it's daylight and to be asleep during the nighttime—are disturbed, usually by flying across time zones. Fresh air and exercise for the whole family are vital to resetting your body clocks, as is getting back into a normal pattern—going to sleep in the evening and resting at least six to eight hours—as quickly as possible. Allow at least a day for you and your children to get reoriented into your familiar surroundings and to adjust to your time zone at home.

Upon returning, your goal should be to help your child recover from jet lag as quickly as possible before restarting her normal school, home, and extra-curricular activities. The first stretch is always the most difficult. Expect your child to wake in the middle of the night, utterly discombobulated and unable to get back to sleep. In my family, since I'm an early riser, this means I do the early shift, getting up with whichever of our children wakes first. I will crash in the early evening, at which point my husband takes over keeping the kids awake at least until their normal bedtimes.

Reading and snuggling in your child's bedroom will help reinforce the fact that it's still nighttime. As children get older, encourage them to stay in their beds, listening to music or reading, at least until dawn. These quiet activities can help a child fall back to sleep, which will make it easier for her to stay awake during the day. Slowly, this will move her into the right time zone. During these first few days, limit daytime naps as much as you can.

Post-Trip Depression • LF

After a trip, life presents itself all too suddenly, with work, bills, cooking, homework hassles, PTSA meetings, and the endless trips to play dates, music lessons, and sports matches. Your life has to speed up again to deal with everything coming your way. It can be a tough transition from relaxation or fun-filled adventure to suddenly having numerous responsibilities again. Particularly if you vacationed somewhere sunny and return home to colder, less appealing weather, the differences between time away and the realities of home can be magnified. Post-trip depression is a very real dilemma many of us face.

Kids often feel a letdown after traveling, too. For them, going on a trip usually means carefree, exciting experiences, with something new and interesting every day. Perhaps they were allowed more freedom too, on the road. Or, if they're young, maybe they really enjoyed full days spent with their parents. Upon returning, it's understandable that they might feel grumpy at having to be responsible for chores and homework again. Plus, your kids will likely be worn out and will need a quiet day with time for reading or napping, to readjust.

Hanging on to That Trip Glow • LF

It's important to try to hold fast to the joys of travel as long as possible, to help everyone make the smoothest transition. There are a number of ways to make this work.

Now's the time to try to recreate that favorite, exotic dish in your own kitchen. It can be a lot of fun to find recipes through an online search, and then to work alongside your kids as you relive the culinary experience of your trip. You can always stop by the grocery store or a deli for ready-made ethnic fare, too.

Regardless of whether or not foreign cuisine is on the menu, dinnertime is ideal to revisit vacation memories—and to learn more about what each family member particularly savored. Doing so not only helps children process the experience, it also provides you with a roadmap for future trips. You'll learn what was successful and what activities didn't live up to expectations.

To stay in a "vacation" mindset, spend time in places where you'll encounter friendly people. Choose to shop in smaller, independently owned stores, and spend your money locally whenever possible, much as you most likely did while on the road.

Trip Memories • LF

Have friends or neighbors over for a "picture show" following the trip. This will give your children the opportunity to talk about their experiences with interested listeners. At our house, we create a digital slideshow, and everyone gathers around a laptop to view the images.

Hot Tip! Most kids tend to talk at length about a single image. By setting a laptop slideshow to a several-second setting, you can whiz through the shots without unnecessarily boring your visitors.

Upload your trip photos to an online photo-sharing and processing service—and single out the best images of your kids to print and frame. These sites make it easy to create a poster of

335

your trip—or to make one poster each year with its highlights, including journeys.

Another way to collect and display memories is to have a bulletin board in each child's bedroom, where she can display her treasured pictures, train tickets, or other memorabilia.

Your kids can even take their memories to school with them. Elementary-age children can tell classmates about their trip during show-and-tell; most would jump at the opportunity to be a star for a day. If they check with their teachers, older kids may be able to make a presentation to their classmates. Touch base before you leave about scheduling the presentation.

During your trip, you'll need to keep your eyes open for easily portable tokens that can serve as props. At home later, help your child color in a map of the country or region as a visual device, and send her off to school with the souvenir kachina dolls from Arizona, maracas from Mexico, or miniature castle from Germany.

"When I have the time, I make a scrapbook of the trip, and Eden takes it to her school," Laura F. says. "She also brings back little coins or other mementos to give to her friends. She loves being able to share."

For middle-schoolers, think about scheduling a play date or sleepover with a few buddies that centers on the place you visited. It might include a short travel video or family movie, and a dinner that features a specialty food from your destination. If you think ahead, be sure your kid buys a small souvenir for each friend. The gift can help make the experience special for the visiting children, as well.

Treasures left by nature make great trip reminders. Lesli B. and her husband take their three young daughters on spring break each year to a Gulf Coast island, where the beach is heaped high with seashells. "They ask you not to take anything that's alive, but there are so many shells, they actually crush the shells as they grade the beach a couple of times a week," she says. "My girls collect the shells, and when we come home, we make picture and mirror frames, and gifts for grandparents."

If you provide your kids with travel-size blank-page journals, their entries will form a lasting memento that they can read again and again. The pages at the end are ideal for pasting pictures and small, flat memorabilia.

Lisa M.'s kids keep journals in which they record their experiences, draw, and paste maps and photos that they cut from travel brochures. In addition, every evening Lisa sets aside time to talk to her kids about the day's highlights, and they jointly create a travel poem by adding a few lines each day. "My mom started this ritual when the kids were quite young, and we treasure our collection of poems," Lisa says. "We come up with a rhyming two-liner for each experience of the day. By the end of the trip, the poem might be two pages long."

On a trip to Belize, Lisa and her children wrote a poem that included:

At Yugadah Café the fish and rice tasted fine,
And Rosie our waitress sang like Patsy Cline.
Soursop ice cream was our Belizean treat
so nice and cold in the tropical heat!
We rode horses through the jungle and saw a boa
Juan suddenly trotted and Vivian said, "Whoa!"

"Now we have a whole binder full of trip poems. It's a reminder of who we met and what we did," Lisa says.

15. RETURNING HOME

Another sure way of staying in a vacation frame of mind is to get out the family calendar and plan your next trip with your kids. It's a cliché, but it's true that children grow up so fast. You'll want to experience as much as possible with them before they leave home. There's nothing quite as satisfying as the closeness, the laughter, and the fun you can have while exploring the world together!

WEBSITE RESOURCES

A Ferry UK	www.aferry.co.uk
AAA	www.aaa.com
Accor Hotels	www.accorhotels.com
Adventure Cycling Association	www.adventurecycling.org
Adventure Travel	www.adventure.travel
Airports Council International	www.airports.org
Alaska Airlines	www.alaskaair.com
Alaska Department of Transportation & Public Facilities	www.dot.state.ak.us
All About Houseboats	www.allabouthouseboats.com
AlluraDirect	www.alluradirect.com
Amazon	www.amazon.com
American College of Obstetricians and Gynecologists	www.acog.org/publications/patient_education
Arm's Reach	www.armsreach.com
Artcyclopedia	www.artcyclopedia.com
Association of Children's Museums	www.childrensmuseums.org
Audible	www.audible.com
Audio-Technica	www.audiotechnica.com
Avent	www.avent.com
Avis	www.avis.com
A-Z Map Company	www.a-zmaps.co.uk
BabyBjörn	www.babybjorn.com
Baby's Away	www.babysaway.com

Banjercito	www.banjercito.com.mx
BC Ferries	www.bcferries.com
Beco Baby Carrier	www.becobabycarrier.com
BedandBreakfast.com	www.bedandbreakfast.com
Bicycle Germany	www.bicyclegermany.com
Bite Blocker	www.homs.com
Blogger	www.blogger.com
BnBFinder.com	www.bnbfinder.com
Boating Holidays	www.boatingholidays.com
Bose	www.bose.com
Budget	www.budget.com
California Whitewater Rafting Association	www.c-w-r.com
CallingCards.com	www.callingcards.com
Canadian Automobile Association	www.caa.ca
Carbon Footprint	www.carbonfootprint.com
Car-Safety.org	www.car-safety.org
Centers for Disease Control	www.cdc.gov
Charter World	www.charterworld.com
Chowhound	www.chowhound.com
Club Med	www.clubmed.com
Cooking.com	www.cooking.com
Coolibar	www.coolibar.com
CouchSurfing	www.couchsurfing.com
Council on Standards for International Educational Travel	www.csiet.org
Coupon Divas	www.coupondivas.com
Cross-Country Ski World	www.xcskiworld.com
Cruise Critic	www.cruisecritic.com
Cycle New Zealand	www.cyclenewzealand.com
Cycletourer	www.cycletourer.co.uk
Cycling in Switzerland	www.cycling-in-switzerland.ch
Delicious Baby	www.deliciousbaby.com

Dive Booty	www.divebooty.com
Divers Supply	www.divers-supply.com
Dorling Kindersley	www.dk.com
Dot Girls	www.dotgirlproducts.com
Drugstore.com	www.drugstore.com
Easyjet	www.easyjet.com
Elderhostel	www.elderhostel.org
Ergo	www.ergobabycarrier.com
ExOfficio	www.exofficio.com
Expedia	www.expedia.com
Facebook	www.facebook.com
Family Friendly America	www.familyfriendlyamerica.com
Farecast	www.farecast.live.com
Federal Aviation Administration	www.faa.gov
Ferrylines.com	www.ferrylines.com
Festál (Seattle)	www.seattlecenter.org /Festal.htm
Flickr	www.flickr.com
Fodor's	www.fodors.com
Frommer's	www.frommers.com
Gap Adventures	www.gapadventures.com
Global Buddies	www.globalbuddies.net
Global Volunteers	www.globalvolunteers.com
Google Blog Search	www.blogsearch.google.com
Google Maps	maps.google.com
Gordon's Guide	www.gordonsguide.com
Gordon's Guide to Whitewater Rafting	www.whitewateradventures.com
Gorp	gorp.away.com
Graco	www.gracobaby.com
Greek Ferries	www.greekferries.gr
Happy Cow	www.happycow.net
Hog Wild Toys	www.hogwildtoys.com
HomeAway	www.homeaway.com
HomeExchange	www.homeexchange.com

Hostelling International	www.hihostels.com
Hotels.com	www.hotels.com
Hotwire	www.hotwire.com
Houseboating.org	www.houseboating.org
Hybrid Rental Car	www.hybrid-rental-car.com
iHealthRecord	www.ihealthrecord.com
Indian Railways	www.indianrailways.gov.in
InMotion	www.inmotionpictures.com
International Association for Medical Assistance to Travelers	www.iamat.org
International Narcotics Control Board	www.icnb.org
ionKids	www.ionkids.com
itunes	www.itunes.com
Japan-guide	www.japan-guide.com
JetBlue	www.jetblue.com
JohoMaps	www.johomaps.com
KaBOOM! Playspace Finder	kaboom.playspace.com
Kayak	www.kayak.com
KidCo	www.kidco.com
KidsFlySafe	www.kidsflysafe.com
Kiplinger	www.kiplinger.com
Klutz	www.klutz.com
Know Your Trade	www.knowyourtrade.com
Kwikpoint	www.kwikpoint.com
La Leche League	www.llli.org
Lands' End	www.landsend.com
Let's Go	www.letsgo.com
Little Acorns Treehouse	www.littleacornscds.blogspot.com
Local Hikes	www.localhikes.com
Lonely Planet	www.lonelyplanet.com
Lonely Planet Thorn Tree	www.lonelyplanet.com /thorntree
Maclaren	www.maclarenbaby.com
Mad Libs	www.madlibs.com

Magellan's	www.magellans.com
Medela	www.medelabreastfeedingus.com
Medical Summary	www.medicalsummary.com
Mommy I'm Here	www.mommyimhere.com
Moon	www.moon.com
Mountain Travel Sobek	www.mtsobek.com
Mountaineers Books	www.mountaineersbooks.org
Museums in the USA	www.museumca.org/usa
Museumstuff	www.museumstuff.com
Muzzy	www.early-advantage.com
MySpace	www.myspace.com
National Geographic	www.nationalgeographic.com
National Highway Traffic Safety Administration	www.nhtsa.dot.gov
National Park Service	www.nps.gov
Nature Conservancy	www.nature.org
NCY & Company	www.nycvisit.com
Nomadic Matt	www.nomadicmatt.com
Only in San Francisco	www.onlyinsanfrancisco.com
Orbitz	www.orbitz.com
Owner Direct	www.ownerdirect.com
Pacific Yurts Inc.	www.yurts.com
Parks Canada	www.pc.gc.ca
Passport Canada	www.ppt.gc.ca
Patagonia	www.patagonia.com
Peugeot	www.peugeot-openeurope.com
Priceline	www.priceline.com
Radtouren in Osterreich (Cycle Tours in Austria)	www.radtouren.at
Recreation.gov	www.recreation.gov
REI	www.rei.com
Renault	www.renaultusa.com
ResortQuest	www.resortquest.com
Roller Coaster DataBase	www.rcdb.com
Rosetta Stone	www.rosettastone.com

Rough Guides	www.roughguides.com
Ryanair	www.ryanair.com
SafeFit	www.safefit.com
Saferoads.org	www.saferoads.org
Sassy Baby	www.sassybaby.com
Sea Bands	www.seaproductsonline.com
Servas	www.servas.org
Shutterfly	www.shutterfly.com
Sittercity	www.sittercity.com
Sixintheworld	www.sixintheworld.com
Ski.com	www.ski.com
Slow Travel	www.slowtrav.com
Snack Trap	www.snacktrap.com
Snapfish	www.snapfish.com
Southwest Airlines	www.southwest.com
Spot Me ID	www.spotmeid.com
Streetwise Maps	www.streetwisemaps.com
Sun Precautions	www.sunprecautions.com
Surfing America	www.surfingamerica.org
Teacher's Discovery	www.teachersdiscovery.com
Technorati	www.technorati.com
The First Years	www.learningcurve.com / thefirstyears
Theme Park Critic	www.themeparkcritic.com
Theme Park Insider	www.themeparkinsider.com
Thomas Cook	www.thomascookpublishing.com
Thomson Family Adventures	www.familyadventures.com
Tinytotsaway	www.tinytotsaway.com
Trails.com	www.trails.com
Transportation Security Administration	www.tsa.gov
Travel for Kids	www.travelforkids.com
Travel Insurance Review	www.travelinsurancereview.net / family-travel-insurance
Travel Savvy Mom	www.travelsavvymom.com

TravelBand International	www.travelband.com
TravelBlog	www.travelblog.org
Traveling Mamas	www.travelingmamas.com
TravellersPoint	www.travellerspoint.com
Travelocity	www.travelocity
Travels with Children	www.minnemom.com
TravelSmith	www.travelsmith.com
Trento Bike	www.trentobike.org
Tripadvisor	www.tripadvisor.com
TripSketch	www.tripsketch.com
Tufts	www.tufts.edu
United Nations Educational, Scientific and Cultural Organization	www.unesco.org
UrbanRail.net	www.urbanrail.net
US Department of State	www.iafdb.travel.state.gov
Vacation Rental by Owner	www.vrbo.com
Vayama	www.vayama.com
ViaMichelin	www.viamichelin.com
Virgin America	www.virginamerica.com
WanderMom	www.wandermom.com
Washington State Ferries	www.wsdot.wa.gov
Washington.org	www.washington.org
Waterparks.com	www.waterparks.com
Weather.com	www.weather.com
WebWiseKids	www.webwisekids.com
What to Expect	www.whattoexpect.com
World Wide Opportunities on Organic Farms	www.wwoof.org
Yelp	www.yelp.com

INDEX